VC[partially obscured by label]

OF THE FIRST WORLD WAR

ROAD TO VICTORY 1918

VCs OF THE FIRST WORLD WAR

ROAD TO VICTORY 1918

GERALD GLIDDON

First published 2004
This new edition first published 2014

The History Press
The Mill, Brimscombe Port
Stroud, Gloucestershire, GL5 2QG
www.thehistorypress.co.uk

British Library Cataloguing in Publication Data.
A catalogue record for this book is available from the British Library.

ISBN 978 0 7509 5361 0

Typesetting and origination by The History Press
Printed in Great Britain

Contents

Acknowledgements

I would like to thank the staff of the following institutions for their assistance during the research for this book: the Commonwealth War Graves Commission, the Imperial War Museum, the National Army Museum and the National Archives. In addition, I would like to thank the archivists and curators of the many regimental museums and libraries who have replied to my requests for information.

Where recently taken photographs have been used, their owners have been acknowledged with the individual illustration. As with my previous books in the *VCs of the First World War* series, Donald C. Jennings of Florida has been very kind in allowing me to reproduce many of the pictures of graves or memorials used in this book. Many of the maps used have been taken from regimental histories or from the *British Official History of the War: Military Operations in France and Belgium, 1914–1918*, edited by J.E. Edmonds, Macmillan / HMSO, 1922–49.

Other individuals who have been of great help in many ways included Peter Batchelor, John Bolton, John Cameron, Jack Cavanagh, Colonel Terry Cave CBE, D.G. Gage, Ray Grover, Peter Harris, Chris Matson, Dick Rayner and Steve Snelling. Other people who provided additional material but whose names are not mentioned here have been acknowledged in the list of sources at the end of the book.

Preface to the 2014 Edition

The History Press has decided to reissue the *VCs of the First World War* series in new editions and I have taken advantage of this decision by revising and updating the texts of the current volume.

Since the initial research for this book was carried out fourteen years ago there has been an increasing interest in and awareness of the stories and lives of the men who were awarded the nation's and the Commonwealth's highest military honour. Evidence of this can be found in the number of new books being published on the subject; the re-issuing of servicemen's records by the National Archives and the accessibility of other records of family history, which are now available via *Ancestry*, the family history magazine, and from other sources. The Internet has also played a major part although information received using this method should always be verified by cross-checking. Finally, the founding of the Victoria Cross Society in 2002 by Brian Best has encouraged further research and publication of informative articles on the holders of the Victoria Cross.

While this book was being prepared the British Government announced plans for commemorating the First World War centenary from 2014 to 2018. One of the ideas put forward is directly linked with the commemoration of the servicemen who won a Victoria Cross during the Great War. It was decided that for men born in the UK a special paving stone would be installed at an appropriate place in the town or district most associated with them. As for VC winners born abroad, it is hoped that their governments might also take up the paving stone scheme or an act of commemoration in their honour.

In addition, the Commonwealth War Graves Commission has an active programme of placing visitors' information panels in cemeteries where VC holders are buried or memorials where they are commemorated.

Gerald Gliddon
November 2013

Introduction

The previous volume to be published chronologically in this series, *VCs of the First World War*, was one that dealt with the German spring offensive. The book ended on a note of optimism for the Allies as they prepared for their great counter-blow, which led to the end of the war within a hundred days from the beginnings of their new offensive on 8 August 1918.

The German Army had not exactly given up all hope of winning the war, but after their March offensive had failed to deliver the hoped-for 'knock-out blow', their leaders must have considered that their best chance of victory had now passed. In addition, American troops and equipment were beginning to contribute substantially to the Allied cause.

The British commander Field Marshal Sir Douglas Haig now firmly believed that the war on the Western Front could be finished by the end of 1918. And this despite it not being long since some members of the British Government and military hierarchy thought the war might drag on until 1920. Whatever reason Haig had given to his detractors in the previous three years as Commander of the British Expeditionary Force, there was no doubt that by the beginning of August 1918 he had acquired a new-found confidence and belief in the ability of the Allied armies to at last push the Germans out of France and Belgium. There is also little doubt that British and Dominion troops had learnt the lessons of the previous four years of relative stalemate and had now mastered the art of dealing with an enemy which was beginning to face manpower and equipment shortages in addition to the beginnings of loss of morale and confidence associated with a losing army.

On 8 August the first blows of the Anglo-French offensive fell on the German Second and Eighteenth Armies to the east of Amiens, and were delivered by General Sir Henry Rawlinson's Fourth Army and the French First Army under General Debeney. Great care was taken to deceive the enemy as to the real whereabouts of the Canadian Corps prior to 8 August, and it was a ruse that appeared to have fooled the enemy. In addition, the Allies now integrated their weaponry of aircraft, artillery, tanks, armoured cars and motorised machine guns. Battlefield communication had also been much improved. In particular the small light tank known as the Whippet was found to be able to work easily with the cavalry when the possibilities of exploitation occurred. The brilliantly executed Allied victory at Hamel in early July, when tanks and infantry combined so successfully, was a glimpse of the future of land warfare. After the initial Allied success on 8 August, the 'Black Day of the German Army', there was an inevitable slow-down with the planned advance. However, the writing was clearly on the wall for the German Army, as within a few days of the beginning of the new offensive, German representatives made official peace overtures to the Allies via President Woodrow Wilson of the USA.

Although the British Army had a good August it was thought that their French colleagues were not pulling their weight in the operations. The British Third and First Armies entered the campaign on 21 August and at the end of the month the Australian Corps captured the stronghold of Mont St Quentin, the protective gateway to the important town of Péronne, which subsequently fell to the victorious Australians.

A few days later, on 2 September, further to the north, the Canadian Corps achieved astonishing success with their breaking of the heavily defended Drocourt–Quéant Line known by the enemy as the Wotan Line. In a matter of twelve days the BEF had advanced 14 miles on a front of 28 miles and had also taken more than 45,000 German prisoners. On 4 September the New Zealand Army made an important contribution by forcing another part of the German defensive line, the Canal du Nord. Later in September further north the Second and Fifth Armies made substantial progress between the La Bassée Canal and Ypres. All these campaigns were accompanied by considerable heroism and gallantry, resulting in the winning of sixty-four VCs between 8 August and 26 September.

It will not come as a surprise to find that the Canadian and Australian Dominion troops figured very highly in the tally of VCs won in this seven-week period. No fewer than eleven VCs were won in the period 8–9 August, six more in the fighting for Mont St Quentin and twelve at the time of the fall of the Drocourt–Quéant Line on 2–3 September. Another dramatic day was the final day of the Battle of Épéhy, when six more Crosses were won. The following day, on 19 September, the British Army began to approach the Hindenburg Line and a week later they were lined up against it.

The last man to be covered in the previous book in the series was the New Zealander Dick Travis, who won his VC on 24 July, close to Hébuterne, and who died the following day. This book covers the fifty days of the Allied Advance from 8 August 1918 to 26 September, and the first two men covered are Herman Good and John Croak, both members of the Canadian Expeditionary Force, who won their VCs in the fighting at Hangard Wood on 8 August. The sixty-fourth man to win the VC covered by this book was Donald Dean in the period 24–26 September. The next book in the series will cover the period from the Battle of the Canal du Nord on 27 September to 6 November 1918, when the last VC on the Western Front was won. Five days later the Armistice was signed on 11 November 1918.

H.J. Good

Hangard Wood, France, 8 August

The great Franco-British Offensive began on 8 August 1918 and within one hundred days the Allies had defeated the German Army, resulting in the signing of the Armistice on 11 November. The Allied plan for the Battle of Amiens included a major role for the Australian, British and Canadian Forces who, with fifteen divisions, were to be very heavily engaged. It was the Canadian and Australian Corps who were to spearhead the advance.

The major offensive was to take place to the east of the city of Amiens and plans were laid to use various ruses and deceptions in order to confuse the enemy about Allied intentions. Units of the Canadian Expeditionary Force were sent northwards to the Ypres Salient and were put into the line on the Kemmel Front, where they were duly identified by the enemy. Corps headquarters was prepared and casualty clearing stations were set up in places where they could be seen. Wireless activity was also stepped up on the First Army Front and the impression was given to the enemy of a great concentration of tanks gathering in the area of St Pol. Training operations, too, were carried out, which in turn were noted by enemy reconnaissance. The rumour that the British were about to begin a large offensive on the Northern Front quickly spread.

While the decoy units were busy near Ypres, the whole of the Corps – nearly 100,000 men – were being moved secretly from the Arras sector to Amiens, some 50 miles to the south-west. Preparations for the advance were carried out as much as possible during the hours of darkness and sounds of tanks or troop movements were muffled by either aerial or artillery activity. The assault began in the early hours of 8 August with a well-timed artillery barrage, combined with the use of several hundred tanks accompanied by troops from Canadian, Australian and French troops moving forward. It was the beginning of the end of the war and the day was later described by the German commander Field Marshal von Ludendorff as the German Army's 'Black Day'.

The 3rd Brigade (Canadian 1st Division) had to cover a front which was originally nearly 2 miles in width, and which was later reduced by a quarter of a mile. The brigade was the spearhead of the 1st Division together with the 4th Tank Battalion, which had forty-two Mark V tanks at its disposal. The first Canadian troops swept forward, regardless of hostile posts, which they left for the following infantry to deal with.

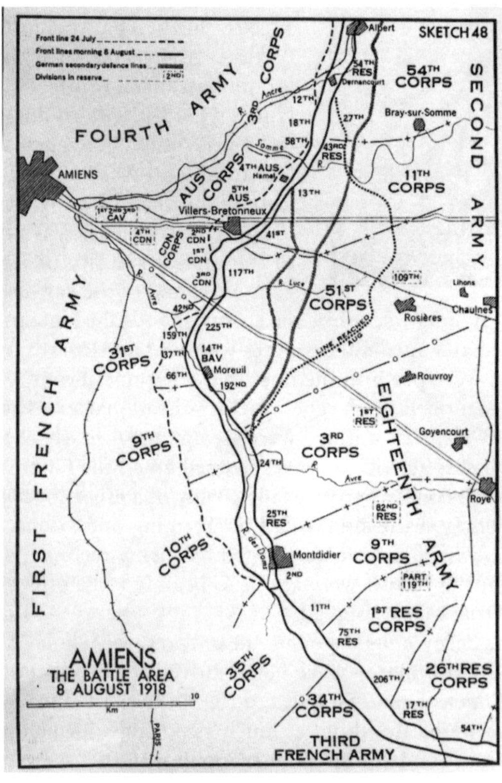

Corporal Herman Good was a member of the 13th Battalion Quebec Regiment (Royal Highlanders) of this Brigade and was a member of 'D' Company. Although in the early morning of 8 August the barrage began very accurately, it later caused casualties to the Battalion when shells began falling short. However, despite this, the Canadian advance was very swift and the village of Aubercourt to the east of Hangard was soon reached. Twenty out of an original twenty-eight tanks in this area reached the high ground and moved off ahead of the 13th and 14th Battalions of the 3rd Brigade. The tanks demoralised the enemy, but the Germans still put up a stout resistance. Their supports were duly dealt with and, according to the British *Official History*, 'the fighting went on simultaneously all over the field'.

Machine-gun nests in Hangard Wood put up considerable resistance and it was in dealing with these nests that Pte Croak and Cpl Good won their VCs. Good's VC was gazetted on 27 September 1918 as follows:

> For most conspicuous bravery and leading when in attack his company was held up by heavy fire from three machine guns, which were seriously delaying the advance. Realizing the gravity of the situation, this N.C.O. dashed forward alone, killing several of the garrison and capturing the remainder. Later on Corpl. Good, while alone, killing several of the garrison and capturing the remainder. Later on Corpl. Good, while alone, encountered a battery of 5.9 inch guns, which were in action at the time. Collecting three men of his section, he charged the battery under point-blank fire and captured the entire crews of three guns.

Having overcome the machine-gun nests in Hangard Wood, the 13th Battalion moved swiftly, killing numbers of the enemy and capturing several German batteries. However, at a position called Croates Trench, the Royal Highlanders were held up for forty-five minutes by some enemy machine guns which proved to be very stubborn. A shortage of bombs was giving the battalion great concern and according to the *Regimental History*:

> Rifle fire was ineffective and two tanks, which went forward in response to the Infantry's request for aid, were put out of commission as soon as they got astride the trench and before they could deal with the occupants. Eventually, two Stokes' guns were brought up and opened fire. After a few rounds from these had burst in the enemy position, a shirt, once white, appeared on the end of a rifle and the German garrison surrendered. By 8 a.m.

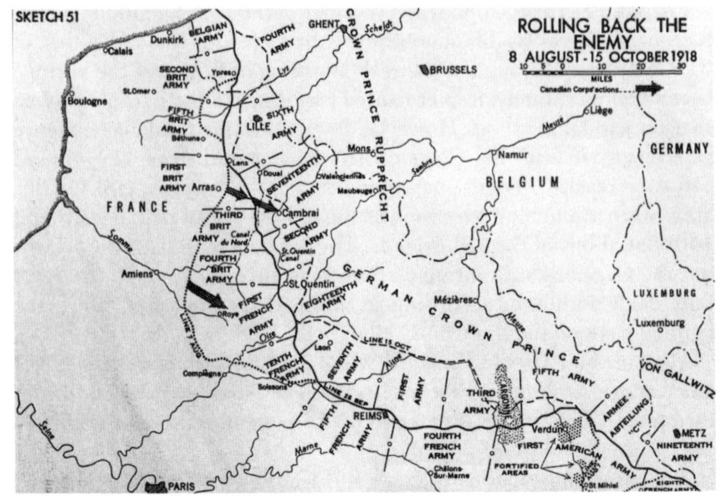
SKETCH 51
ROLLING BACK THE ENEMY
8 AUGUST - 15 OCTOBER 1918
MILES
Canadian Corps' actions
CROWN PRINCE RUPPRECHT
GERMAN CROWN PRINCE
VON GALLWITZ
FRANCE
BELGIUM
GERMANY
LUXEMBURG
Calais
Dunkirk
BELGIAN ARMY
FOURTH ARMY
GHENT
Scheldt
BRUSSELS
SECOND BRIT ARMY
Ypres
St.Omer
Boulogne
Lys
FIFTH BRIT ARMY
Béthune
SIXTH ARMY
LILLE
Liège
Meuse
Lens
Mons
Namur
Sambre
FIRST BRIT ARMY
Arras
Douai
SEVENTEENTH ARMY
Valenciennes
Maubeuge
THIRD BRIT ARMY
Cambrai
Canal du Nord
SECOND ARMY
Somme
St.Quentin Canal
FOURTH BRIT ARMY
Amiens
St.Quentin
EIGHTEENTH ARMY
FIRST FRENCH ARMY
Roye
Mézières
Luxemburg
Oise
LINE 7 AUG
LINE 15 OCT
Laon
SEVENTH ARMY
Aisne
TENTH FRENCH ARMY
Compiègne
Soissons
LINE 26 SEP
FIRST ARMY
THIRD ARMY
ARGONNE
FIFTH ARMY
ARMEE-ABTEILUNG "C"
Seine
FIFTH FRENCH ARMY
REIMS
FOURTH FRENCH ARMY
Verdun
FIRST AMERICAN ARMY
METZ
NINETEENTH ARMY
Marne
Châlons-Sur-Marne
FORTIFIED AREAS
St Mihiel
PARIS
EIGHTH FRENCH ARMY

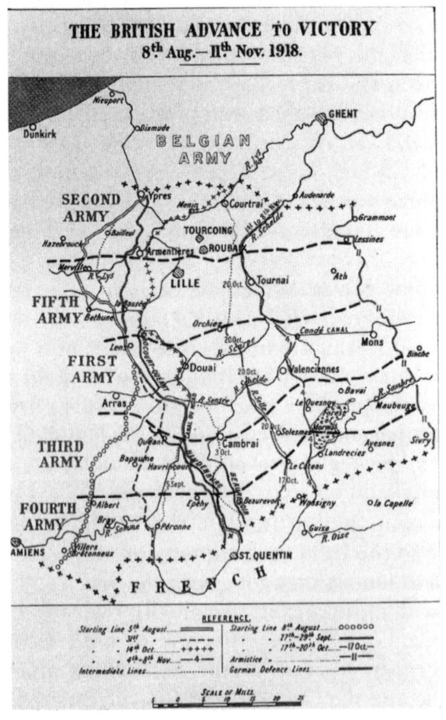
THE BRITISH ADVANCE to VICTORY
8th Aug.—11th Nov. 1918.
Nieuport
Dunkirk
Dixmude
GHENT
BELGIAN ARMY
R. Lys
SECOND ARMY
Ypres
Menin
Courtrai
Audenarde
Grammont
Bailleul
TOURCOING
Hazebrouck
Armentières
ROUBAIX
R. Schelde
Lessines
Merville
R. Lys
LILLE
20.Oct.
Tournai
Ath
FIFTH ARMY
Bethune
La Bassée
Orchies
Condé CANAL
Mons
Lens
R. Scarpe
Binche
FIRST ARMY
Douai
Valenciennes
R. Schelde
Bavai
R. Sambre
Arras
R. Sensée
Le Quesnoy
Maubeuge
Forêt de Mormal
Quéant
Cambrai
Solesmes
Avesnes
Sivry
THIRD ARMY
Bapaume
Havrincourt
3.Oct.
Landrecies
Le Cateau
5.Sept.
17.Oct.
FOURTH ARMY
Albert
Epéhy
Beaurevoir
Wassigny
la Capelle
Bray
R. Somme
Péronne
Guise
R. Oise
AMIENS
Villers Bretonneux
ST. QUENTIN
FRENCH
REFERENCE.
Starting Line 5th August
Starting Line 8th August
31st
27th–29th Sept.
14th Oct.
17th–20th Oct.
4th–8th Nov.
Armistice
Intermediate Lines
German Defence Lines
SCALE OF MILES

> the 3rd Bde. had reached nearly three miles into enemy territory and the objective, the Green Line had been reached. Here the battalion halted and consolidated and the 2nd Bde. passed through their lines in order to continue the attack. It was at this point that the British Cavalry made an appearance. The day had been a great success.

Good was presented with his VC by the King on 29 March 1919 in the Ballroom of Buckingham Palace.

Herman James Good was one of six brothers and eight sisters, children of Walter and Rebecca (*née* Sealy) Good. He was born in South Bathurst, Gloucester County, New Brunswick, Canada, on 29 November 1887, where he attended Big River School. After leaving school he was involved in lumbering operations in the Bathurst area. By this time he had developed into a heavily built man, just under 6ft in height, with sandy hair and blue eyes.

On 29 June 1915 Good joined the Canadian Army in Sussex, New Brunswick, and was given the service number 445120. He left for Europe on the SS *Corsician* on 30 October and arrived in England on 9 November. He joined the 5th (2nd Pioneer) Battalion and later transferred to the 13th Battalion on 15 April 1916. Over a period of three years he served in the 55th, 2nd Pioneer and 13th Battalions. He was wounded three times, the first time when he was shot in the buttocks on 5 June 1916, and was subsequently moved to the 2nd Canadian Field Ambulance.

Six weeks later he rejoined his unit but nearly three months after that he was suffering from shell shock and was sent to the Convalescent Depot for Shell Shock Cases at Le Treport on 6 October. He spent some time at base and rejoined his unit on 11 November. A few weeks later he was back in hospital and rejoined his unit on 6 January 1917. Towards the end of May he caught a severe bout of mumps and was sent to a general hospital and on recovering returned to base once more. By now he wore three wound stripes. On 29 August 1917 he was made an acting lance-corporal, and this rank was confirmed four months later, on 29 December. On 18 May the following year he was made a full corporal and on 25 September 1918 he was promoted to lance sergeant after winning his VC.

When Lance Sergeant Good returned on the *Olympic* he was met by his parents from Big River and the Mayor of Bathurst, a town close by, on 22 April 1919 and given a hero's welcome. Four days later he was discharged at Saint John, New Brunswick.

Much of his later life was spent in lumbering operations in the Bathhurst area and he later became a warden for game and fish, as well as acting as fire warden in the same district, a position he held for nearly twenty years.

Ten years after the war he travelled to London for a dinner hosted by the Prince of Wales and Admiral of the Fleet Earl Jellicoe, President of the National Executive Council of the British Legion, on 9 November 1929, in honour of all holders of the VC. The dinner took place in the Royal Gallery of the House of Lords. Dress was lounge suits with medals. As a souvenir of this famous dinner each winner of the VC was presented with a copy of the *Legion Book*, signed by the Prince of Wales, and copies of this book and signature have subsequently become highly collectable. They can be found in second-hand shops, but usually with the autograph removed.

Good was a modest man and made one of his rare public appearances in August 1962 when he laid the cornerstone of a new Legion building on St Peter Avenue, which was subsequently named after him. He was also made a life member of the Gloucester branch which was renamed 'Herman J. Good, V.C. Branch No. 18.' in September 1966. He was also a member of St George's Anglican Church.

On 13 April 1969 Good suffered a stroke and died five days later at home in Bathurst. His body was taken from the hospital to rest at Elhatton's Funeral Home, St George Street, Bathurst, before it was placed in the West Bathurst Protestant Receiving Vault until later in the spring. His funeral service took place in St George's Church with full military honours, being attended by the CO of the Black Watch, Royal Highland Regiment of Canada, Lt Col G.S. Morrison, together with six other officers, a firing party of one sergeant and fourteen other ranks. A band with pipes and drums was also in attendance and took part in the service. Good was laid to rest in St Alban's Cemetery, Sand Hill, Bathurst, where later a cairn was put up to his memory at the Salmon Beach Road entrance to the cemetery.

Good had three sons, Frank, Alfred and Milton (who died in childhood); he bequeathed his VC to Frank. His wife, Martha, predeceased him in 1941.

A second person from New Brunswick to win the VC was a great friend of Good's, Dr Milton F. Gregg; Good named one of his sons after him.

Good's decorations, including the VC, British War Medal (BWM), Victory Medal (VM) and Coronation Medals for 1937 and 1953, were acquired by the Canadian War Museum in December 2013.

J.B. CROAK

Hangard Wood, France, 8 August

Private John Croak, like Cpl H. Good VC, was a member of the 13th Battalion Quebec Regiment (Royal Highlanders of Canada) (3rd Brigade, 1st Division) and he also gained his VC at Hangard Wood. The village of Hangard is to the north of the Amiens–Roye road and, on the morning of 8 August, the Canadian Corps' front line ran roughly north to south through Hangard Wood West to a line to the west of Hangard village. The 1st Divisional boundary was between the wood and the village.

The 13th Battalion led the attack in a heavy fog at dawn, with the 16th Battalion to their right and the 14th to the left. A huge barrage was set down, which was the prelude to a charge across No-Man's-Land into the German positions. During the advance, accompanying tanks found themselves blinded as a result of the barrage. During the attack Pte Croak took on a German machine-gun nest with a supply of grenades, which resulted in seven Germans being captured. Although he was wounded in the arm during the action, Croak led the group of prisoners to company headquarters and, once there, was instructed to have his arm attended to. Ignoring this order he took on a second machine gun which was targeting the Canadian command post. Croak rallied some of his colleagues and together they charged the enemy position, managing to overcome it with the bayonet. During this second deed Croak was mortally wounded and died within a few minutes.

Croak became the first man born in Newfoundland (not then part of Canada) to win the VC; his citation was published in the *London Gazette* on 27 September 1918:

> For most conspicuous bravery in attack when, having become separated from his section, he encountered a machine gun nest, which he bombed and silenced, taking the gun and crew prisoners. Shortly afterwards he was severely wounded, but

> refused to desist. Having rejoined his platoon, a very strong point, containing several machine guns, was encountered. Private Croak, however, seeing an opportunity, dashed forward alone, and was almost immediately followed by the remainder of the platoon in a brilliant charge. He was the first to arrive at the trench line, into which he led his men, capturing three machine guns and bayoneting or capturing the entire garrison. The perseverance and valour of this gallant soldier who was again severely wounded and died of his wounds, were an inspiring example to all.

This official citation was added to by Capt. Harwood Steele in his book *The Canadians in France*:

> Private John Bernard Croak distinguished himself greatly. In the early stages of the attack he went hunting by himself, found a machine gun in action and bombed it with such fury that gun and crew became his captures. He then rejoined his platoon, although wounded, and went with it to the attack. Shortly afterwards, a machine gun nest in a trench was encountered. Private Croak led a magnificent charge under heavy fire, was first into the trench, and was largely instrumental in killing or capturing the whole garrison.

John Croak was buried in Hangard Wood British Cemetery, Plot 1, Row A, Grave 9 and it is very close to where he fell. The track leading to the cemetery is close to the No-Man's-Land crossed by the 1st Canadian Division on 8 August and between the two sections of Hangard Wood.

On 23 November 1918, Lieutenant-Governor Grant of Nova Scotia presented Croak's VC to his mother, Mrs James Croak, at a ceremony at Government House, Halifax, Nova Scotia. Mrs Croak, who was accompanied by her husband and daughter, was also awarded a second medal, that of the International Order of the Allied Mothers in Suffering.

At the conclusion of the proceedings, the Croak family were presented with two 'handsome and valuable chairs' by their son's former employers, Local No. 7. The opening address from Local No. 7 to Mr and Mrs James Croak began with the following sentence:

> We are here to-night to tender you the sincere and heartfelt congratulations of the officers and members of Local No. 7 A.M.W. of Nova Scotia, New Aberdeen on the high honour and distinction just conferred upon you in memory of the noble and valiant deeds of your brave boy, who made the supreme sacrifice in the service of his King and Country.

At Mr Croak's request a Mr McAulay expressed the thanks of the family for the gifts and tributes on their behalf. A musical interlude then followed and the function ended with the playing of the National Anthem. In addition to receiving a letter of condolence from the 13th Battalion Chaplain, Mrs Croak also received a letter of sympathy from Brig.-Gen. G.S. Tuxford of the 3rd Canadian Infantry Brigade.

John Croak was the son of James and Cecilia Croak and born in Little Bay, Green Bay, Newfoundland, on 26 January 1892 and baptised into the Roman Catholic Church the same day. His name in Newfoundland was spelt Croke but he preferred Croak as the spelling of his name. Some records suggest he was born on 18 May in the same year. His parents moved to Glace Bay in 1894 and John attended St John's High School, New Aberdeen, and later Aberdeen Public School in Glace Bay. He left school at the age of fourteen when he became a miner, working in Dominion No. 2 colliery at Glace Bay.

In 1915 Croak joined the Canadian Army in Sussex, New Brunswick, and was given the service number 445312. He volunteered for overseas service with the 55th Canadian Battalion, which left for Europe in November 1915. After training, Croak was transferred to the 13th Battalion Quebec Regiment (Royal Highlanders of Canada). He served in France and Flanders between 1917 and 1918, and saw action on the Somme, at Vimy, Arras, Hill 70 and Passchendaele.

After his death Croak was commemorated by Branch 125 of the Royal Canadian Legion in New Aberdeen being named after him but, owing to lack of funds, the branch was wound up. A chapter of the Imperial Order of the Daughters of the Empire was also named after him, but it too became defunct. After that a school was named after him in St John's, Newfoundland, only to be later closed down. Much later, though, Croak was commemorated with a plaque, hewn out of a block of Cape Breton rock to symbolise the 'unpolished virtue' of the character of Pte Croak of Glace Bay. This was placed in the Memorial Park in Glace Bay, which is also named after him. The site was formerly the grounds of the former Dominion No. 2 Colliery reservoir. The plaque was unveiled on Croak's centenary, on 18 May 1992, and the ceremony was preceded by a Memorial Mass at St John the Baptist Church in New Aberdeen. Croak's decorations were presented to the Army Museum at the Citadel, Halifax, by Bernard Croak, a nephew, on 19 August 1972. Apart from the VC, they incuded the BWM and the VM and are now on display at the Canadian War Museum in Ottawa.

A.E. GABY

Villers-Brettoneux, France, 8 August

On 8 August 1918, to the north of the Canadian Corps, the Australian Corps operated together with four divisions in the area of Villers-Brettoneux. A fifth Australian division entered the battle the following day. The 7th Australian Brigade of the 2nd Australian Division consisted of the 26th, 27th and the 28th (West Australian) Battalions which, together with the 5th Brigade, were involved in fighting to the north of the village of Marcelcave. According to an account based on the battalion diary published in the book *They Dared Mightily* the following occurred:

> Soon after midnight movement extraordinary commenced behind our lines, columns of troops in fighting order, ably led to the jumping-off tapes by guides, were seen everywhere, and everything pointed to this great attack – the biggest in history to the Australians ... Whilst on the tapes, the attacking troops were subjected to a very heavy barrage, but no casualties ... at 4 a.m. a very heavy mist fell ... covered all movement ... everything was in order and quietness reigned. At 4.23 our artillery put down a terrific barrage on the enemy lines and at 4.25 the infantry moved forward to the assault ... according to plan. In the attack many lively combats ensued and feats of great daring [were] performed by numerous members of this Battalion ...

The attack, which began on the eastern outskirts of Villers-Brettoneux, was to cover the southern section of the 2nd Australian Division between the 4th Canadian and 5th Australian Brigades. It moved in a slightly south-easterly direction preceded by twenty-three tanks, one of which broke down. The attackers were broken up by Allied 'friendly fire' and the Australian survivors moved in small groups towards the Marcelcave railway line. In having to keep up with an accurate barrage, and with the tanks in their first real battle outing, it was inevitable that there would be accidents.

As the Australians moved forward they came across several enemy machine gun posts which had to be dealt with. As the attackers neared a small wood called Card Copse, to the north of the railway line, they hit a wire entanglement. A gap in the wire was spotted and the attacking Australians made for it, only to be shot at from an enemy strongpoint 40yds beyond the position. The attack, which had not yet been supported by tanks in this part of the advance, came to a swift halt. Visibility was described as being misty, made more dense by the dust from a continous barrage. Sections could not even see those sections next to them. It was at this point that, after emptying his revolver into a German garrison, Lt Gaby (Acting Commander of D Company) persuaded a company of fifty Germans armed with four machine guns to surrender. It was Gaby who had found the gap in the wire in the first place. After this capture the tanks that should have preceded the attack finally showed up and any further resistance failed. Gaby, who would not have known of his VC, was killed three days later when carrying out a similar deed east of Framerville. His VC was gazetted on 30 October 1918:

> During the attack east of Villers-Brettoneux, near Amiens, on the morning of 8 August 1918, this officer led his company with great dash, being well in front. On reaching the wire in front of the enemy trench, strong opposition was encountered. The enemy were holding a strong point in force about 40 yards beyond the wire, and commanded the gap with four machine guns and rifles. The advance was at once checked. Lieut Gaby found another gap in the wire, and entirely by himself approached the strong point, while machine guns and rifles were still being fired from it. Running along the parapet, still alone, and at point-blank range, he emptied his revolver into the garrison, drove the crews from their guns, and compelled the surrender of 50 of the enemy, with four machine guns. He then quickly reorganised his men, and led them on to his final objective, which he captured and consoildated. On the morning of the 11 August 1918, during an attack east of Framerville, near Amiens, Lieut Gaby again led his company with great dash to the objective. The enemy brought heavy rifle and machine gun fire to bear upon the line, but in

the face of this heavy fire Lieut Gaby walked along his line of posts, encouraging his men to quickly consolidate the line. While engaged on this duty he was killed by an enemy sniper.

Alfred Edward Gaby was born in Springfield, near Ringarmma, Tasmania, on 25 January 1892, the seventh son of Alfred and Adelaide (*née* Whiteway).

He was educated at Scottsdale and after leaving school worked on the family farm. He served for three years with the militia in the 12th Infantry Regiment (Launceston Regiment) and two of his elder brothers served in the Boer war.

In 1914 Gaby left Tasmania and went to Katanning in Western Australia where he worked as a labourer until he enlisted at Blackboy Hill Camp on 6 January 1916 as a private with the 28th Battalion (Western Australia) AIF where he trained at Blackboy Hill Camp. He was posted to the 10th reinforcements to the 28th Battalion and sailed on a troopship to France, and joined his battalion on 6 August. He became a lance corporal and then corporal, progressing rapidly through the ranks until he was commissioned on 7 April 1917. On 26 September he was promoted to lieutenant and during a gas attack in October was wounded. His battalion was then part of the 7th Brigade of the 2nd Division.

Three days after the action in which he won his VC Gaby was killed and was buried in Plot V, Row E, Grave 14 in Heath Cemetery, Harbonnières, close to the busy Amiens–St Quentin road. He is buried in the same cemetery as Pte Robert Beatham who gained a posthumous VC on 9 August.

Alfred Gaby Senior was presented with his late son's VC on 19 July 1919 by the Governor in Launceston, Tasmania and it was later given to Reginald, another son. A tablet to his memory was unveiled in Katanning, Perth, in December 1920. In addition, a portrait of him was unveiled in the Scottsdale HQ of the Returned Soldiers Sub-Branch. Gaby's decorations, including the VC, BWM and VM are owned by the Tasmanian Museum and Art Gallery in Hobart. He is commemorated at Canberra in the Australian War Memorial. In addition his name is one of ninety-six Australian VCs won in the Great War, commemorated in Victoria Cross Park Memorial in Canberra and dedicated in July 2000, 100 years after Australia received its first VC. The same ninety-six names are also commemorated in the Victoria Cross Memorial in the Queen Victoria Building in Sydney.

H.G.B. Miner

Démuin, east of Hangard, France, 8 August

Corporal Harry Miner won a posthumous VC at Démuin, to the east of Hangard on 8 August 1918 when he took on enemy machine gun and bombing posts single-handed, despite being wounded. He was a member of the 58th Battalion (2nd Central Ontario Regiment, 9th Brigade, 3rd Canadian Division). The 9th Brigade also included the 43rd, 52nd and 116th Battalions. The 43rd was responsible for capturing Rifle Wood, to the west of the Démuin–Moreuil road, which they duly accomplished by 7.30 a.m. The 116th attacked Hamon Wood from the north and Miner's battalion, which had also been involved in the fighting at Rifle Wood, pushed on to Démuin and had cleared the hamlet of Courcelles, north-east of Démuin, by 7.05 a.m. It was during this fighting that Miner was severely wounded in the head, left arm and face. He later died from these wounds and was awarded a posthumous VC, which was gazetted on 26 October 1918 and presented to his parents by His Excellency, the Duke of Devonshire, Governor-General of Canada. The citation was as follows:

> For most conspicous bravery and devotion to duty in attack, when, despite severe wounds, he refused to withdraw. He rushed an enemy machine gun post single-handed, killed the entire crew and turned the gun on the enemy. Later, with two others, he attacked another enemy machine gun post, and succeded in putting the gun out of action. Corpl. Miner then rushed single-handed an enemy bombing post, bayoneting two of the garrison and putting the remainder to flight. He was mortally wounded in the performance of this gallant deed.

Miner was buried at Crouy British Cemetery, 10 miles north-west of Amiens, Plot V. Row B. Grave 11. The commanding officer of the 58th Battalion, Maj. R.L. Smythe, wrote a letter of sympathy to his parents, as did several of the officers in his unit.

Harry Garnet Miner, the son of John and Orphra Miner, was born on 24 June 1891 in Cedar Springs in Ontario. He attended school at Selton and continued his schooling in Highgate School in Oxford Township, Ontario. After leaving school he went into farming and at some point lived in Ohio and Detroit in the USA. He enlisted in the Canadian Army on 1 December 1915 and was posted to the 142nd Battalion, being promoted to lance corporal on 1 October 1916. He arrived in Britain on 25 October when he became a member of the 161st (Huron) Battalion and also asked for his rank to be altered to private, acting lance corporal, in order that he could join the 58th Battalion, 2nd Central Ontario Regiment. He then trained for six weeks before transferring to the 58th Battalion in France in November 1916. He was made a full corporal on 1 January 1918. As a lance corporal he had won the French Croix de Guerre for deeds carried out in the St Emile sector between Hazebrouck and Lens in 1917.

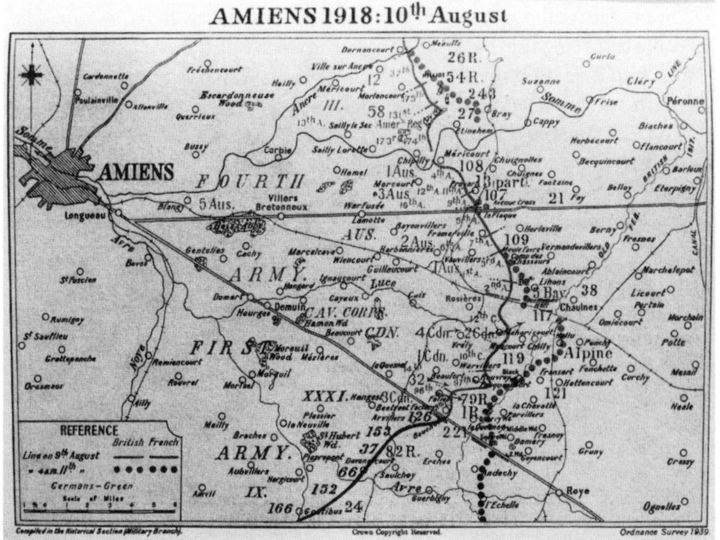

His citation reads as follows: 'During the night of 30–31 December 1917, being in charge of a wiring party, he did excellent work, by his example and energy, in keeping his men together for seven hours in spite of enemy machine guns which were firing on his position.' On 22 September 1963 a historical plaque to his memory was unveiled in Cedar Springs, Miner's birthplace. This plaque was one of several which commemorate the Canadian holders of the VC. The idea was instigated by the provincial Department of Travel and Publicity who acted on the expertise and advice supplied by the Archeological and Historic Sites Board of Ontario.

This particular ceremony was organised and sponsored by the local branch of the Royal Canadian Legion. The legion invited various local dignitaries to the unveiling, which included a legion drum head service. The plaque itself was unveiled by Mr Ross Miner, a brother of Cpl Harry Miner. It was dedicated by the Revd A. Meecham of Blenheim United Church, Ontario.There is also a plaque to Miner's memory in the United Church in Cedar Springs.The branch 185 of the Royal Canadian Legion in Blenheim was also named after him.

Harry Miner's decorations, including the VC, BWM, VM and Croix de Guerre, are kept in the Huron County Museum, Goderich.

J. Brillant

Near Wiencourt, France, 9 August

Between 8 August 1918, the first day of the Battle of Amiens, and 11 August, no fewer than eleven men gained the VC, of whom eight were serving with Canadian Forces. One of the Canadians, who in fact was a French Canadian, was Lieutenant Jean Brillant of the 22nd Canadian Infantry Battalion (5th Brigade, 2nd Canadian Division). On 8 August his battalion was operating south-east of Villers Bretonneux, engaged in mopping-up operations to the west of the village of Wiencourt-L'Équipée, during which he rushed an enemy machine-gun post which was holding up the left flank of his company. He killed two machine gunners but in doing so was injured in his left arm.

At 10 a.m. the following day his battalion moved from Wiencourt and, supported by artillery, proceeded in a south-easterly direction towards the village of Caix and took over enemy positions after very arduous fighting in the village of Vrély to the south of Rosières-en-Santerre. The enemy had entrenched machine gun positions close to the village of Vrély and any advance over open ground would prove to be very costly. Companies were organised into groups which used the cover of ditches and sunken roads. By 3.15 p.m. the leading groups had managed to progress through Vrély and beyond, and proceeded to consolidate 500yds east of Méharicourt, which they reached by 5.30 p.m. By then they were too far ahead and had to wait for their neighbours to catch up, which they did two hours later. Although the battalion had been successful it came at a very high cost in casualties of six officers and 176 other ranks either killed, wounded or missing.

During the attack on Vrély, athough Brillant was already wounded, he led a group of two platoons using bombs and grenades in a skirmish which led to the capture of no fewer than fifteen machine guns together with 150 prisoners. During this action he was wounded again, this time in the head, yet still managed to organise a party to capture an enemy four-inch gun which was engaging the battalion over open sights. It was for this bravery during this fighting, in addition to his work the previous day, that Lt Jean Brillant won his VC. In two days of hard fighting he had been wounded three times but tragically succumbed to his injuries on 10 August. His citation was published in the *London Gazette* of 27 September 1918:

> For most conspicuous bravery and outstanding devotion to duty when in charge of a company which he led in attack during two days with absolute fearlessness and extraordinary ability and initiative, the extent of the advance being twelve miles. On the first day of operations, shortly after the attack began, his company's left flank was held up by an enemy machine gun. Lieut. Brillant rushed and captured the machine gun, personally killing two of the enemy crew. While doing this he was wounded, but refused to leave his command. Later on the same day his company was held up by heavy machine gun fire. He reconnoitred the ground personally, organised a party of two platoons, and rushed straight for the machine gun nest. Here 150 enemy and fifteen machine guns were captured, Lieut. Brillant personally killing five of the enemy, and being wounded a second time. He had this wound dressed immediately, and again refused to leave his company. Subsequently this gallant officer detected a field-gun firing on his men over open sights. He immediately organised and led a 'rushing' party towards the gun. After progressing about 600 yards he was again seriously wounded. In spite of this third wound he continued to advance for some 200 yards more, when he fell unconscious from exhaustion and loss of blood. Lieut. Brillant's wonderful example throughout the day inspired his men with an enthusiasm and dash which largely contributed towards the success of the operations.

Brillant's last words were said to have been: 'I am through. Take charge of the company because I know I won't be here long.' He died of his wounds and loss of blood on 10 August and was buried in Villers-Bretonneux Military Cemetery, Plot VIa, Row B, Grave 20, to the left of the Cross of Sacrifice. His posthumous VC was presented to his father in Rimouski, Quebec, on 16 December 1918 by His Excellency The Duke of Devonshire, Governor-General of Canada.

Jean-Baptiste-Arthur Brillant, a French-Canadian, was born of a military family, in Assametquaghan, Matapadia Co., Quebec, on 15 March 1890. His father was Joseph, a railway maintenance worker and his mother Rose-de-Lima Raiche Brillant. He studied at St Joseph University, Memramcook, New Brunswick, and later at the Seminaire de Rimouski (1904–05). He became a railway telephone operator. In 1903 he volunteered to serve in 89th (Temiscouata & Rimouski) Regiment (which in 1920 was renamed les Fusiliers du St Laurent) and claimed later to have been a member for thirteen years, becoming a lieutenant. He quit his job on 20 March 1916 when he applied to join the CEF. After six months' training at Valcartier he attested at the camp on 20 September and sailed for Liverpool three days later on board SS *Lapland*. When he attested, his address was Bic. Co., Rimouski, Quebec.

Arriving in England on 6 October he became a member of the 69th Infantry Battalion on the 9th and left for France from the same port on the 29th having become a member of the the only French-Canadian Infantry Unit serving in the field at that time, the 22nd Battalion, Quebec Regiment (Canadian Français), CEF who were part of the 2nd Division. On arrival in France he proceeded to his new battalion at Bully-Grenay.

In 1917, between 9 and 14 April, Brillant took part in the fight for Vimy Ridge and subseqently spent a few days in hospital with trench fever. Three months later he was wounded briefly and became a patient in the Duchess of Westminster Hospital in Le Touquet on 17 July and was transferred to 51st General Hospital in Etaples the following day. After two months he was discharged to base on 18 September.

Brillant won the MC for his work during the night of 27–28 May in the vicinity of Boiry-Besqerelle, 110 miles north of Paris when he was called to assist in the silencing of an enemy outpost defended by two machine guns and fifty men. During the attack he spied a small of group of five Germans making their escape. He managed to despatch four of them and captured a fifth and took him back to battalion headquarters for interrogation. During the fighting Brillant was wounded. On 6 July he was able to go to Paris for a week for what was to be his last leave. Four weeks later he was mortally wounded on 9 August and died of wounds the following day.

His posthumous MC was gazetted on 16 September, eleven days prior to his VC. Apart from these two decorations, his medals included the BWM, VM and King George Vth Coronation Medal of 1911. They became the property of his regiment and were displayed at the Royal 22 Regiment Museum at Citadel, Quebec, together with a Dead Man's Penny and other related items to his life. In addition, his name was the first to be listed on the Rimouski War Memorial, and a park in Montreal was named after him. Streets are also named after him in Rimouski and Montreal, and his name was also used by the Royal Canadian Legion Branch in Quebec City. Unusally his name has also been used for a retirement home group.

R.M. Beatham

Rosières, France, 9 August

On 8 August 1918, the first day of the Franco-British summer of 1918 offensive, four Victoria Crosses were won by members of either the Canadian or Australian Armies. The Dominion troops had to fight in order to overcome well-sited and tenaciously defended German machine-gun posts. Time after time this was what had to be done. Although the first day of the offensive had begun very successfully for the Allies, the second day was not well planned or coordinated and, in the words of the Australian historian C.E.W. Bean, 'will probably furnish a classic example of how not to follow up a great attack'.

The advance continued with the 1st and 2nd Australian Divisions attempting to wrest the high ground from the enemy to the west of Chaulnes. It was the Canadian and French Armies accompanied by cavalry who were to create a southern flank for the Australians. The 7th and 8th Australian Battalions moved off from close to Harbonnières under heavy German artillery fire from Lihons to the south-east. Lihons had a protective hill in its north-west corner. During the advance, tanks accompanying the Australian move forward were gradually knocked out, but the 8th (Victoria) Battalion managed to push on uphill towards Lihons – it was during this fighting that Pte Robert Beatham of the 8th Battalion (2nd Brigade 1st Division) carried out his first deed of the day which led to him winning a VC. His action took place at the village of Rosières where his battalion was south of the Lihons road and the commander of its left company, Capt. A.G. Campbell, worked his way forward until they were in a position to enfilade the enemy positions. It was probably at this time that Pte Beatham, accompanied by Pte W.G. Nottingham, bombed and captured the crews of four machine guns which were holding up the advance. Nottingham also managed to turn two of the captured guns on the enemy. Later in the day the 8th Battalion had got too far forward and was expecting to be counter-attacked at any moment. However, Australian gunners had galloped up to some new positions near Vauvillers to the north, and the sight of the guns encouraged the enemy to withdraw from the crest. Even so there were still strong pockets of resistance covering enemy machine-gun positions and it was during this fighting that Beatham continued rushing enemy strongpoints, but this time lost his life in doing so. The historian C.E.W. Bean concluded that the attacking Victorians were as yet unaware that they had taken on a powerful reinforcement, in that they had been pushing back remnants of the German 109th Division.

Beatham's posthumous VC was gazetted on 14 December 1918 as follows:

> For most conspicuous bravery and self-sacrifice during the attack north of Rosières, east of Amiens on 9 August 1918. When the advance was held up by heavy machine gun fire, Private Beatham dashed forward, and, assisted by one man, bombed and fought the crews of four enemy machine guns, killing 10 of them and capturing 10 others, thus facilitating the advance and saving many casualties. When the final objective was reached, although previously wounded, he again dashed forward and bombed a machine gun, being riddled with bullets and killed in doing so. The valour displayed by this gallant soldier inspired all ranks in a wonderful manner.

The officer commanding A Company of the 8th Battalion AIF, wrote to a Mr J. Hounsby on 12 September 1918 about the circumstances of Beatham winning the VC and being mortally wounded:

> Yes, it is quite true, he was killed in action on Aug. the 11th. I was with him at the time.
>
> He was a hero, and if ever a V.C. was earned, one was earned by him that day. First our advance was held up by ten enemy Machine Guns but this did not deter him, he worked up an old communication trench & knocked the M.G.'s out, killing & taking prisoners all the crews of same.
>
> Later, the enemy were in the same trench as us, we were both bombing our way along the trench when the enemy jumped out of the trench & began shooting at us from the top. BEATHAM jumped up & killed them, but as he was getting back into the trench, he was sniped through the head. Death was instantaneous.

We have recommended him very strongly from here & if these decorations [are] fairly awarded he is certainly to get the V.C.

It must be an awful blow to his people & I assure you it was a terrible blow to his comrades. Any praise that I could give would not be high enough for his magnificence, tenacity and courage.

The whole of the Battalion unite with me in expressing the very deepest sympathy for the Dear relatives of this magnificent soldier in their very sad bereavement.

Believe me to be
ys in very deepest sympathy
R.W. Dowling, Lieut.,
'A' Coy., 8th Batt. A.I.F. France

Beatham's body was buried in Heath Cemetery, Harbonnières, close to the main road in Plot VII, Row J, Grave 13. In the same cemetery is the grave of Lt Alfred Gaby who won the VC on 8 August. Beatham's VC was presented to his widowed mother in the Ballroom of Buckingham Palace on 8 March 1919.

Robert Matthew Beatham, the son of John and Eléabeth (*née* Allison) was born in Glassonby, an East Fellside village near Penrith, Cumberland, on 16 June 1894, although some accounts state that his date of birth was 11 August. He came from a large family of nine boys, and his father worked as a foreman for a paper manufacturer. Robert attended Maughanby Church of England School, and at the age of 14 left to work on a local farm before emigrating to Australia which he did with one of his brothers in 1913. Robert then worked as a labourer in Geelong, Victoria.

At the age of 20 Beatham enlisted in the Australian Army on 8 January 1915 and was allocated the service number of 2742. He was posted to the 8th Reinforcements for the 8th Victorian Battalion. He arrived in Suez in October and in November was officially taken on the strength of the battalion and served briefly in Gallipoli in December. He later sailed with them to France. In August he was wounded close to Pozières and was evacuated for six weeks. He was again wounded during the Third Battle of Ypres in October 1917 and returned to England to recover. His time in England included spending a short time in Glassonby during November.

Robert was the third of seven sons who served in the forces to die within a period of five months. Another brother, Walter Beatham, who emigrated with Robert to Australia, was taken prisoner in August 1916 after service in Gallipoli, later dying in 1918. A second brother, John Wilfred, died in the Salonika campaign.

Robert Beatham is commemorated on the war memorial in Glassonby, Cumbria, and by a brass plaque at Addingham-with-Gamblesby Church, in Yorkshire. The plaque records the names of men who died from that parish, and includes the three Beatham brothers from the smaller parish of Glassonby. The three former Sunday School boys are also listed on a small brass plaque on the wall of a Wesleyan Chapel in Glassonby. His portrait used to be on display at his former school at Maughanby.

Beatham is also commemorated at Canberra on the Australian War Memorial. His name is also one of ninety-six Australian VCs won in the First World War, commemorated in Victoria Cross Park Memorial in Canberra. The same ninety-six names are also commemorated in the Victoria Cross Memorial in the Queen Victoria Building in Sydney.

Beatham's VC was sold by the Beatham family in 1967 by J.B. Hayward for £700 and is at present in private hands, having been sold again in March 1999 for £73,000 at Spink's, in Melbourne. The VC is on loan to Queensland Museum, South Bank, Brisbane and the First World War trio of the 1914–15 Star, BWM and VM are kept privately.

J.E. Tait

Beaucourt Wood, France, 8–11 August

Lieutenant James Tait of the 78th Battalion (Winnipeg Grenadiers) (12th Brigade 4th Canadian Division) won his VC over a period of three days between 8 and 11 August. By late afternoon of 8 August 1918 the Canadian advance to the south-east of Amiens had reached Beaucourt, near Le Quesnel and north of the road to Roye. To the south of Beaucourt Wood the landscape was very open and devoid of cover. Because of this the Canadians lost heavily from machine-gun fire coming from the direction of Fresnoy-en-Chaussée as well as the northern edge of Le Quesnel. As a result any idea of a frontal attack was ruled out. The right flank of the 12th Brigade in particular was strongly attacked by fire coming from Beaucourt Wood and it left a company from each of the the 38th and 78th Battalions in order to deal with it. The 78th Battalion took on the enemy machine guns at the north end of the wood and with artillery and tank support overcame them when they then formed a defensive flank. It was during this action that Lt Tait, in command of C Company, won his VC when he knocked out an enemy machine-gun post single-handed. In addition, his men captured a dozen machine guns and twenty prisoners. The 72nd Battalion, despite heavy rifle and machine-gun fire, succeeded in passing through the lines of the 78th Battalion to reach its final objective at about 6.15 p.m., a dozen miles from its starting point.

The rest of the 12th Brigade dealt successfully with enemy resistance and reached the southern edge of the wood to the south of Caix at about 4.45 p.m. In this section of the battlefield the day had been a most successful one, with considerable territorial gains and the capture of 13,000 prisoners.

Lieutenant Tait's citation was gazetted on 27 September 1918 as follows:

> For most conspicuous bravery and initiative in attack. The advance having been checked by intense machine gun fire, Lieut. Tait rallied

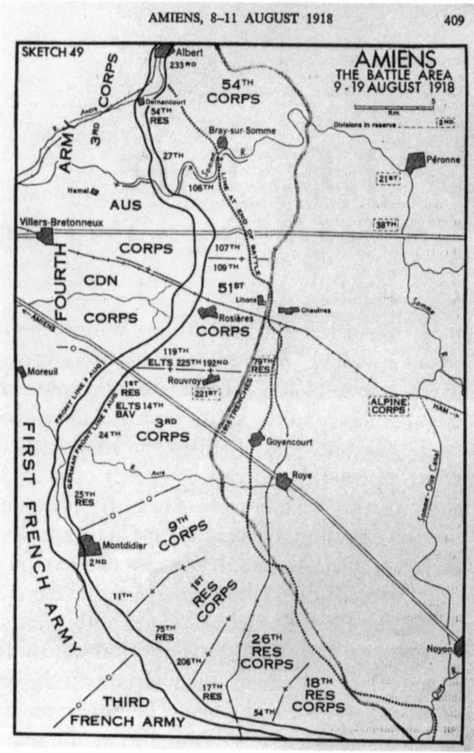

his company and led it forward with consummate skill and dash under a hail of bullets. A concealed machine gun however, continued to cause many casualties. Taking a rifle and bayonet, Lieut. Tait dashed forward alone, and killed the enemy gunner. Inspired by his example, his men rushed the position, capturing twelve machine guns and twenty prisoners. His valorous action cleared the way for his battalion to advance. Later, when the enemy counter-attacked our positions under intense artillery bombardment, this gallant officer displayed outstanding courage and leadership, and, though mortally wounded by a shell, continued to direct and aid his men until his death.

Tait died in action at Hallu on 11 August 1918 and was probably first buried in the village prior to being moved to Fouquescourt British

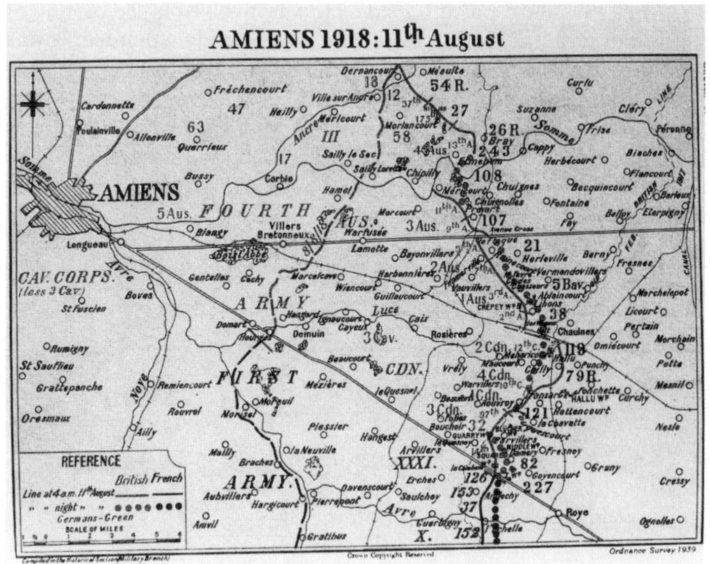

Cemetery where he is believed to be buried. He has a headstone which is number eight of a section of similar casualties but gives his age as 31 and not 32. The village of Fouquescourt is 16 miles south of Albert, to the south-west of Hallu, and the cemetery is just outside the village which was captured by the Canadian Corps in August 1918. Tait's VC was presented to his widow Jessie by His Excellency the Lieutenant Governor of Manitoba.

James Edward Tait was the son of James Bryden and Mary (*née* Johnstone) and born in Greenbrae, Dumfries, Scotland on 27 May 1886, although some accounts say his birthplace was Kirkcudbrightshire. He attended Laurieknowe School, Maxwelltown, and later Dumfries Academy. He later emigrated to Canada where he trained as a surveyor. In 1915 he joined the 100th Battalion (Winnipeg Grenadiers) and arrived in England in 1916. In September he became a member of the 78th Battalion in France. Before gaining his posthumous VC he also won the MC when taking part in the capture of Vimy Ridge in April 1917, and he published an article called 'The Vimy Ridge' on 28 July

1917 in a periodical called *Canada*. He was involved in the capture of a German post and during the action was severely wounded. It was probably when he was convalescing in England that he married Jessie Spiers from California.

His decorations, consisting of the VC, MC, BWM and VM, are in the collection of the Glenbow Museum, Calgary, Alberta and he is commemorated on the Laurieknowe School War Memorial and on the Maxwelltown Memorial in Scotland.

A.P. BRERETON

Hatchet Wood, France, 9 August

On 9 August, north of the Amiens–Roye road, the 2nd Canadian Brigade (1st Division) advanced against the villages of Warvillers and Vrély across a flat and open landscape covered with growing corn. After the euphoria of the great Allied advance the day before, the 8th Canadian Battalion (Winnipeg Rifles), Manitoba Regiment (2nd Brigade, 1st Division), unsupported by either artillery or tanks, neverthless played a full role in coping with enemy machine-gun nests at Hatchet Wood and adjacent copses to the north-west of the village of Warvillers to which it provided the key. To their right was the 5th Battalion which had flat ground covered with crops to pass through, which they did in short rushes.

Although the enemy was waiting for them and hidden in woods and copses, the Canadians, after hard fighting, still managed to occupy Hatchet Wood before dusk and then the battalion struck forward to the north of Warvillers. During this fighting Cpl Alex Brereton of the 8th Battalion gained a VC as a result of dealing with one of the machine-gun positions single-handed. The citation for his VC was gazetted on 27 September 1918 and told the story as follows:

> For most conspicuous bravery during an attack, when a line of hostile machine guns opened fire suddenly on his platoon, which was in an exposed position and no cover available. This gallant N.C.O. at once appreciated the critical situation, and realised unless something was done at once his platoon would be annihilated. On his own initiative, without a moment's delay and alone, he sprang forward and reached one of the hostile machine

> gun posts, where he shot the man operating the machine gun and bayoneted the next one who attempted to operate it, whereupon nine others surrendered to him. Corpl. Brereton's action was a splendid example of resource and bravery, and not only undoubtably saved many of his comrades' lives, but also inspired his platoon to charge and capture the five remaining posts.

Brereton was decorated by the King at Buckingham Palace on 24 October 1918 together with Sergeant Coppins of the same battalion who won his VC in the same action. A third Canadian, Sgt R.L. Zengel of the neighboring 5th Battalion, also won the VC.

Alexander Picton Brereton was born in Oak River, Alexander, Manitoba, on 13 November 1892, the son of a farmer Cloudesley Picton Brereton and his wife Annie Frazer (*née* Black). Alexander was one of six children; four sons and two daughters and went to school in Oak River. After leaving school he worked on a farm.

On 31 January 1916 Brereton enlisted in the Canadian Army, giving his occupation as barber. He was allocated the service number of 830651. He left for England in September and arrived in France in January 1917 where he joined the 8th Battalion Manitoba Regiment (2nd Brigade, 1st Canadian Division), with whom he remained for twenty-two months.

At the end of the war he returned to Canada and was welcomed home by his parents and other members of his family, as well as Lt Col A.W. Morley and other officers from the 144th Battalion. During his stay he spent a few days with friends before returning home to a hero's welcome in the town of Violadale, Manitoba. He was discharged from the Canadian Army in 1919 and returned to farming, eventually acquiring 640 acres of farmland in the Elnora district of Alberta, which is where he made his home. On 17 June 1925 he married Mary Isabel McPhee and the couple had three children, one son and two daughters. Four years later Brereton attended the November 1929 VC Dinner in the House of Lords.

During the visit of the recently crowned King George VI and Queen Elizabeth to Canada in 1939, Brereton was presented to them in Edmonton on 2 June. Three months later the Second World War broke out when when he rejoined the army serving as a company quartermaster sergeant at an army training camp in Red Deer, Alberta. After he was discharged in 1944 he ran a butcher's shop at Bashan for a short period and later a general store at Newbanan, until he returned to his farm at Elnora in early 1946. He was then responsible for only a small section of the family farm and his son Mac was responsible for the rest. The farm boasted a fine herd of Aberdeen Angus cattle.

In June 1956 Brereton attended the Hyde Park VC/GC Review, in London. He later moved to Fort St John in British Columbia.

Brereton's wife predeceased him by four years, dying in 1972, and Alex himself died in the Colonel Belcher Hospital Calgary, on 11 June 1976. His funeral took place at Knox United Church, Three Hills, four days later. He was buried in Elnora Cemetery.

Alex Brereton was survived by his son, Mac, of Three Hills and his two daughters, Mrs Betty McPhee of Edmonton and Mrs Gwen Wik of Fort St John, British Columbia. After his death the only Alberta man left who had won the VC in the First World War was Brig. F.M.W. Harvey. Alberta had produced no fewer than eighteen VC winners during the war.

Brereton's decorations are on display in the Lord Ashcroft Gallery in the IWM, London. Apart from the VC, they include the BWM, VM, Canadian Volunteer service Medal (1939–45), War Medal 1939–45 and Coronation Medals for 1937 and 1953. He is also commemorated at Elnora with a Royal Canadian Legion Post named after him.

F.G. Coppins

Hatchet Wood, France, 9 August

On 9 August 1918 Cpl Frederick Coppins gained the VC on the same day as his colleague Cpl Alex Brereton. Both men were members of the 8th Canadian Battalion (Winnipeg Rifles), Manitoba Regiment (2nd Brigade, 1st Division). As the battalion moved forward over the flat agricultural plain in the direction of Warvillers, the enemy was waiting for them and held its fire to the last moment. The battalion faced serious resistance from the enemy when they began to fire out of Hatchet Wood and adjoining copses to the north. The Manitoba Battalion found itself in a precarious position against an overwhelming German force, but far from shirking danger, Corporals Coppins and Brereton courted it and became the means of saving many lives and of materially helping achieve military objectives. Coppins' citation was published on 27 September 1918 as follows:

> For most conspicuous bravery and devotion to duty when during an attack his platoon came unexpectedly under fire of numerous machine guns. It was not possible to advance or retire, and no cover was available. It became apparent that the platoon would be annihilated unless the enemy machine-guns were silenced immediately. Corpl. Coppins, without hesitation and on his own initiative, called on four men to follow him, and leaped forward in the face of intense machine gun fire. With his comrades he rushed straight for the machine guns. The four men with him were killed and Corpl. Coppins wounded. Despite his wounds, he reached the hostile machine guns alone, killed the operator of the first gun and three of the crew, and made prisoners of four others, who

> surrendered. Corpl. Coppins by this act of outstanding valour, was the means of saving many lives of the men of this platoon, and enabled the advance to be continued. Despite his wound, this gallant N.C.O. continued with his platoon to the final objective, and only left the line when it had been made secure and when ordered to do so.

The 117 graves provide the mournful evidence of the losses from the 8th Manitoba Battalion in the nearby Manitoba Cemetery, revealing the high human cost paid for by the Canadians in order to reach their objectives on 9 August 1918.

Together with Cpl Brereton, Cpl Coppins was decorated in the Ballroom of Buckingham Palace on 24 October 1918 when both men were then wearing their sergeant's stripes.

Frederick George Coppins was born in London on 25 October 1889 and spent four years with the Royal West Kents before emigrating to Canada where he joined the 19th Aberta Dragoons. He then enlisted in Valcartier Camp, Quebec, on 23 September 1914 and his height was 5ft 6in. He was allocated the service number of 1987 and served in France with the 8th Manitoba Regiment and was promoted to corporal and then sergeant.

Between the wars he was involved in a collision between police and strikers in Winnipeg, when serving as a special constable, when he was dragged off his horse and severely injured.

He later lived in California and worked for the Pacific Gas and Electric Company in Oakland as a construction foreman. At the end of 1942, during the Second World War, he enlisted in Angel's Camp in Averas. Co., California, but we have no details of what role he played.

At the age of 73 Frederick Coppins died on 30 March 1963 in the US Administration Hospital in Livermore, California. Three days later his funeral took place in Oakland and his ashes are kept in the Chapel of the Chimes Crematorium, where his name is listed on a vault. His VC was originally presented to the Valour Road Branch of the Royal Canadian Legion, Winnipeg, on 26 September 1965. It had, though, been bequeathed to the 8th Battalion Association, and is now in the collection of the Royal Winnipeg Rifles (Little Black Devils) Museum. His other decorations were the BWM, VM and Coronation Medals for 1937 and 1953.

R.L. ZENGEL

Near Warvillers, France, 9 August

On 9 August 1918 the 2nd Canadian Brigade of the 1st Canadian Division attacked over open farmland in its advance against the villages of Vrély and Warvillers. Serious opposition came from hidden German machine-gun nests and Sgt Raphael Zengel gained a VC to the east of Warvillers, when serving with the 5th Battalion (Saskatchewan Regiment). According to the *Official History*:

> The 5th Battalion reached the enemy's front line, capturing twenty machine guns, and then halted for half an hour for the 8th Battalion to come up. An attempt by a squadron of the 16th Lancers (3rd Cavalry Brigade) to charge and round up a party of German machine gunners holding out in a copse after the Canadian infantry has passed by, completely failed. When the advance was continued Warvillers village and wood were captured about 4.30 p.m. though at the cost of heavy casualties.

Zengel was the third member of the CEF to win the coveted medal on the same day in the area of Warvillers and Beaufort. He won the decorations to the east of Warvillers, in what was known as 'the triangle', which consisted of an area of land flanked by three roads to the south-west of the village. At first the advance had been pretty rapid, but later Zengel's platoon was pinned down by a machine-gun nest in a wheatfield. Zengel then decided to go it alone and crawled along a gully, which led him indirectly to a position from which he was able to observe a party of the enemy retreating towards a white château. At the same time he found himself close to the enemy machine-gun nest which had been causing all the trouble. After firing from the hip and killing the officer, Zengel managed to shoot two members of the gun crew; the remaining man rushed at him, but Zengel disposed of him with his bayonet. After this success Zengel waved his platoon on and they continued the advance. By late afternoon the assaulting 2nd Brigade had reached ground near the Méharicourt–Rouvroy road.

At the end of the action only sixteen men were left out of the original thirty-one.

The citation of Zengel's VC was gazetted on 27 September 1918 as follows:

> For most conspicuous bravery and devotion to duty when protecting the battalion right flank. He was leading his platoon gallantly forward to the attack, but had not gone far when he realised that a gap had occurred on his flank, and that an enemy machine gun was firing at close range into the advancing line. Grasping the situation, he rushed forward some 200 yards ahead of the platoon, tackled the machine gun emplacement, killed the officer and operator of the gun, and dispersed the crew. By his boldness and prompt action he undoubtably saved the lives of many of his comrades. Later, when the battalion was held up by very heavy machine gun fire, he displayed much tactical skill and directed his fire with destructive results. Shortly afterwards he was rendered unconscious for a few minutes by an enemy shell, but on recovering consciousness he at once continued to direct harassing fire on the enemy. Sergt. Zengel's work throughout the attack was excellent, and his utter disregard for personal safety, and the confidence he inspired in all ranks, greatly assisted in bringing the attack to a successful end.

Zengel was decorated at Buckingham Palace on 13 December 1918.

Raphael (Ray) Louis Zengel was born in Faribault, Minnesota, USA on 11 November 1894. At some point he and his mother moved to a homestead near Plunkett in Saskatchewan, and when war broke out he was working on a farm near Virden in Manitoba. In December 1914, as an American citizen he enlisted in the 45th Battalion and was provided with the service number of 424252. When he reached France after training he transferred to the 5th Battalion and took part in several trench raids, including one at Passchendaele where he probably won his MM in November 1917, which was gazetted on 13 March 1918.

After the war he worked for a short time as a fireman in Calgary before moving to Rocky Mountain House, where he took up farming again. In November 1929 he travelled to London for the VC dinner at the House of Lords, but this visit appears to be the only time that he visited London after the war.

During the Second World War Zengel held the rank of sergeant-major at Suffield Experimental Grounds, Alberta. He remained there throughout the war in charge of military components which were attached to civilian scientific groups involved in wartime experiments. In 1966 he married a second time, a lady called Myrtle.

The Royal Canadian Legion allocated numbers to the various areas covered by their branches and in 1968 Zengel's local Branch No. 8 was renamed as a tribute to him, becoming the R.L. Zengel VC Wing of the Alberta command. After he moved and arrived in the Legion's District 69 he became a member of Parksville Branch No. 49 and in 1975 was made an honorary president.

Two years later Raphael Zengel died in Nanaimo Regional Hospital, Victoria Island, British Columbia, on 27 February 1977 and was buried at Pine Cemetery, Rocky Mountain House, Alberta. Later a commemorative plaque to his memory was set up outside the Pine Cemetery. There is also a plaque in his homestead at Rocky Mountain House in memory of him and a mountain is named after him in Jasper National Park, Alberta.

His decorations, apart from the VC and MM, include the BWM, VM, Canada Volunteer Service Medals (1939–45) and Centenary Medals (1967) and they are held in the Royal Canadian Legion Post, Rocky Mountain House.

T.J. Harris

West of Morlancourt, France, 9 August

On the night of 8–9 August 1918 the British 37th Brigade (12th Division) formed up west of Morlancourt, south-west of Albert, ready to move through the lines of 35 Brigade and advance to the Old Outer Amiens Outer Defence Line, the divisional objective. Start-time was set at 4.30 a.m., but at midnight the time was put back to 5.30 p.m., but unfortunately this information didn't reach brigade headquarters until after battalions had begun to move off. By 6.20 a.m. the 6th Royal West Kents were to be north-west of Morlancourt villages. The 1st Cambridgeshires together with three tanks were then to carry out mopping up duties. The news of the postponement did finally reached the battalions and the start of the operation was duly begun at 5.30 p.m., twelve hours later. Despite the postponement it was carried out according to plan although with hindsight the advance would have been easier if it had taken place during the small hours.

The advance was accompanied by a creeping barrage and three tanks but the 6th Royal West Kents, on the left of the brigade, came up against enemy machine guns concealed in shell-holes hidden in standing crops which then held up their advance. At this point Sgt T. Harris, at the head of his section, took matters into his own hands and charged one of the guns, but twice more the advance was checked in the same way, and twice more Harris rushed the machine guns causing the hold-up. On the first occasion he was successful, capturing the gun and killing the entire crew single-handed, but tragically he was shot and killed when taking on the second. By his courageous example though he had inspired other troops who enabled the battalion to reach its objective

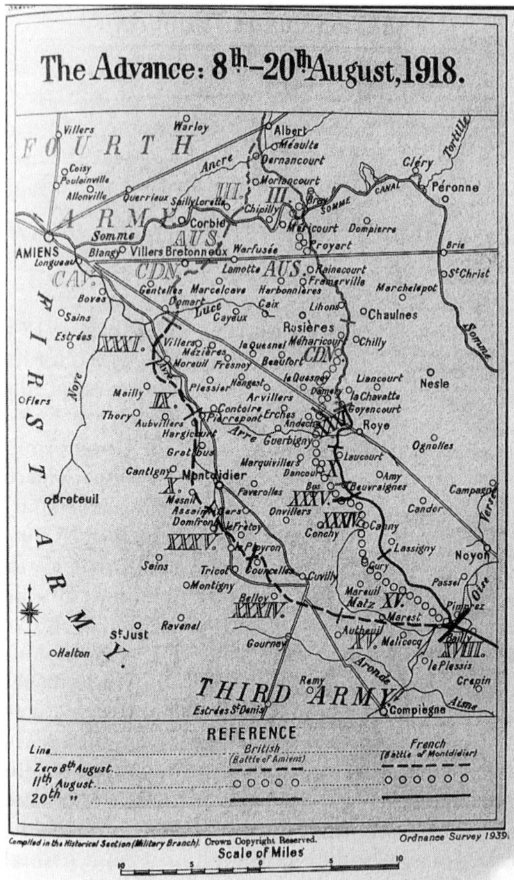

and establish itself. The site of his death was about a mile from Ville-sur-Ancre.

Harris' citation was gazetted on 22 October 1918 as follows:

> For most conspicuous bravery and devotion to duty in attack when the advance was much impeded by hostile machine guns concealed in crops and shell-holes. Sergt. Harris led his section against one of these, capturing it and killing seven of the enemy. Later, on two successive occasions, he attacked single-handed

> two enemy machine guns which were causing heavy casualties and holding up the advance. He captured the first gun and killed the crew, but was himself killed when attacking the second one. It was largely due to the great courage and initiative of this gallant N.C.O. that the advance of the battalion was continued without delay and undue casualties. Throughout the operations he showed a total disregard for his own personal safety, and set a magnificent example to all ranks.

Harris was buried 2 miles south of Albert in Dernancourt Communal Cemetery Extension, Plot VIII, Row J, Grave 20. His VC was presented to his parents in the Quadrangle of Buckingham Palace on 17 May 1919.

Thomas James Harris was born at 6 Manor Terrace, High Street, Halling, Kent on 30 January 1892 and was the son of William John Harris and Sarah Ann from Rochester. The town of Halling is on the River Medway, south of Rochester, and Manor Terrace is on the High Street to the north of St John the Baptist Church. Although Manor Terrace still exists the houses have been renumbered as the houses have been incorporated into the High Street.

Thomas was the seventh of nine children and began his schooling in the Halling Board School in July 1896. On leaving school he may have worked at the local Hilton & Anderson's Manor Cement Works. He enlisted on 27 August 1914 at the age of 22 and became a member of 6th Battalion the Queen's Own Royal West Kent Regiment with whom he reached France on 1 June 1915. The battalion was part of the 37th Brigade (12th Eastern Division). He was promoted to lance corporal on 9 July 1915 and to corporal on 1 June 1916 and during the same year was wounded on two occasions: 26 February and 2 July. After he was first wounded, followed by a few days in hospital, he returned to duty on 12 March. On 2 July he received a shrapnel wound on his right side and was sent home to hospital in England where he was a patient from 8 July to 25 August. He returned to France on 23 May 1917 and ten months later was promoted to acting sergeant on 28 March 1918. March was also probably the time when he won the MM when involved in fighting near Authuille during the German Spring Offensive. The citation for the medal was published in the *London Gazette* three months later on 12 June.

After the war Harris' VC and MM were mounted in a glass-fronted case and on 20 July 1969 were presented by Thomas's brother

Frederick to the Queen's Regimental Association. The presentation was made during a service of Remembrance and reunion in Maidstone, Kent, during which Harris' decorations were handed over to Major-General Tarver. Apart from the VC and MM, the medals included the 1914–15 Star, BWM and VM. The glass-fronted case was first given to Major-General Tarver and then taken around the parade in order to allow everyone to see it. It was then handed over to the curator of the Maidstone Museum, who placed it on display during the afternoon. At the service, which took place in All Saints' Church, a page of the Regimental Book of Life was turned by Harris' nephew Frank, and the page referred to his uncle. Another holder of the VC was in attendance, Col Donald Dean of the 8th Royal West Kents.

Harris used to live opposite The Black Boy Pub in Upper Halling and was later commemorated there by the display of a memorial plaque and an oil painting. On 30 January 1971 a block of houses sponsored by Strood Rural District Council and named Harris House was officially opened in his memory as a home for elderly people. The idea for the complex, built on the site of an old cement factory, was suggested in 1968 in order to provide a sheltered housing complex where elderly people could enjoy living under a single roof. They would still have their own self-contained accommodation, together with communal recreational facilities. The complex took ten months to build at a cost of just over £59,000 and is opposite the police station and close to the Plough Inn. The houses are now independently owned.

On 6 October 2008 what had originally been the car park for Harris House to the south of the church was named by MHS Homes Ltd after Thomas Harris and a memorial stone to his memory was also unveiled. Thomas's name is also included in the list of names on the Roll of Honour, which takes the form of a three-panel oak memorial in St John the Baptist Church, Halling. In the same church there is also a memorial stained glass window to the fallen. After the First World War a German field gun was displayed outside the church in Halling to commemorate Harris, but was later taken away for scrap.

T. DINESEN

Parvillers, France, 12 August

Private Thomas Dinesen was a member of the 42nd Battalion (Royal Highlanders of Canada), 7th Brigade, 3rd Division, and won the VC at Parvillers, north-west of Roye, on 12 August 1918. On 8 August the Canadian Corps had some of its greatest successes and the advance continued until 14 August when Sir Douglas Haig decided to break off the battle. Before this, though, on 12 August, the 7th Canadian Brigade was sent to the vicinity of the village of Parvillers and here the 42nd Battalion was involved in a fierce battle. The battalions went into the line with orders to keep up pressure on the enemy which was fighting a rearguard action. The Canadian battalions were to be involved in clearing miles of enemy trenches which linked up the villages of Fouquescourt, Parvillers and Damery. About 1½ miles behind this defensive system was another which connected the villages of Hattencourt, Fresnoy and Goyencourt. The fortified village of La Chavatte was at a point midway between the two systems of defence.

Spread across the landscape were the remains of many derelict tanks which were often adapted by the enemy as suitable cover for machine guns. Communication trenches on the battalion front connected the German frontal positions with those of the La Chavatte defences. The task of capturing these heavily defended villages presented a very strong task for the 42nd Battalion. On the left of the battalion the 44th Battalion (10th Brigade, 4th Canadian Division) penetrated the German line and managed to capture Fouquescourt. It was then decided to attempt to take the trench system at Parvillers to the south by using a bombing attack from the northern flank. The method used was to send men over in pairs, as it was hoped they would not attract enemy observation. The trenches to be attacked were defended by heavy wire and by deep timbered dugouts.

In the middle of the afternoon of 12 August, the enemy, although taken by surprise at the Canadians' attack, fought on stubbornly. During the fighting the 16th Platoon under Lt Adam Sheriff Scott reached so far forward into enemy lines, at least 1,500yds, that they became cut off. They had reached the railway crossing on the outskirts of Fransart. Owing to strong opposition, the small group had to retire, and at first they had to cross a section of trench which was in a very exposed position. They were then in danger of becoming trapped between the railway embankment and the road, nearly a mile from their objective. Their successful withdrawal was greatly assisted by the action of three privates, including Thomas Dinesen, who not only sniped the enemy, but managed to keep the German heads down by showering bombs over the railway embankment. Dinesen's two colleagues were both killed in this covering defence. Later in the day Scott's platoon was again in trouble and at some point H.A. Manning Scott was wounded. Again, he took a hand to protect the platoon while the officer was removed to safety. A report written by Maj. D.B. Martyn MC (and included in the unit history) notes the as follows:

> There never was greater dash nor perseverance shown by men than that by the Company of the 42nd who cleared about four miles of a network of trenches and fought steadily and at deadly close range for ten hours. The spirit was such that throughout the men continually cheered. Every man played his part ...

Throughout the action Dinesen was an outstanding figure and according to the unit history he was the 'spearhead' of C Company's thrust into the German lines. According to Martyn again:

> ... he led the way into the midst of groups of the enemy, wielding bayonet and clubbed rifle with irresistible effect. Repeatedly, also, he rushed forward alone in the face of machine gun fire from which it seemed impossible to escape unhurt and personally put the machine guns out of action ...

On 10 October the 42nd Battalion moved to the Quéant area and stayed there for ten days. On 17 October they were visited by the Prince of Wales. By the time the war ended on 11 November the battalion found themselves in the city of Mons and set up outposts on the outskirts of the eastern side of the city. Battalion headquarters was in the Hôtel de Ville in the Grand Place.

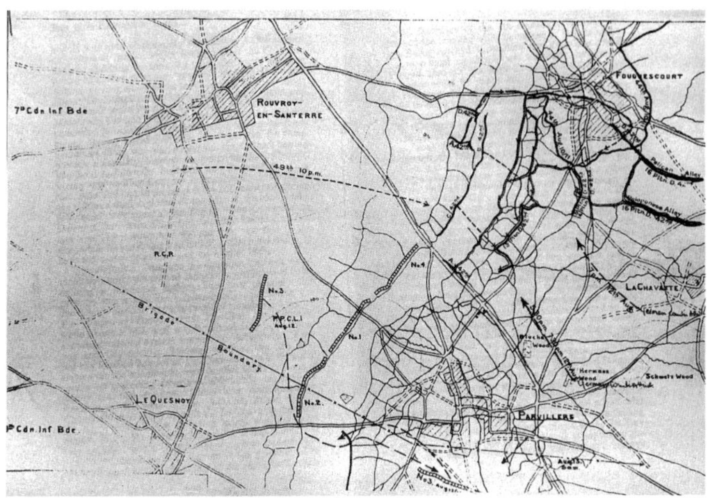

The citation for Dinesen's VC was gazetted on 26 October:

> For most conspicuous and continuous bravery displayed during ten hours of hand-to-hand fighting, which resulted in the capture of over a mile of strongly garrisoned and stubbornly defended enemy trenches. Five times in succession he rushed forward alone, and single-handed put hostile guns out of action, accounting for twelve of the enemy with bomb and bayonet. His sustained valour and resourcefulness inspired his comrades at a very critical stage of the action, and were an example to all.

Dinesen was almost immediately promoted to lieutenant in the field and was decorated by the King at Buckingham Palace on 13 December.

Thomas Dinesen was born in Rungsted, Denmark, on 9 August 1892, into a well-off Danish family of army officers and landed gentry. He was educated at the local state school, followed by the Polytechnical School, Copenhagen, where he graduated in civil engineering in 1916. He was keen on sports, including hunting and sailing.

On the outbreak of the war there was a very real invasion threat from Germany, which encouraged him to try and join up on the Allied side and he approached the British and French legations in Copenhagen with a view to joining one of their armies, but they told him that only their own nationals could join up – a ruling which was not to last for the duration of the war. After a great deal of difficulty, he finally achieved his wish and joined up in the Canadian Recruiting Office in New York City. He was allocated the service number of 2075467.

On entering the Canadian Army, Dinesen was first sent to Guy Street Barracks in Montreal as a member of the Black Watch reinforcement unit. Three months later he recrossed the Atlantic to England, where he trained at Bramshott and then Aldershot. It was not until March 1918 that he was sent to France. During the spring and early summer, his 42nd Battalion was not involved in any major battle, but they were in a very active part of the Canadian Corps front and Dinesen volunteered to take part in as many trench raids as possible.

After Dinesen was discharged he returned to Denmark and moved in the early 1920s to Kenya, where he took up farming, civil engineering and writing. He remained there for five years before returning to Denmark for good in 1925. He continued with his writing, combining this activity with extensive farming and forestry interests. These were based on his home at 'Leerbeck', his estate in Jutland.

He wrote ten books including *Merry Hell! A Dane with the Canadians* first published in 1930, translated from the Danish title of *No Man's Land*, and it was this book which dealt with his war experiences. It was reprinted in 2005. In it he wrote the following fatalistic comments: 'When I was sent to the front from England last year I did not expect to come back any more ... Once and for all, I shook off the fear of Death by looking death straight in the face'.

Describing the day he received his VC from the King at Buckingham Palace he has this to say in his book:

> At Buckingham Palace the King gave me the Victoria Cross. There were three others who received the cross at the same time. One was to be given to a sergeant who had been killed, so his parents had come to get it in his place – two old, frail people. The King said a few gracious words to each of us. We saluted and stepped back. That afternoon I went for a long tramp through the rain across Hampstead Heath and came home in the evening deadly tired, sick of the whole world.

On his time spent in training in England, he made some scathing comments about his military training:

> We might have learned how to find our way about after dark, to judge distances and recognise objects and people in the dark or in moonlight. It seems almost too stupid a thing to be recorded, but never once in Bramshot did we try to load or fire rifles unless it was in broad daylight, nor did we practice in the dark any of the jobs a soldier has to do at night such as putting up wire entanglements, putting on gas masks or thrusting with the bayonet.

Although Dinesen had lived in Canada for only three months, during his army training, he always retained a soft spot for the country and in particular the comrades who he had met while serving with the 42nd Battalion. He kept in touch with them and visited Canada several times, for reunions and other meetings. Apart from the VC, his decorations included the Croix de Guerre (France) and he was awarded with a Knight of the Order of Dannebrog by the King of Denmark.

Dinesen was a fine-looking man and also a very brave one: after all, having been born in a country which was not even directly involved in the war, he didn't have to get involved at all.

He had a sister, Karen, Baroness Blixen, who wrote under the name of Isak Dinesen. One of her most famous books was *Out of Africa*, which was based on her life in Kenya and which was turned into a film starring Robert Redford and Meryl Streep. Thomas and his sister would have been in active partnership in the early 1920s in Kenya and one of her business interests was called Karen Coffee Company. She had also met the German general Paul von Lettow-Vorbeck, when he was on the same boat to East Africa at the end of 1913, and they struck up a friendship. In 1958 she visted the former enemy general in Hamburg in 1958; he died six years later when he was in his early nineties.

Thomas Dinesen attended the House of Lords VC Dinner in November 1929 and the VC centenary review in London in June 1956 and was a guest at the Canadian Victoria Cross and George Cross holders' reunion in Ottawa in 1967. He died at the age of 86 at his home in Leebaek, Denmark, on 10 March 1979 and was buried in the family plot at Horsholm Cemetery, Rungsted, near København, Denmark. His decorations were in private hands until December 2013, when they were acquired for the Lord Ashcroft collection held at the Imperial War Museum.

R. Spall

Near Parvillers, France, 12–13 August

During the period 12–14 August 1918 the 3rd Canadian Division, which had taken over the right of the Canadian Corps front, was involved in clearing the strongly held German trenches between the villages of Fouquescourt and Parvillers, to the north-west of Roye. Except for the 32nd Division's advance south-west of Damery on 11 August the enemy was still holding their trench network system between the Roye road and Fouquescourt.

The 7th and 9th Canadian Brigades, working in tandem, pushed close up to Parvillers and it was during this period that Pte Thomas Dinesen and Sgt Robert Spall, both of the 7th Brigade, won their VCs. Spall was a member of the No. 3 Company of Princess Patricia's Canadian Light Infantry in former trenches immediately behind Nos 2,1 and 4 Companies. They were to the north-west of Parvillers.

At 3.30 in the afternoon of 12 August the neighbouring 42nd (East Lancashire) Division attacked Parvillers from the north. The CO of the PPCLI organised a supporting bombing attack to the south of the village in which Spall's No. 3 Company, under the leadership of Capt. C.M. MacBrayne, were to be used. At 8 p.m. they attacked across the Parvillers–Damery road and it was during the fierce fighting that Robert Spall gained a posthumous VC while involved in clearing the enemy trenches. His citation was gazetted on 26 October 1918 and tells the story briefly as follows:

> For most conspicuous bravery and self-sacrifice [13 August] when during an enemy counter-attack, his platoon was isolated. Thereupon Sergt. Spall took a Lewis gun and, standing on the parapet, fired upon the advancing enemy, inflicting severe casualties. He then came down from the trench, directing the men

> into a sap seventy-five yards from the enemy. Picking up another Lewis gun, this gallant N.C.O. again climbed the parapet, and by his fire held up the enemy. It was while holding up the enemy at this point he was killed. Sergt. Spall deliberately gave his life in order to extricate his platoon from a most difficult situation, and it was owing to his bravery that the platoon was saved.

On the next day the Princess Patricia's Canadian Light Infantry managed to gain an entry into Parvillers but were quickly forced out; however, the village was finally taken the following day.

The former Chief Justice and 12th Lieutenant Governor of Quebec, the Hon. Sir Charles Fitzpatrick, presented Spall's VC to his father Charles Spall, at Château Frontenac, in Quebec City, on 13 December 1918. Robert has no known grave and his name is listed on the Vimy Ridge Memorial, one of 11,000 Canadian servicemen who died during the war who have no known grave.

Robert Spall was the son of Charles and Annie Maria (*née* Morgan) and born in the district of Brentford at the Royal India Asylum, Ealing on 5 March 1890. Charles worked as a gardener in the grounds of the asylum, which had been set up for the benefit of infirm pensioners who had worked for the East India Company. Two years later when the asylum closed the Spall family emigrated to Montreal in Canada with Robert and three other sons and two daughters. Charles took up gardening work once more.

Robert was a pupil at Aberdeen school and later, prior to the war, he worked in an office in Winnipeg as a customs broker. In around 1910 he moved to Winnipeg and on 28 July 1915, when working as a custom broker he joined a draft of the 90th Winnipeg Rifles and was given the service number of 475212; he then served in the Canadian Army Service Corps. He was 5ft 6in tall, with a chest measurement of 34in. He arrived in England on 6 September and was posted to the 11th Battalion. On 29 November he transferred to the Canadian Army Service Corps (CASC) at their training depot. Spall proceeded to France on 16 February 1916. Once in France, he joined the CASC unit at the headquarters of the Canadian Cavalry Brigade. Impressing the authorities Spall was made acting sergeant in the field. On 14 May, wishing to be part of a fighting unit and reverting to being a private, he joined the 'Princess Pat's', a new Canadian light infantry regiment formed in August 1914. The regiment attracted volunteers from all over Canada and gave preference to those men who had already served in the army. After initial training, he joined his new regiment in the field at Courcelette on 18 September 1916. They later fought in the battle for the Ancre Heights and in April 1917 took an active part in the Battle of Vimy Ridge. Seven months later this was followed by service at Passchendaele and also in the Battle of Amiens in August 1918. By 29 December 1917 he was acting sergeant once more.

An article by Dr N.J. Skinner was published in the *Suffolk Roots* (Journal of the Suffolk Family History Society), page 156, vol. 23, in November 1997, in which the writer tries to find out more about Robert Spall, who had a familiar surname in the county of Suffolk. Skinner writes that Spall was born in Ealing on 5 March 1890, and that his parents were Charles and Annie Maria Spall (*née* Morgan), who had married in South Kensington on 11 July 1882. Charles was a gardener and at the time of Robert's birth he was working for the East India Company at their Royal India Asylum for infirm pensioners in Ealing. Three years later a Neville Skinner wrote an extended article in *Stand To!* No. 59.

The Royal British Legion, Brentford branch, organised a special service on 1 November 1998 when Spall's name together with two others were added to those names already included on the cenotaph. In what is a memorial garden Spall's name is commemorated at the foot of the front of the Brentford War Memorial close to the local public library in Boston Manor Road, Brentford. The Canadian maple leaf and badge of the Princess Pat's are featured as well.

Spall's decorations were donated to his regiment in Calgary by his sister Mrs Isobel Stoneman in 1969 and consisted of the VC, the BWM and VM, and are held in the Museum of the Regiments in Calgary, Alberta.

P.C. STATTON

Proyart, France, 12 August

While Private Dinesen and Sergeant Spall were winning VCs in the Canadian advance on 12 August, an Australian, Percy Statton, was gaining the same honour at Proyart to the north of the Amiens–St Quentin road. Statton was a sergeant in the 40th Battalion (Tasmania), (10th Brigade, 3rd Australian Division) AIF and on 12 August the battalion's objective was a valley to the south of the Proyart–Chuignes road. Their sister and supporting battalion, the 37th, was later to move through Proyart to a line beyond the railway to the north of the Proyart–Chuignes road. In order to reach these positions it was necessary for the 40th Battalion to move across about 1,400yds of open ground, which was under direct observation from the enemy on high ground to the east of the village. After about 875yds the advance was held up by intense artillery fire but A Company did manage to enter Proyart village and with the help of Sgt Statton and his Lewis gun reached the objective. The remainder of the 40th Battalion followed.

In the evening the advance of the 37th Battalion from the village to its own objective was held up by very severe machine-gun fire and Sgt Statton could see their predicament and the line of enemy machine guns and a patrol of a dozen men attempted to advance anyway and were destroyed even before reaching the first enemy guns. With the assistance of three colleagues and together with the use of two Lewis guns he came to their rescue. Following the bank of the Chuignies road, Statton led his men over 70yds of open ground and into the German trench. The group despatched two guns, together with their crews, with Statton accounting for most of the crews with his revolver. Running out of ammunition, he then used a German rifle as a bayonet. The group intended to take on another two guns but their crews had fled, though they were later killed by guns that Statton had already set up. By now one of his men, Private Styles, was dead and Cpl Upchurch badly wounded and Statton then crawled back to the 37th Battalion lines and Statton went out later that night to bring the wounded man to safety and also collected the body of Private Styles.

The citation for Statton's VC was gazetted on 27 September 1918 as follows:

> For most conspicuous bravery and initiative in action when in command of a platoon which reached its objective, the remainder of the battalion being held up by heavy machine gun fire. He skilfully engaged two machine gun posts with Lewis gun fire, enabling the remainder of his battalion to advance. The advance of his battalion on his left had been brought to a standstill by heavy machine gun fire, and the first of our assaulting detachments to reach the machine gun posts were put out of action in taking the first gun. Armed with only a revolver, in broad daylight, Sergt. Statton at once rushed four enemy machine gun posts in succession, disposing of two of them, and killing five of the enemy. The remaining two posts retired and were wiped out by Lewis gun fire. Later in the evening, under heavy machine gun fire, he went out again and brought in two badly wounded men. Sergeant Statton set a magnificent example of quick decision, and the success of the attacking troops was largely due to his determined gallantry.

By 8 p.m. the whole of A and C Companies had reached the valley which had been their original objective; the ground on the eastern side of the valley consisted of a row of solid dugouts. Beyond the valley was flat ground towards St Martin and Matto Woods, to the south-west of Chuignes. The following day the Australians were relieved by the 17th (Northern) Division and returned to their original bivouac area of Reginald Wood.

On 27 September the announcement of Statton's VC was made at a battalion parade by the CO, Lt Col John Lord. Statton was given three cheers and carried shoulder high through the ranks to the accompaniment of a band. Three weeks later Statton was granted ten days' leave in Paris and he returned briefly to his battalion before leaving for England on 5 November. In December he was granted two more weeks' leave. He returned to France on 27 January 1919 and worked with the headquarters of the Australian Base Depot. He left for Engand in June and was presented with his VC by the King on the seventh in the Quadrangle of Buckingham Palace. After more leave he left for Australia on 24 September and the troopship arrived in Tasmania on 26 November. He was finally discharged on 18 January 1920.

Percy Clyde Statton was the son of Edward Statton, a miner formerly of Bendigo, Victoria and Maggie Lavinia (*née* Hoskins). He was born in Beaconsfield, Tasmania, on 21 October 1890 and attended the Zeehan State School. When still only 16 years old he married Elsie May Pearce and the couple had one son and two daughters. Elsie warned her husband that if he joined up she would divorce him. Statton later worked as a farmer in Tyenna before ignoring his wife's pleas: he enlisted on 29 February 1916 in Claremont, when he was allocated the service number 506.

He joined the 40th Battalion (Tasmania) which became part of the 10th Infantry Brigade of the Australian 3rd Division, and embarked from Hobart with them on 1 July. They arrived in Devonport in mid August and after three months training in England the battalion arrived in Le Havre on 23–24 November. The 40th Battalion was transferred to Flanders in early 1917.

Statton had been made a lance corporal on 22 May and on 19 November was made a full corporal. On 16 January 1917 he was made a temporary sergeant, which was confirmed on 23 April. Statton won his MM (*LG* 16 August 1917) when the 40th Battalion was involved when leading carrying parties during operations in Messines in the period 7–9 June. The citation read as follows: 'performing exceptionally fine service under heavy artillery and machine-gun fire, in supervising and conducting carrying parties to the most advanced troops.' On 12 October, during the Third Battle of Ypres, Statton was wounded in the shoulder and was sent to several hospitals until 28 January 1918 when he was granted a fortnight's leave. He left again for France on 1 May and rejoined his battalion on the 13th. While in action at Villers-Brettoneux he was wounded during a gas attack and spent time with the 10th Australian Field Ambulance followed by a stay with the 40th CCS. He was fit enough to rejoin his battalion on 24 June but was seconded to 10th Brigade HQ and later the American 3rd Battalion. He was back with his own battalion on 27 July.

Statton returned to Australia in November 1919 on the troopship *Pnkoba* and was given a hero's welcome in Hobart, Tasmania. He was discharged on 18 January 1920 when his wife, sticking to her promise, duly divorced him, on 1 October 1920. Percy lived for many years in

Fitzgerald, Tasmania, where he worked in the timber industry before taking up farming. On 21 December 1925 he married Eliza Grace Hudson (*née* Parker) in Hobart.

In 1934 Statton had played a prominent role in coming to the rescue of several families who were cut off by severe bushfires in the Derwent Valley. His own home had been destroyed in similar circumstances during the 1920s. In the Second World War he enlisted with the Volunteer Defence Corps and was commissioned as a lieutenant on 18 June 1942. He served throughout the war with the 5th Battalion VDC until his discharge on 9 Janury 1946. After his wife's death in January 1945 he married, again in Hobart, Monica Enid Effie Kingston, a school teacher and Baptist, on 16 December 1947. They were to have one son.

In the last years of his life Statton and his family lived at Ouse, where he worked as a commercial agent, and he was also a member of the local council. He and Monica later moved to Brighton and his last job was with the Australian Newsprint Mills. In June 1956 Statton attended the Hyde Park VC Review.

Just over three years later, at the age of 69, Percy Statton died of stomach cancer on 5 December 1959 in the Repatriation Hospital, Hobart, Tasmania, and was given a full military funeral, followed by a cremation at Cornelian Bay, Hobart, where there is a plaque to his memory. He is also commemorated in Canberra in the Australian War Memorial and his name is also one of ninety-six Australian servicemen who won the VC who are commemorated in Victoria Cross Park Memorial in Canberra. The same list of men is also commemorated in the Victoria Cross Memorial in the Queen Victoria Building in Sydney.

However, it doesn't end there, as Statton is commemorated with a monument on the Lyell Highway, Ouse 7120, an area where he farmed in Tasmania. His name is also remembered with the names of two streets in Canberra named after him. His service decorations are in the Australian War Memorial collection. Apart from the VC and MM, they consist of the BWM, VM, and Coronation Medals for 1937 and 1953.

D.M.W. Beak

South of Bapaume, France, 21–25 August and 4 September

T/Cdr Daniel Beak of the Drake Battalion (63rd (RN) Division) gained his VC over a period of several days to the south of the town of Bapaume during what was known as the Battle of Albert, which lasted for eight days from 21 August to 29 August 1918.

General Sir Julian Byng's Third Army Front stretched from Miraumont in the Somme southwards to Moyenville and much bitter fighting had recently taken place in the area of Achiet-le-Petit and Logeast Wood. On 21 August the enemy, close to Logeast Wood, repelled the Royal Naval Division which was lacking artillery support. Although the division did have the use of several tanks they quickly became disabled. The result was that the troops in the centre of the divisional front fell back to positions east of Logeast Wood, which in turn led to retirement on the two flanks.

However, the Anson and Drake Battalions maintained advance posts and the night was a quiet one. The next day the enemy made three determined counter-attacks. But the divisional artillery was now contributing their support and by the following day, 23 August, the enemy was back on a line Grévillers–Loupart Wood–Warlencourt. The aim of the Allies was to cut the Albert–Bapaume road and thus prevent German attacks from the north-west. On 24 August Loupart Wood was attacked by the 37th Division and the New Zealand Division, and also for some distance on each flank. The wood was then captured but isolated posts on the eastern side were holding out and the enemy continued to occupy Grévillers and Warlencourt. Orders were then issued to the Royal Naval Division to assist the New Zealanders in making an attack on Grévillers to drive out the enemy. The roll of Daniel Beak during this fighting covered the events between 21 and

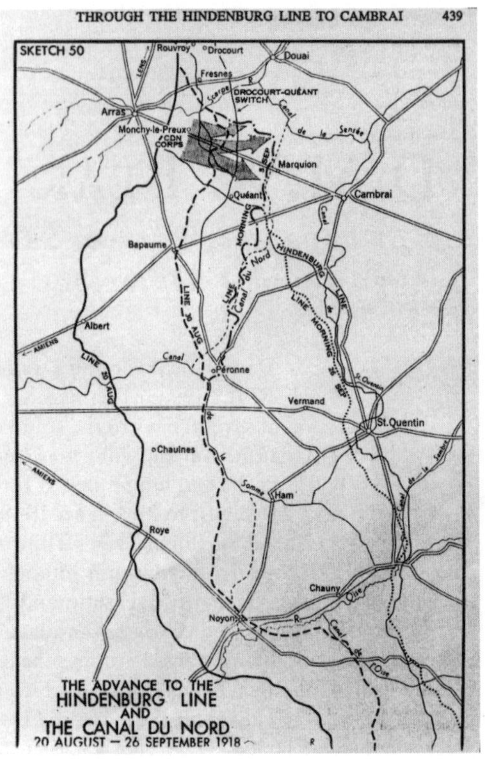

25 August, as well as those on 4 September, and was gazetted on 15 November 1918 as follows:

> For most conspicuous bravery, courageous leadership and devotion to duty during a prolonged period of operations. He led his men in attack, and, despite heavy machine gun fire, four enemy positions were captured. His skilful and fearless leadership resulted in the complete success of this operation and enabled other battalions to reach their objectives. Four days later, though dazed by a shell fragment, in the absence of the brigade commander, he reorganised the whole brigade under extremely heavy gun fire and led his men with splendid courage to their objective. An attack having been held up, he rushed forward, accompanied by only one runner,

> and succeeded in breaking up a nest of machine guns, personally bringing back nine or ten prisoners. His fearless example instilled courage and confidence in his men, who then quickly resumed the advance under his leadership. On a subsequent occasion he displayed great courage and powers of leadership in attack, and his initiative, coupled with the confidence with which he inspired all ranks, not only enabled his own and a neighbouring unit to advance, but contributed very materially to the success of the Naval Division in these operations.

Beak was presented with his VC by the King in Vincent Barracks, Valenciennes on 6 December 1918.

Daniel Marcus William Beak was born at No. 42 Kent Road, St Denys, Southampton, on 27 July 1891, the son of Mr and Mrs W.H. Beak, formerly of West End House, Donhead St Mary, Wiltshire. He attended St Denys School and later Taunton's School in Southampton. He left school in order to train as a schoolteacher, but changed his mind and then tried his hand at being a private secretary to a clergyman in Bristol. He was rescued by the war and on 2 February 1915 he joined the RNVR as an ordinary seaman and rose to become a Petty Officer, gazetted on 8 May as a sub-lieutenant. He was to spend most of his career in the war as a member of the Drake Battalion of the 63rd RN Division, although he also served for a short time with the Anson and Howe Battalions. In the same year he was posted to the Mediterranean Expeditionary Force and briefly served in Gallipoli and was present at the evacuation in January 1916. In May he arrived in France and he was appointed adjutant to the Drake Battalion on 2 March 1917.

Beak was promoted from sub-lieutenant to acting commander of Drake Battalion on 19 March for the period up to 3 April and on relinquishing command he was attached to headquarters. Towards the end of the year Beak attended a Senior Officers' Course in Aldershot and was promoted to temporary commander and commander of the Howe Battalion on 31 December 1917. He remained with the Howe Battalion until its disbandment in February 1918. He then transferred to command the Anson Battalion for a short period and on 12 March 1918 he was put in command of the Drake Battalion. A few days later he won a DSO for a skilful operation carried out during the night of

23–24 March 1918, and for a successful rearguard action on the Ytres–Bus road on the morning of 24 March. He had already been awarded the MC, gazetted on 26 January 1917, and a bar, which was gazetted on 17 July 1917. He was mentioned in despatches twice, on 7 April 1918 and on 21 December 1918.

On 2 April 1919 the Freedom of the County Borough of Southampton was conferred upon him. Two months later he was demobilised, in June 1919, and in the same month the Prince of Wales attended a large parade of members of the division in Horse Guards Parade, London. Cdr Beak was in command of the Drake Battalion at the ceremony. At the end of the war the RND had been disbanded and a memorial was later erected in Greenwich.

Probably owing to an extremely active war, Beak found that he was unable to settle to civilian life and in 1920 he enlisted in the army and was commissioned in the Royal Scots Fusiliers as a captain. He served in Eire, taking part in the Irish War of Independence. In 1923, on 5 September, he married Miss Frances Wallace, only daughter of Lt Col Wallace, DSO, of Busbie, Cloncaird Castle, Maybole, and of the late Mrs Wallace in the parish church in Ayr. Frances died seven years later when Beak was left with two sons to bring up. In 1929 he was given a brevet promotion to the rank of major, which was confirmed in 1932. In the same year he was transferred to the King's Regiment with the rank of major and served in India for a time.

Promoted to lieutenant colonel in 1935, he took the 1st Battalion South Lancs Regiment, the Prince of Wales's Volunteers, to France in 1940. After the fall of France he became an acting major-general. In 1942 he became general officer commanding troops in Malta during one of the island's toughest times during the Second World War. Later Field Marshal Montgomery gave him the sack.

Daniel Beak finally left the army in 1945 when he made his home at Sheepdrove Lodge, Lambourn, Berkshire. He died in Princess Margaret Hospital, Swindon, on 3 May 1967 and had a private funeral. He was buried in grave 222960 in St Gabriel's Avenue, Brookwood Cemetery, Woking. There was no headstone to his grave, but his name is included on the memorial tablet to his wife at the New Cemetery, Ayr, Wall Section, Lair 52. On his death he left £12,000, and his decorations are part of Lord Ashcroft's collection on display in the Imperial War Museum. They consist of the VC, DSO, MC & Bar, 1914–15 Star, BWM 1914–20, VM,1939–45 Star, Africa Star & clasp '8th Army', War Medal (1935–45) & MiD Oakleaf, King George V Silver Jubilee Medal 1935 and Coronation Medals for 1937 and 1953.They were sold on behalf of the family at Spink's on 5 November 2003 for the then record price of £178,250. On 27 September 2006 a plaque to Beak's memory was unveiled at the War Memorial in Cheltenham which was sponsored by the magazine *This England*. The inscription included the additional information that at one point Beak was the secretary of the local branch of the YMCA.

E.B. SMITH

Beauregard Dovecot, France, 21–23 August

Prior to the Battle of Albert, which began on 21 August 1918 the 1/5th Lancashire Fusiliers (125th Infantry Brigade) 42nd East Lancashire Division assembled in positions west of Beaumont Hamel-Puiseux, in preparation for a major attack the following day. They had three objectives: Hill 140, better known as The Lozenge, south of Puiseux, which was known to be full of machine guns; the high ground further to the east; and Beauregard Dovecot, astride the junction of five roads which overlooked Miraumont and the Ancre.

At 4.45 a.m. the battalion moved forward under a heavy artillery barrage and in a thick mist. These conditions were in their favour and they managed to capture the first objective with only light casualties. By 7 a.m. the second objective had also been taken, but this time the casualties were much heavier. It was with the capture of the Dovecot that L/Sgt Smith was to be most heavily involved, when he killed at least six of the enemy. When the Germans counter-attacked, Smith led a section forward and was able to restore part of the line.

For his courageous actions L/Sgt Smith was awarded the VC for gallantry during the fighting between 21 and 23 August which was gazetted on 22 October 1918 as follows:

> For most conspicuous bravery, leadership and personal example during an attack and in subsequent operations. Sergt. Smith, while in command of a platoon, personally took a machine gun post, rushing the garrison with his rifle and bayonet. The enemy, on seeing him advance, scattered, to throw hand grenades at him. Regardless of all danger, and almost without halting in his rush on the post, this N.C.O. shot and killed at least six of the enemy.

> Later, seeing another platoon requiring assistance, he led his men to them, took command of the situation, and captured the objective. During the enemy counter-attack on the following day he led a section forward and restored a portion of the line. His personal bravery, skill and initiative were outstanding, and his conduct throughout exemplified magnificent courage and skill, and was an inspiring example to all.

Smith was decorated in the Ballroom of Buckingham Palace on 9 November 1918.

Edward (Ned) Benn Smith was born at 1 North Quay, Maryport, on 10 November 1898 and was the son of Charles Henry Smith and Martha (Benn). Charles was a seaman in the Royal Naval Reserve and was later to take part in the Dardanelles campaign in 1915 and Martha came from two generations of lifeboatmen in Maryport, which is on the north-west coast of Cumberland. The town was best known for its fishing and coalmining industries.

Edward, one of three brothers and two sisters, was educated at the local National School and later worked at the Oughterside Coliery, near Maryport. When only 17 years of age he attested on 11 December 1915, but owing to his youth he was transferred to the reserves. He enlisted with the Lancashire Fusiliers in July 1917. He was sent to France on 10 December to join the 1/5th TF Lancashire Fusiliers of the 125th (Infantry Brigade) 42nd East Lancashire Division and was soon promoted serving in the Givenchy area. Eight months later he was awarded the DCM for an action on 10 August 1918 to the south of Hébuterne. Major-General A. Solly-Ford, Commanding Officer of the Division, wrote the following report:

> On 10 August, south-east of Hébuterne, this N.C.O. led a daylight patrol. By skilful handling and use of cover he examined two points of the enemy line about which information was required. This information he obtained. When on the point of returning, Sgt Smith noticed a party of forty of the enemy coming forward from their main line of resistance, obviously to take up night outpost dispositions. Sgt Smith decided to wait for the enemy, and engage them, though outnumbered. He inflicted heavy casualties on the enemy, who at once scattered. His initiative and determination to inflict casualties on the enemy was a fine example.

Having won the VC less than a fortnight later when still 19 years old, it was said that Smith was the youngest VC holder in the army. At the time of his VC action he was promoted to sergeant.

When he returned home on leave to Maryport, he was greeted by 6,000 people and given a civic welcome. Complimentary speeches were made in his honour in the local marketplace. Edward and his parents received various gifts, including a long case clock, a silver tea-set, and £200 in war bonds, as well as a gold watch with chain, a gold brooch and a Meerschaum pipe. Men of the Home Defence Corps escorted him back to his home in North Quay.

After the war Smith had given up on a career in the mines and re-enlisted on 5 May 1919 in the Cameron Highlanders, having previously left the army when the war ended a few months before. He was with the Highlanders for a brief time before transferring to the 1st Lancashire Fusiliers at Blackdown. He was made drum-major in 1920 and in the following year he was one of the holders of the VC invited to the King's Garden Party held at Buckingham Palace on 26 June 1920. In 1924 he was promoted to company sergeant-major and in 1926 was sent to Malaya, where he instructed Malaya volunteer forces for three years.

On 29 July 1932 he was made regimental sergeant-major and served with the 1st Battalion in Colchester; Shanghai and Tientsin. In 1938 he left the army with a pension and joined the Corps of Commissionaires in London, but on the outbreak of the second war he rejoined the army and this time was granted a Short Service Commission as lieutenant and quartermaster. He was sent to France with the 2nd Battalion Lancashire Fusiliers (42nd (East Lancashire) Division in early 1940 and was involved in the fighting south-east of Bethune, near Bucquoy, when he was discovered in his store, shot in the head, having possibly taken his own life. Another version of his death was that he was killed accidentally by 'friendly fire', which of the two options seems less likely. Sadly he died of his wounds on 12 January and was buried in Beuvry Communal Cemetery Extension, Pas-de-Calais in Plot I, Row B, Grave 7. On 13 January Charles and Martha Smith received a War Office telegram informing them that their son had been 'killed in action'. On the same day an unamed colonel (see Cumbrian local press) also wrote to them informing them that their son had died the day before from 'a bullet in the head'.

Later in the war Mrs Smith presented her son's First World War uniform to the army for the use of another serviceman.

On 23 November 1977 Smith's nine decorations were put up for sale by his family and purchased at Sotheby's by a private collector for £7,000. They were offered for sale again on 12 March 1996, and this time fetched £19,000. The suggested price given by Spink in its catalogue was £18,000–£20,000 and the buyer was Lord Ashcroft. The decorations are in his collection in the Imperial War Museum. Apart from the VC and DCM, they include the BWM, VM, 1939–45 Star, Silver Jubilee 1935, Coronation Medals for 1937 and 1953 and an Army Long Service and Good Conduct Medal. Edward's name is commemorated on the Maryport War Memorial.

R.A. West

Near Lagnicourt, France, 21 August and 2 September

The Battle of Albert took place between 21 and 23 August 1918, and the aim of the Third Army's attack was to extend its front line from the village of Moyenneville to the River Ancre. In order to achieve this, the first objective was to be the line of the Albert–Arras railway which ran from Moyenneville to Achiet-le-Grand and Miraumont in the Ancre valley. On the following day the Fourth Army was to take part in the operations and come into line between the Ancre and the Somme. On 23 August the Australians were to renew their advance.

The 2nd Tank Brigade was on the left of the Third Army and was made up of the 12th and 15th Heavy Battalions, and the 6th Light Battalion, which used Whippet light tanks. The 3rd Tank Brigade was in reserve with the 9th, 11th and 14th Heavy Battalions, and the 1st Tank Brigade was in the centre with 7th and 10th Heavy Battalions, the 3rd Light Battalion, and the 17th Armoured Car Battalion.

Canon Lummis, the compiler of records of holders of the VC, was a captain in the Suffolk Regiment and was a witness of much of the activity that took place in the Third Army attack on 21 August. He was able to meet up with A/Lt Col Richard West, attached to the 6th Tank Corps, on the left of the advance. West was destined to win a VC, firstly for his actions on 21 August, and secondly for those on 2 September. The Allied attack began in a thick fog; smoke shells added to the heavy mist, which became so bad that it was difficult to see one's own colleagues, let alone the enemy.

Lummis's orders were to proceed at about 5 a.m. from the east of Courcelles-le-Comte, as far as the north–south railway which ran between the village and the village of Gomiécourt. On the way to Courcelles while in the valley below Caruson Copse, Lummis, leading his company, met up with A/Lt Col West. The two men spoke briefly for a few minutes and when West's horse became entangled in some barbed wire it was Lummis who managed to set the horse free. Lummis then progressed with his company which, owing to the heavy mist, became reduced to one platoon. The group encountered a few of the enemy in the mist and managed to overcome them. It was for this action, as well as for his subsequent role in a night attack, that Lummis was awarded the MC. As Lummis proceeded to look for them, his 'missing platoons' turned up, and they then came across two tank officers whose tanks had been knocked out close to the railway line. At this point the Suffolk Battalion was under fire from the right flank and from trench mortar to the front. Lummis could see a machine gun being set up on the far side of the railway and sent a message to the Tank Brigade, suggesting that they should deal with the machine-gun position. A small group of Whippet tanks managed to come down from the left, using the railway track as a road. The tanks were quickly knocked out by an anti-tank gun, but even so the enemy resistance was weakening.

On 2 September Lummis again witnessed part of Col West's actions when he was holding a company on a line near Vaulx-Vraucourt. He came across stragglers of the 1st Royal Scots Fusiliers and 7th (S) Battalion King's Shropshire Light Infantry, who were delaying progress of the division. During this time Lummis saw an officer on horseback, who could only have been Col West.

On the night of 1–2 September nine Whippet tanks had left the village of Gomicourt to attack in an easterly direction towards Lagnicourt. As the tanks had been overused and under-serviced, it was found that many of them were not ready by zero hour. The commanding officer, Lt Col West, left the tank camp on horseback on the morning of 2 September, accompanied by two orderlies. It was his intention to accompany the Whippets in the journey towards Lagnicourt. He arrived at the front line in time to see the beginning of a strong enemy counter-attack. The subsequent VC citation, gazetted on 30 October 1918, tells what happened on 21 August and 2 September:

> For most conspicuous bravery and leadership 21 Aug. at Courcelles, and self-sacrifice 2 Sept. 1918. During an attack, the infantry having lost their bearings in the dense fog, this officer at once collected and reorganised any men he could find,

> and led them to their objective in face of heavy machine gun fire. Throughout the whole action he displayed the most utter disregard of danger, and the capture of the objective was in a great part due to his initiative and gallantry. On a subsequent occasion it was intended that a battalion of Light Tanks, under command of this officer, should exploit the initial Infantry and Heavy Tank attack. He therefore went forward in order to keep in touch with the progress of the battle, and arrived at the front line when the enemy were in process of delivering a local counter-attack. The Infantry Battalion had suffered heavy officer casualties, and its flanks were exposed. Realizing that there was a danger of this battalion giving way, he at once rode out in front of them under extremely heavy machine gun and rifle fire and rallied the men. In spite of the fact that the enemy were close upon him, he took charge of the situation and detailed non-commissioned officers to replace officer casualties. He then rode up and down in front of them in face of certain death, encouraging the men and calling to them, 'Stick it, men; show them fight, and for God's sake put up a good fight'. He fell riddled by machine gun bullets. The magnificent bravery of this very gallant officer at the critical moment inspired the infantry to redoubled efforts, and the hostile attack was defeated.

West was buried the same evening in Mory Abbey Military Cemetery 4 miles north of Bapaume in Plot III, Row G, Grave 4. His posthumous VC, and the bar to his DSO, were presented to his widow at Buckingham Palace on 15 February 1919.

Richard Annesley West was fourth son of Augustus George West of White Park, County Fermanagh. His mother, Sara West (*née* Eyre), was the daughter of Canon Richard Both Eyre, a rector at Eyre Court in County Galway. Richard was born on 26 September 1878 at No. 1 Oxford Street, Cheltenham, and later the family moved to Cleveden. West was educated at Channel View School, Clevedon, and Monkton Combe School, Bath.

West served in the South African War between 1900 and 1902 as a trooper in the 45th Irish Hunt Company, which was part of the Imperial Yeomanry. He was later a trooper NCO and lieutenant in the 2nd Battalion, Kitchener's Fighting Scouts. In November 1901 he was promoted to lieutenant and later became a superintendent in the Transvaal Repatriation Department. In early 1904 he was assistant adjutant of the Transvaal Horse Artillery Volunteers, serving with the regiment for eight years. He then moved to the Transvaal Reserve of Officers.

For his service in South Africa West was awarded the Queen's South Africa Medal with three clasps and the King's South Africa Medal with two clasps.

While in Pretoria, Transvaal, he married Maude Ethel, daughter of Henry William Cushing of London, on 16 July 1909. At the outbreak of the Great War he joined the North Irish Horse, Cavalry Special Reserve, and was made a lieutenant on 11 August 1914. He was a member of one of their squadrons during the retreat from Mons, and was later attached to the North Somerset Yeomanry. He was promoted to captain and on 18 November 1915 was made temporary major. On 11 April 1917, during the Battle of Arras at Monchy-le-Preux, when the enemy resistance had begun to stiffen, West was awarded a DSO, which was gazetted on 1 January 1918 as follows:

> ... his squadron was sent forward to reinforce the right flank of the Brigade under very heavy shell and machine gun fire. By his excellent example, rapid grasp of the situation and skilful disposition of his squadron, he did much to avert an impending German counter-attack. He had shown great ability in command since July 1915...

On 18 January 1918 West was made an acting major in the Tank Corps and on 8 August 1918 was awarded a MC, which was gazetted in November 1918:

> During the advance [east of Amiens] on 8 August at Guillencourt [Guillaucourt], in command of a company of Light Tanks, he displayed magnificent leadership and personal bravery. He was able to point out many targets to his Tanks that they would not otherwise have seen. During the day he had two horses shot under him, while he and his orderly between them killed five of the enemy and took seven prisoners. On the 10th he rendered great services to the Cavalry by personally reconnoitring the ground in front of Le Quesnoy, and later in the day, under very heavy machine-gun fire, rallied and organised the crews of the Tanks that had been ditched, withdrawing them after dark.

He was awarded a bar to his DSO for action on 21 August (*London Gazette*, 7 November 1918) near Courcelles:

> In consequence of this action being fought in a thick mist, this officer decided to accompany the attack to assist in maintaining direction and cohesion. This he did mounted, until his horse was shot under him, then on foot until the final objective was reached. During the advance, in addition to directing his Tanks, he rallied and led forward small bodies of Infantry lost in the mist, showing throughout a fine example of leadership and a total disregard of personal safety, and materially contributed to the success of the operations. Major West was in command of the battalion most of the time, his Commanding Officer having been killed early in the action. The consistent gallantry displayed by this officer throughout the operations since 8 Aug. has been remarkable.

On 22 August 1918 West was made acting lieutenant colonel and was in command of the 6th Light Battalion. In addition to his decorations, West was mentioned in despatches, including those of Sir John French (7 September 1914) and Sir Douglas Haig (in his despatches of 7 November 1917 and of 8 November 1918), for gallant and distinguished service in the field.

Shortly after her husband's death Maude, his wife, gave birth to a daughter, the couple's only child, who was named Gertrude Annesley and born on 17 November 1918, in Hove.

West's decorations at one time were on loan to the Tank Museum in Bovington and at some point were purchased by Lord Ashcroft and are now part of the VC collection in the Imperial War Museum. Apart from the VC and South African medals, they consist of: a DSO and Bar, MC, 1914 Star clasp 5 August–22 November 1914, BWM, VM (1914–19) and MiD Oakleaf.

West's name is commemorated on the family headstone at Coolebrooke Churchyard, County Fermanagh, Northern Ireland; on a memorial at Belfast City Hall; on the war memorial at Enniskillen, County Fermanagh; and with a memorial at St Ronan's Church, also in Enniskillen. Finally a blue plaque to his memory was unveiled at his birthplace by the Mayor of Cheltenham at No. 1 Oxford Street, Cheltenham on 11 September 2009.

G. Onions

South of Achiet-le-Petit, France, 22 August

In the area of IV Corps, L/Cpl George Onions, 1st Devons (95th Brigade, 5th Division) won a VC south of Achiet-le-Petit on the morning of 22 August 1918 on the second day of the Battle of Albert. At around 5 a.m. the enemy appeared to be making a strong attack on the positions of the 42nd Division, the division which had recently replaced the New Zealand Division in front of Miraumont in the Ancre valley. The fire from the enemy bombardment did not reach the Devons' front, but two of their scouts were ordered to investigate the situation. The two men moved forward in the early morning mist and reached a former trench which they found to be empty. However, much to their surprise, a large group of Germans suddenly jumped into it. They then opened fire and the Germans, unable to assess how many attackers they faced, quickly surrendered to the two scouts who took charge of all 242 of them! The names of the two men were L/Cpl George Onions, who was awarded the VC (*London Gazette* 14 December 1918), and his colleague, Pte H.J.C. Eades, who was awarded the DCM for his part in the action:

> Having been sent out with one man at Achiet-le-Petit on 22 Aug. 1918, to get in touch with the battalion on the right flank, he observed the enemy advancing in large numbers. Realizing his opportunity he boldly placed himself with his comrade on the flank of the advancing enemy, and opened rapid fire when the target was most favourable. When the enemy were about 100 yards from him, the line wavered and some hands were seen to be thrown up. L.-Corpl Onions then rushed forward, and with the assistance of his comrade took about 200 of the enemy prisoners, and marched them back to his company commander.

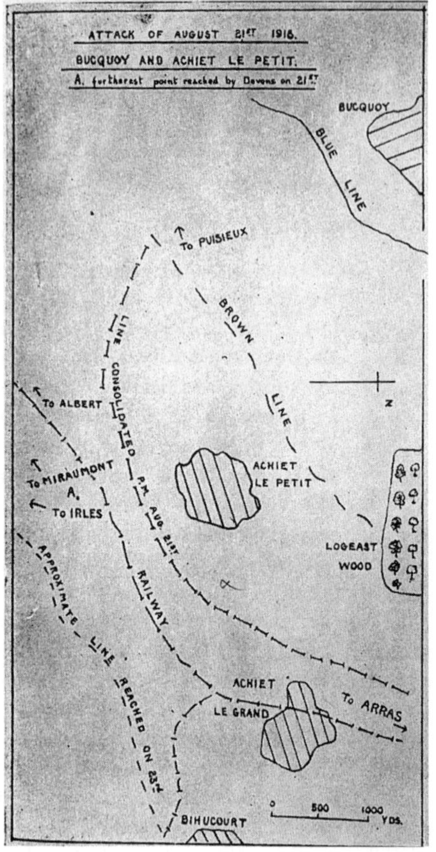

After achieving this tremendous bluff, Onions was badly gassed later on the same day, and was invalided home to a hospital in Liverpool. Later the same day, the Devons were ordered into reserve.

Onions, accompanied by his wife and son, was decorated with his VC in the Ballroom of Buckingham Palace on 13 February 1919. As a special award he was commissioned for the same day into the Rifle Brigade, in recognition of his valuable services, and was allowed to wear the uniform on appropriate occasions. He was demobilised the following day.

George Onions was the son of Mr Z. Webb Onions, of White Lodge, Edgbaston, Birmingham, and Amy S. Onions (*née* Skemp). George's mother was a descendant of Jan Ridd, the hero of *Lorna Doone*. George was born on 2 March 1883 in Bilston, Staffordshire, and he had six sisters and one younger brother, but sadly their mother died in 1884. The Onions family were well known in the iron and steel industry, both father and grandfather having been ironmasters. The family moved to Monmouthshire where George attended the West Monmouthshire Grammar School in Pontypool. When he left school he entered the steel industry as an iron and steel merchant, as well as becoming a manufacturer's representative.

He decided to emigrate to Australia, and in 1907 he married Florence McFarlane in St Paul's, Brisbane, Queensland. The couple had one son, named George, born on 2 November 1909. Returning to England, Onions enlisted in the 3rd (King's Own) Hussars on 5 September 1914, and was allocated the service number of 21378. He served in France in 1915 and in the same year his family moved to Sale in Cheshire, then in 1916 he was stationed in Ireland with the 9th Reserve Cavalry Regiment at the time of the Irish Rebellion. On 14 April 1917 Onions, by now a corporal, was transferred to the Devonshire Regiment, when his service number became 63514. In August 1918 he was badly gassed while serving in France.

After he was demobilised he returned to the steel industry, becoming a manager for a firm of ironmasters and merchants. By then the family had moved to Northumberland.

George's younger brother, Tpr A.R.F. Onions, enlisted in the Dragoon Guards in August 1914 and served in France between 1915 and 1918 in the 4th and 7th Dragoon Guards, winning the DCM.

On 26 June 1920 George attended the VC Garden Party at Buckingham Palace and also the House of Lords Dinner on 9 November 1929. His father had died in 1921.

During the Second World War Capt. Onions, as he had by then become, served with the Royal Defence Corps in Birmingham from 1939 and was made acting major in December. As the equivalent of the Home Guard, the members of the unit guarded bridges and other important points against sabotage. All of the men involved had served in the First World War and the unit was attached to the Royal Warwickshire Regiment. On 19 May 1942 Onions was promoted to major but he later resigned his commission and served in the South Staffordshire zone Home Guard before ill health forced his permanent retirement. His civilian job at this time was publicity agent for the Colliery Guardian Company in London.

George Onions, whose home was then at No. 4, Hagley Court, Edgbaston, died on 2 April 1944 in Edgbaston Hospital, Birmingham, and was buried in Quinton Cemetery four days later. His grave, part of the family plot, is in section six of the cemetery, number 7364.

His VC, 1914–15 Star, BWM, VM and 1937 Coronation Medal are with the Devonshire an Dorset Regimental Museum, in Dorchester, Dorset where there is also a portrait of him on display.

As a culinary coincidence Theodore Veale won his VC in July 1916 during the Battle of the Somme and Thomas Sage won a VC during the battle for Passchendaele in October 1917.

W.D. Joynt

Plateau Wood, France, 23 August

On 23 August 1918, as part of the Battle of Albert, the Fourth Army continued the attack it had launched the previous day, extending it southwards to the Somme to take in the Australian Corps. The British 32nd Division was under the command of this corps and based in positions north of the Amiens–St Quentin Road and the objective was the high ground east of Chuignes, about 3 miles distant. General Monash, the Australian commander, decided to use the 32nd Division on the right and the 1st Australian Division on the left. The first phase of the objective was the line Herleville–Plateau Woods.

The 2nd Australian Brigade, together with tank support, had to advance over a landscape which had been very well adapted by the enemy for defence purposes. According to the *Official History* the land was 'intersected by deep gullies and sunken roads, besides old trenches, and dotted with woods with the Herleville valley beyond it'. Although tanks had not arrived by zero hour, the Australian infantry were ordered to move forward anyway, but they were covered by an excellent barrage. The forward Australian battalion, the 6th, was however slowed by intense fire and this led to the attack falling behind schedule. To the left, the 5th Battalion encountered resistance from near St Martin's Woods, which was dealt with assistance from the 7th Battalion. By 5.15 a.m. the 6th Battalion was also in trouble from the direction of St Denis Wood to the right and the ground to the east of it. Soon this wood was captured, but the enemy still held out in St Martin's Wood itself. By this time, after heavy officer casualties, the tanks had finally arrived and one tank knocked out twenty machine guns in front of St Martin's Wood. But the remaining posts in the wood continued to delay the advance and it was at this point that

Lt William Joynt, of the supporting 8th Battalion, saw what was happening and went forward with his batman, Pte T. Newman. They assisted the 6th Battalion to reform in some dead ground of a sunken road and Joynt urged them on, but they were later held up by intense fire from Plateau Wood. At this point Joynt was joined by Lt L.C. McGinn from his own battalion, together with fifteen more men, and McGinn's Lewis gunner managed to put a dangerous machine gun out of action.

Joynt and his group then crossed the road safely and, capturing fifty Germans on the way, they decided to attack Plateau Wood which had become the main point of danger. Requesting covering fire from the left of the 6th Battalion he instructed his men to open fire on Plateau Wood.

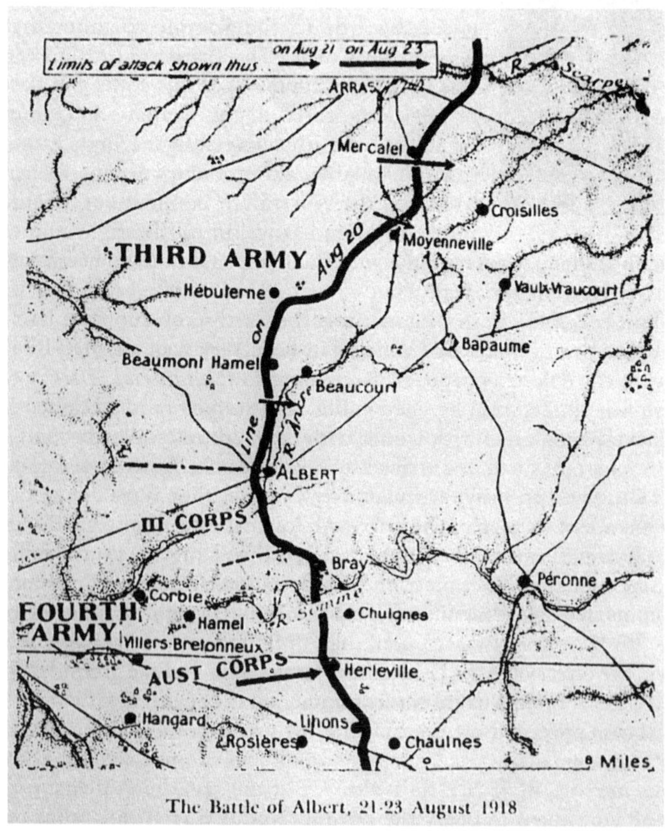

The Battle of Albert, 21-23 August 1918

Joynt and McGinn then paused for a while, before moving through a trench full of abandoned machine guns plus both dead and living Germans, many of whom had lost interest in fighting. Joynt managed to capture a party of twenty Germans by himself. He then spread his men out in this trench facing the wood, planning to attack from that position. However, the site of another enemy machine gun was discovered, so he then searched for – and found – a trench which led into the wood and in turn to the position of the machine gun. The wood was taken by 7.30 a.m., with the Australians getting their adversaries on the run, and the 2nd Brigade reached all of its objectives. Seven tanks also reached the wood and later nine rallied after the action.

Lieutenant William Joynt gained the VC for his work on 23 August which was gazetted on 27 November 1918:

> For most conspicuous bravery and devotion to duty, during the attack on Herleville Wood, near Chuignes, Péronne, on 23rd Aug. 1918. His company commander having been killed early in the advance, he immediately took charge of the company, which he led with courage and skill. On approaching Herleville Wood, the troops of the leading battalion, which his battalion was supporting, suffered very heavy casualties and were much shaken. Lieut. Joynt, grasping the situation rushed forward under very heavy machine gun and artillery fire, collected and reorganised the remnants of the battalion, and kept them under cover, pending the arrival of his own company. He then made a personal reconnaissance, and found that the fire from the wood was checking the whole advance and causing heavy casualties to troops on his flanks. Dashing out in front of his men, he inspired and led a magnificent frontal bayonet attack on the wood. The enemy were staggered by this sudden onslaught and a very critical situation was saved. Later at Plateau Wood, this very gallant officer again, with a small party of volunteers, rendered invaluable service, and after severe hand-to-hand fighting turned a stubborn defence into an abject surrender. His valour and determination was conspicuous throughout, and he continued to do magnificent work until badly wounded by a shell.

Joynt was always in the thick of the battle, and was badly wounded in the buttock on 26 August during another attack near Péronne.

He was presented with the VC on 19 July 1919 in the Quadrangle of Buckingham Palace.

William Donovan Joynt was the younger son of Edward Kelly Joynt, late of Ballina, County Mayo, and Alice Joynt (*née* Woolcott) of Exeter, Devon. Alice's father was a prominent solicitor in Melbourne, and William was born at Elsterwick, Melbourne, Victoria, on 19 March 1889. He was educated at the Grange Preparatory School and later at Melbourne Church of England Grammar School (1904). Although he studied accountancy (1906–07), he later decided to go into farming. He sailed from Rockland in Queensland and later boarded a steamer bound for Cairns and took up farm work in Northern Queensland, gaining experience in cattle-, sheep- and wheat-farming. He worked in the Victorian Mallee and in Western Australia, and while he was working in Flinders Island, Bass Strait, off Tasmania, the war broke out.

He left his work to enlist in Melbourne before joining the Army on 21 May 1915, initially as a member of the Victorian Rifles. He was commissioned on Christmas Eve 1915 and served in Gallipoli before moving to France in May 1916. Once there, he was posted to the 8th Battalion in July. During the time that he was in France it was said that Joynt took part in every single major operation but one that his battalion was involved in. He fought on the Somme in 1916 and was wounded in the shoulder on 30 September during a raid on enemy trenches in the Ypres sector at a ravine close to The Bluff. He was evacuated to England and subsequently mentioned in divisional orders and promoted to lieutenant in December.

He was absent from his battalion until 15 January 1917. Other engagements that he took part in included the advance to the Hindenburg Line, Bapaume, in the spring of 1917, and the fighting at Lagnicourt and Bullecourt, followed by the Third Battle of Ypres, Polygon Wood, Broodseinde Ridge and Passchendaele in the second half of 1917. During the Battle of Lys in the spring of 1918 he fought in the Nieppe Forest. On 29 October 1918 he was promoted to captain and in March 1919 he was posted to AIF Headquarters in London.

It was not until after the war was over that Joynt recovered from the two wounds that he suffered during the war. In February 1920 he returned to Melbourne and was discharged on 11 June 1920. Before Joynt left Britain he had set up a scheme whereby other former Australian soldiers should receive some agricultural training in the English farming methods while they awaited repatriation. H.W. Murray, another VC holder, took over this work from him. Then for a few years Joynt farmed 100 acres near Berwick, Victoria, under a Soldier Settle Scheme.

Unfortunately, this admirable farming venture failed, mainly because of droughts, and a few years later Joynt moved to Melbourne, where he changed his career completely and founded a printing and publishing firm instead. He was an innovative printer over sixty years and despite economic highs and lows, seemed to have survived.

In 1923 in Melbourne Joynt was a founder member of a small group of ex-servicemen who included Lt-Gen. Sir Stanley Savige, who formed a movement with the name of Legacy, a group whose aims were to care for veterans' widows and their children. As founder members, Savige and Joynt attended a meeting in Melbourne of war widows at which their ideas were set out. Joynt became a member of several committees of legacy and retained an interest in the group for the rest of his life. The group successfully campaigned to have the Melbourne Shrine of Remembrance built in its present form.

Joynt was still very interested in military matters between the two wars and for seven years from 1926 he was an officer in the militia, serving with the 6th Royal Melbourne Regiment. After he was promoted to major in February 1930 he became the regiment's second-in-command.

In January 1932 Joynt was one of the pallbearers at the funeral of Albert Jacka VC who had died on the 17th. Two months later, on 19 March, Joynt married Edith A. Garrett in a civil ceremony and the couple lived at Kallista, Melbourne. The marriage had lasted forty-six years when Edith died in May 1978. They left no children.

After the Second World War began, Joynt returned to full-time soldiering, on 26 September 1939 commanding the 3rd Garrison Battalion at Fort Queenscliff. He was then made commandant of the large training centre at Puckapunyal, and from June 1942 was staff officer and quartermaster at a similar camp nearby at Seymour. On 10 October 1944 he was placed on the Retired List as an honorary lieutenant.

During his business career Joynt became a director of several publishing firms, and was the president of a group called the Old Melbournians. In September 1949 he unveiled a memorial headstone to the memory of Albert Lowerson VC at Myrtleford, which was paid for by the local residents. The ceremony was also by A.C. Borella VC and other ex-servicemen from the district.

In 1956, when Joynt was visiting London for the VC/GC celebrations he was invited to broadcast to Australia at the dinner given by the Lord Mayor of London. The following year, in 1957, together with six other holders of the VC, he attended a memorial service for the late William Dunstan VC, held at Christ Church, South Yarra, on 5 March.

During an Australian royal tour in 1977, the Queen and Prince Phillip met Edward Kenna VC and William Joynt VC. The latter read a note from Rupert Vance Moon VC, who was unable to meet the Queen himself. All three men had been introduced to the Queen in an earlier tour of Australia in 1954.

In 1971 Joynt published his first of three autobiographical books: *To Russia and Back Through Communist Countries*, followed by *Saving the Channel Ports 1918* (1975). Four years later he published *Breaking the Road for the Rest* (1979) which was issued by Hyland House of Melbourne.

During his life Joynt sees to have been a model citizen and was always a great supporter of the VC reunions, which included dinner in Melbourne on Armistice Day 1929, the Hyde Park Centenary Parade on 26 June 1956, the VC and GC Association gathering at Buckingham House and the Mansion House in July 1962, as well as other meetings in London in July 1966.

Donovan, as he was known throughout his life was clearly quite a character; he had the advantage of being on the small side. Bill Gammage has described him as a 'chirpy cock sparrow of a man'. He was also 'self-reliant, dogmatic, conservative, a nominal Anglican, a Freemason from 1924, a dedicated advocate of returned-soldier causes, a special constable during the 1923 Melbourne police strike, a keen club-man and a life member of the Naval and Military Club …'

On 5 May 1986 William Joynt, at the age of 97, the last survivor of the sixty-six Australians who were awarded the VC in the First World War, died at his home in Windsor, Melbourne, Victoria. He was buried with full military honours on 12 May at Brighton Lawn Cemetery. More than 340 soldiers joined the procession that moved down Glen Eira Road, Caulfield, after a funeral service at St Mary's Anglican Church where there had been a congregation of 200 people. His VC was carried together with the rest of his decorations on a blue velvet cushion behind the gun carriage bearing his coffin. Joynt is commemorated in the Australian War Memorial, Canberra, but his medals are in private hands.

In 1992 Joynt's field service diary, which he kept from March to August 1916 with entries in indelible pencil, was offered for sale in Australia. It had marbled green card covers and contained very detailed entries. In it he described the actions and movements carried out by the 8th Battalion, as well as giving his personal observations of the war and people with whom he came into contact.

Joynt's name is one of ninety-six Australian VCs won which are commemorated in Victoria Cross Park Memorial in Canberra and dedicated in July 2000, 100 years after Australia won its first VC. The same ninety-six names are also commemorated in the Victoria Cross Memorial in the Queen Victoria Building in Sydney.

L.D. McCarthy

North of Lihons, France, 23 August

Madame Wood is a very small copse to the north of the village of Lihons, adjacent to a track that leads to the village of Herleville. It was in this area, during the Battle of Albert, that Lt Lawrence McCarthy, D Company Commander of the 16th (SA & WA) AIF (4th Brigade) gained the VC on 23 August 1918 at Courtine Trench.

During the previous night, the British 97th Brigade (32nd Division) had attacked Herleville, managing to capture it with only a small loss. However, this was followed by a hold-up in some woods in a gully, south of the Roman road.

On 23 August, to the south, a subsidiary advance involving the 16th Lancashire Fusiliers (96th Brigade, 32nd Division) and a bombing party of the 16th AIF (4th Brigade) took place. The advance began at 4.45 a.m., with other battalions belonging to the 4th Australian Brigade to the right and the 96th Brigade to the left. The distance they had to cover was only about 300yds, but the two battalions encountered very strong opposition of machine guns and bombs. The Australian bomb supply was running very low and an officer was sent back for more.

It was at that point the Australian Company Commander Lt L.D. McCarthy came up to see what the delay was. Rather than wait for the extra bombs to be brought up, he then gave orders to charge the obstacle, which was a sort of island protected by wire barricades. The enemy covered the Australian trench with machine-gun fire and McCarthy could see other enemy posts within a distance of 50yds. Accompanied by Sgt F.J. Robbins, McCarthy moved quickly around a block and into a sap. Two members of the Lancashire Fusiliers began tunnelling underneath the block in order to make communication easier. At a trench crossing McCarthy shot a sentry and, moving round a corner, found himself face to face with the very machine-gun post that was enfilading the Australian positions. He disposed of the men at the

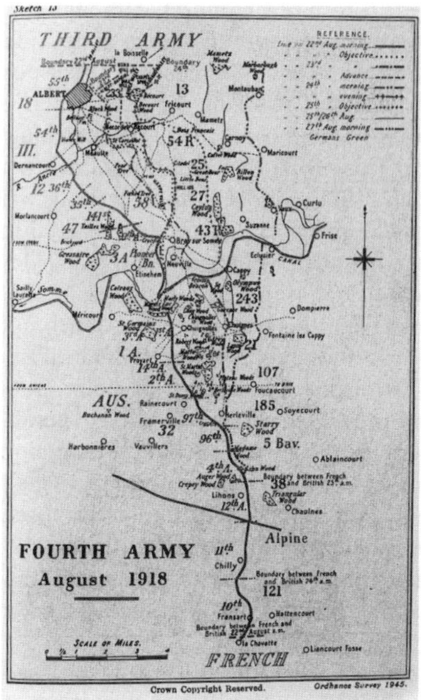

post before moving on to find himself behind a German officer waving his arms at a group of men who were running off in all directions. McCarthy shot this German officer and the rest of the enemy ran into a short narrow sap. The two Australians lobbed their last few bombs into this sap and, acquiring a supply of German bombs, threw these in too! At that point two British soldiers appeared, having emerged from the tunnel. The German heads were kept down by Lewis gun fire.

After a while the sign of surrender, in the form of a bloodstained handkerchief, was displayed from the sap and forty Germans surrendered. Fifteen others had been killed in the fighting. By his personal intervention McCarthy had captured 500yds of enemy front line, although in the end 700yds of captured trench were handed over to the British. As a consequence of McCarthy's valour and audacity the objectives were eventually reached and consolidated. McCarthy's VC was gazetted on 14 December 1918 as follows:

> For most conspicuous bravery, initiative, and leadership on the morning of 23 Aug. 1918, in attack near Madame Wood, east of

> Vermandovillers (north of Chaulnes). Although the objectives of his battalion were attained without serious opposition the battalion on the left flank was heavily opposed by well-posted machine guns. Lieut. McCarthy, realizing the position, at once engaged the nearest machine gun post, but still the attacking troops failed to get forward. This officer then determined to attack the nearest post. Leaving his men to continue the fire fight, he with two others, dashed across the open and succeeded in reaching the block. Although single-handed, as he had out-distanced his comrades, and despite serious opposition and obstacles, he captured the gun and continued to fight his way down the trench, inflicting heavy casualties and capturing three more machine guns. At this stage, being some 700 yards from his starting-point, he was joined by one of his men, and together they continued to bomb up the trench until touch was established with an adjoining unit. Lieutenant McCarthy, during this most daring advance, single-handed killed 20 of the enemy and captured in addition five machine guns and 50 prisoners. By his gallant and determined action he saved a critical situation, prevented many casualties, and was mainly, if not entirely, responsible for the final objective being taken.

According to the battalion history the prisoners closed in on him from all sides and patted him on the back! As well as capturing fifty prisoners and killing twenty Germans he also captured about 460 metres of the German front line. C.E.W. Bean considered this a great individual action which was on a par with Albert Jacka's at Pozières on 7 August 1916. If a reader cares to vist the area today they will find that the A29 Autoroute splits the villages of Lihons and Herleville.

On 18 September McCarthy was one of the officers in charge of attacking companies who were involved in the capture of the Hindenburg Line outpost of Le Verguier. The operation by the 16th Battalion was very successful and they only suffered twenty casualties, but still managed to capture 450 German prisoners along with sixty machine guns, as well as several other guns.

On 21 November McCarthy became ill and was sent back to England to recuperate. He married Florence Minnie Norville at Weston-super-Mare, Somerset, on 25 January 1919, and the couple were to have one son, Lawrence Norville.

On 12 July McCarthy attended the investiture when he received his VC from the King in the Ballroom of Buckingham Palace.

❖❖❖

Laurence Dominic McCarthy was the son of Florence McCarthy of County Cork, Ireland, and his wife Anne McCarthy (*née* Sherry). He was born east of Perth in York, Western Australia, on 21 January 1892. Both of his parents died when he was young and his early years were spent in the Clontart Orphanage and in various Catholic schools. He became a commercial traveller and building superintendent, growing up with an ample frame and acquiring the nickname of 'Fat'.

McCarthy became a member of the 18th Light Horse before moving to Lion Mill where he worked as a contractor. Lion Mill was later called Mt Helena. When the war began in August 1914 he enlisted in the AIF as a private on 16 October and trained at Blackboy Camp. He was an original member of the 16th Battalion, with the number 422. He left Melbourne for Egypt on the *Ceramic* on 22 December 1914, landing at Gallipoli on 26 April 1915 as a member of C Company. He was made a lance corporal on 13 May and promoted to corporal on 19 July and then to sergeant on 1 September. In the same month he became ill and was evacuated, returning to duty in November. He left Gallipoli a second time with the last party of his battalion on 20 December.

The 16th Australian Battalion reached France in June 1916, in time to participate in the heavy fighting around Pozières and Mouquet Farm in August. On 8 March 1917 McCarthy became company sergeant-major, and on 10 April was commissioned second lieutenant. The following day he was wounded in the first battle for Bullecourt, where his battalion was very badly cut up, and he was invalided to hospitals and convalescent homes in England.

It was to be nearly three months before he rejoined his unit on 9 July 1917. On 1 November he was promoted to full lieutenant and on 3 November he received the French Croix de Guerre at Beaumetz. On 31 January 1918 he was posted to the 13th Training Battalion, in Tidworth, England. He returned to his former 16th Battalion in time for the opening offensive on 8 August. He became ill again towards the end of November, being once more evacuated to hospital which is when he learnt of his VC award in December. He was transferred to Reserve of Officers in 1919, returning to Australia on 20 December, and his appointment with the AIF ended on 6 August 1920.

In 1926 McCarthy moved from Western Australia to Victoria, joining the staff of Sunshine Harvester Works as a traveller in the Mallee until he lost his job owing to the depression in 1934. In 1929 he had attended the VC Dinner in Melbourne on 11 November. He obtained a new position in 1935 as a superintendent of The Trustees, Executors & Agency Co. Lt Building, Melbourne. His son, Lawrence Norville, was killed in action at Bougainville, Solomon Islands, in May 1945.

In June 1956 McCarthy was one of the Australian contingent to visit London for the Hyde Park Review and in 1964 he attended the opening of the VC Corner at the Australian War Memorial in Canberra. He also took part in the commemorations of the fiftieth anniversary of the Anzac landings at Gallipoli on 25 April 1965. He was one of seventy-eight Australian and New Zealand veterans who were then aged between 69 and 76 years old. Landing at Anzac Cove (Ari Burnu), instead of being met by deadly fire, they were greeted by Turkish veterans and the former enemies exchanged gifts. The landing party of 'first day men' also included Bill Ruthven VC and Captain Perakaka Taitwi, the only Maori officer to have survived the Gallipoli campaign. The rest of the Anzac contingent, which consisted of 250 Australians and seventy-seven men from New Zealand, were spectators of the 'landing' from a Turkish ship anchored close by. The 'landing' was the culmination of four days of commemoration based on the Turkish capital of Istanbul. In addition to the Anzac men, there was also a group of seventeen men from Newfoundland who had been part of the landing of the British 29th Division. Their expenses had been paid for by their government, but sadly Britain was not represented as the Foreign Office was unable to justify the expenditure of public funds for the trip!

McCarthy was a past president of the 16th Battalion and 4th Brigade Associations. His home was Lorne Parade, Mont Albert. He died on 25 May 1975 at the Heidelberg Repatriation Hospital, Melbourne, where he had been a patient for about three weeks. He was given a funeral with full military honours three days later. A service was held at Wycliff Church, Norfolk Road, Surrey Hills and his remains were then cremated at the Springvale Crematorium, where at the crematorium necropolis there is a plaque which commemorates his life.

McCarthy was survived by his wife Florence, who bequeathed his decorations to the Australian War Memorial where there is also a portrait of him by Charles Wheeler DCM. Apart from the VC, the medals are: the 1914–15 Star, BWM, VM, Coronation Medals for 1937 and 1953 and the Croix de Guerre (France). On the wall of the Mairie at Vermandovillers (north of Lihons) is a plaque which commemorates Lt McCarthy's extraordinary achievement on 23 August 1918. A ward in the Hollywood Repatriation General Hospital was also named after him. He is also remembered with McCarthy Place in Canberra. In April 2007 a branch of the RSL was named after him in York, his home town. His name is also one of ninety-six Australian VCs won which are commemorated in Victoria Cross Park Memorial in Canberra and dedicated in July 2000, 100 years after Australia received its first VC. The same ninety-six names are also commemorated in the Victoria Cross Memorial in the Queen Victoria Building in Sydney.

H. McIver

East of Courcelles-le-Comte, France, 23 August

During the Battle of Albert (21–23 August 1918) the operations on 21 August were sufficiently successful that the decision was made that a planned general attack by the Third and Fourth Armies could now go ahead. On 22 August the 2nd Royal Scots (Lothian Regiment) of the 8th Brigade of the 3rd Division took over front-line positions close to the Arras–Albert railway opposite the village of Gomiécourt to the north-west of Bapaume. They were given high ground to the east as their objective.

Gomicourt was captured by the 76th Brigade, 3rd Division by 5 a.m., and 300 prisoners were taken. The infantry had the assistance of eight tanks in the mopping up operations which included destroying machine-gun nests. It was the 8th Brigade of the same division who, after considerable opposition from enemy machine guns, managed to reach its objective north of the village. This brigade included the 7th (S) King's Shropshire Light Infantry and the 2nd Royal Scots, and one member of the latter battalion was Pte Hugh McIver, who gained a VC during the advance.

According to the *Regimental History* the operation on 23 August began at 4 a.m., proving very successful, and, according to the history:

> ... there was never a hitch, and skilfully controlled by their officers the men brilliantly sustained the reputation of the battalion. 'C' Company at one time seemed to have the prospect of a stiff fight, but the extraordinary daring of the company runner Private H. McIver, converted a potential resistance into an absolute rout. Early in the fray he singled out a German and chased him for 150 yards. The hunted man jumped into a

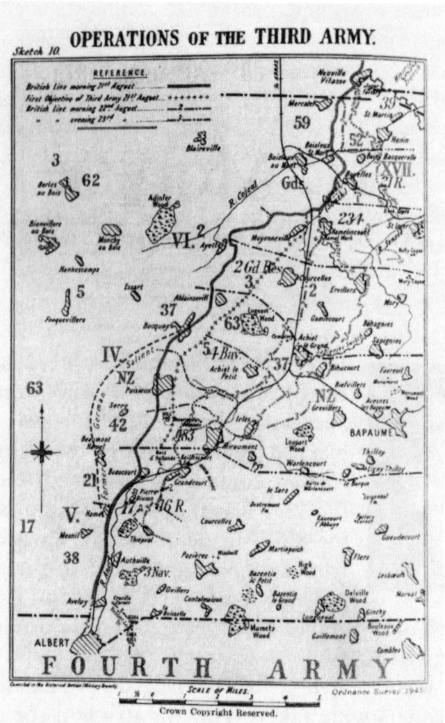

machine gun nest, but Private McIver, who gave no thought to his own safety, immediately followed him and fought like a man possessed against the occupants of the trench. After six Germans had been shot or bayoneted by the daring runner, the remainder of the garrison, about twenty in number, although they were armed with two machine guns, surrendered …

McIver's deed encouraged the rest of C Company to move successfully forward, while at the same time it seemed that the remaining Germans had lost heart. This led to the capture of 284 officers and men, together with several field-guns, howitzers and machine guns. Having reached their objective, the Royal Scots were able to allow a new British division to pass through their lines. The battalion moved back to trenches east of Adinfer and on 29 August it moved to Boiry-St Martin, ready again for action; two days later the battalion took over trenches at Hamelincourt. Orders for a fresh attack were received and after midnight the men, having had to don their gas respirators, passed through Érvillers and Mory to the west of Noreuil and moved into new trenches in readiness for the attack. It was in the subsequent fight that Private McIver lost his life. Casualties were high, but those of the enemy even higher, and in all 384 prisoners were captured. The 2nd Royal Scots, after their involvement in this action, returned to the Hamelincourt area on 3 September, where they received a short period of training before returning to the front line on 16 September. McIver's VC was gazetted on 15 November 1918:

> For most conspicuous bravery and devotion to duty when employed as a company-runner east of Courcelles-le-Comte on 23 August 1918. In spite of heavy artillery and machine gun fire, he carried messages regardless of his own safety. Single-handed he pursued an enemy scout into a machine gun post and having killed six of the garrison, captured twenty prisoners with two machine guns. This gallant action enabled the company to advance unchecked. Later, he succeeded at great personal risk in stopping the fire of a British tank which was directed in error against our own troops at close range. By this very gallant action Private McIver undoubtably saved many lives.

After McIver was killed north of Lagnicourt on 2 September, he was buried in Vraucourt Copse British Cemetery, nearly 5 miles to the north-east of Bapaume in Plot I, Row A, Grave 19. Six days after McIver had been killed Alick Gordon, captain of C Company, wrote a letter of sympathy to his parents:

> I am writing these few lines to try to express, both on my own behalf and also for the men of my company, our greatest sympathy for you in the loss of your son Hugh in the recent fighting.
>
> It came as a great blow to me, as he was my personal orderly, and he was quite close to me when he was killed. We were going up a hill, attacking some machine guns, when he was killed by a bullet, and it may soften your blow a little to know he never felt it.
>
> It is only about ten days since I recommended him for the Victoria Cross, and it is quite likely that it will be awarded to you, and if ever a man deserved the V.C., Hugh did, as he was one of the best and bravest boys in the battalion; in fact, the bravest I have ever known.
>
> I am sending onto you his Military Medal and rose, which I cut off his breast for you. His other personal effects will follow later.

> I can only say, Mrs. McIver, that your son died a hero's death, and he has left a record in the battalion second to none. Again expressing my deepest sympathy to you and yours.

McIver's parents were presented with their son's posthumous VC by the King at Buckingham Palace on 13 February 1919.

Hugh McIver, the eldest of seven children, was born at 30 Napier Street, Linwood, Kilbarchan, Renfrewshire, on 21 June 1890. His parents were Hugh McIver and Mary (*née* Flynn). When Hugh junior was still young the family moved to a mining village close to Glasgow, where their home address in 1918 was 34 Dunlopst, Newton Hallside, Glasgow. Hugh attended St Charles' Roman Catholic school and after leaving school he became a miner at Newton No. 1 Pit. In early 1914 he decided to join the army and became a member of the Highland Light Infantry. However, his behaviour was not up to military requirements and he was discharged in March after barely eight weeks' service.

Two weeks after the war broke out he enlisted in the Royal Scots on 18 August when he was allocated the service number of 12311. He served in France with the 2nd Royal Scots from 11 May 1915 until 19 October 1917 and later from 12 February 1918 until 2 September 1918, the day when he was killed. Among his decorations, which are in the collection of the Royal Scots in Edinburgh Castle, are the 1914–15 Star, the MM (*LG* 19 September 1916) and Bar (*LG* 21 October 1918), BWM and VM. He was unmarried.

On 26 June 2007 after a service in Paisley Abbey a memorial to McIver and four other Renfrewshire VC holders including Captain Arthur Henderson VC was unveiled in Hawkhead Cemetery.

S. FORSYTH

Grévillers, France, 24 August

Towards the end of August 1918 the New Zealand Division of the New Zealand Expeditionary Force was held in readiness to exploit any success made on the IV Corps front. In the very early morning of 24 August the New Zealand 1st Brigade consisted of the 1st and 2nd Battalions, Wellington Regiment, and the 2nd Battalion, Auckland Regiment, who were to move forward via Loupart Wood and Grévillers to the west of Bapaume. This left the 1st Auckland Battalion in reserve. Sergeant Samuel Forsyth, a New Zealand sapper, on attachment to the 2nd Auckland Infantry Regiment, won a posthumous VC on 24 August and was killed in the action.

The New Zealand troops assembled on the east side of the Albert–Arras railway and at about 4.30 a.m. attacked towards their first objective, the village of Grévillers. They were without artillery support as there had been too short a time to arrange it. This was two-edged, for although the brigade had surprise on its side it also found many machine-gun nests intact. Initially the two leading companies of the 2nd Auckland met little opposition, but later a machine gun on the left flank became troublesome, delaying the left platoon while the rest of the attack continued its advance. A supporting company managed to capture the machine-gun nest from the rear, resulting in a quick German withdrawal, and several machine guns together with their crews were captured. The west side of Grévillers was reached by 6 a.m. with only slight casualties. By 7 a.m. the village had fallen, with the enemy garrison taken completely by surprise. Some Germans, apparently, were even having their breakfast when the New Zealanders fell upon them.

The outskirts of the village provided a much stiffer test for the 37th Division, which was on the flank of the New Zealand Brigade. Former British huts on the road to Biefvillers-lès-Bapaume provided very suitable cover for the enemy, who directed heavy fire on the left of the Auckland company when it came into their range of observation. This is where the tanks which had been sent for came into play as they managed to clear out the huts. A company of the 2nd Wellington Battalion crossed the road and pushed on to high ground to the north. Posts were pushed forward to 500yds to the east of Grévillers towards Avesnes-lès-Bapaume.

On the south side of Grévillers troops of the 2nd Auckland Battalion were held up by the enemy, who were providing stiff opposition against the 1st Wellington Battalion from the fringe of Loupart Wood. It was noted that Sgt Samuel Forsyth did good work and showed excellent leadership qualities. He managed to destroy three machine-gun nests almost single-handed. The advance then continued towards the Transloy–Loupart system which guarded the town of Bapaume. The trenches ran in a westerly direction and faced the 1st Brigade, which was subsequently held up by intense fire from enemy positions in sunken roads and hidden pits. The New Zealanders sent for tanks and in time the high ground around the village was captured, thanks in very large measure to Sgt Forsyth. His citation tells the story of what happened very well. Sadly he was killed by a sniper while in action winning his VC and his posthumous decoration was gazetted on 22 October 1918:

> For most conspicuous bravery and devotion to duty in attack. On nearing the objective, his company came under heavy machine gun fire. Through Sergt. Forsyth's dashing leadership and total disregard of danger, three machine gun positions were rushed, and the crews taken prisoner before they could inflict many casualties on our troops. During subsequent advance his company came under heavy fire from several machine guns, two of which he located by a daring reconnaissance. In his endeavour to gain support from a Tank, he was wounded, but after having the wound bandaged, he again got in touch with the Tank, which in the face of very heavy fire from machine guns and anti-Tank guns, he endeavoured to lead with magnificent coolness to a favourable position. The Tank, however, was put out of action. Sergt. Forsyth then organized the Tank crew and several of his men into a section, and led them to a position where the machine guns could be outflanked. Always under heavy fire, he directed them into positions which brought about a retirement of the enemy machine guns and enabled the advance to continue. This gallant N.C.O. was at that moment killed by a sniper. From the commencement of the attack until the time of his death Sergt. Forsyth's courage and coolness, combined with great power of initiative, proved an invaluable

> incentive to all who were with him, and he undoubtedly saved many casualties among his comrades.

Of Sgt Forsyth's actions the *History of the Auckland Regiment* comments:

> ... he moved freely and around a bare and exposed slope organising the new run. Enemy snipers not a hundred yards away were very busy and one of them shot Sergeant Forsyth dead. He had been in front from the moment the advance started and had acted throughout with the most cool and desperate daring. It was quite certain that he would be killed. He has as fine a fighting service as any man in the Division. Enlisting with the main body of Engineers he was one of the few who went right through Gallipoli. In France he had been through every engagement in which New Zealand troops had fought in addition to which he had been in two fights with Australian and one with British troops. His was a wonderful record crowned by a day of glorious deeds ... All were agreed that he was worthy of it and that there was no one who could be in any way equal to him.

Forsyth was buried 7 miles north-est of Albert and about 2 miles from where he was killed, in Adanac Military Cemetery, Plot 1, Row I, Grave 59. His headstone is almost the first grave on the left inside the cemetery which can be found to the south of Miraumont. His VC was presented to Mary his widow in the Ballroom of Buckingham Palace on 23 November 1918. Her address was 79 John Knox Street, Glasgow.

Samuel Forsyth was born to Mr and Mrs Thomas Forsyth in Wellington, New Zealand, on 3 April 1891 and was educated at Thorndon and Terrace Schools in the same city. After leaving school Forsyth took up gold-mining and became an Amalgamator with Monowai Gold Mining company at Thames. He was a practising Christian and a member of the Kent Terrace Bible Class, and also worked hard for the Sailors' Friend Society. His home address was 26 Cottlerville Terrace, Wellington.

As a reservist, when war broke out, Forsyth was among the first men to be called up, joining the army on 13 August 1914. His attestation forms record that he was 5ft 11in tall, weighed 10st 7lb, and had a fresh complexion, hazel eyes and fair hair. He had some military experience, having already served with the Field Engineers for four years.

On 16 October Forsyth left New Zealand for Egypt with the New Zealand Engineers, who were attached to the 2nd Battalion Auckland Infantry Regiment. He was posted to Field Troop as a sapper. His service number was 4/400; the 4 meant that he was an engineer and the 400 stood for the order of enlistment. He landed in Gallipoli on 9 May 1915 but two months later, on 4 July, owing to sickness, he was evacuated to a Cairo hospital. He returned to Gallipoli and in August was slightly wounded in action but remained at duty, staying on the peninsula for three more months before he was evacuated to Mudros to a hospital in Lemnos. He later left Mudros for England and was in hospital in Birmingham in early December. After a short period in Hornchurch, Essex, and still not fit, he was transferred to the New Zealand hospital in Walton-on-Thames, Surrey and from there he returned to Hornchurch before proceeding to France on 14 April 1916.

Forsyth joined the 3rd Field Company, New Zealand Engineers. By this time he was a lance corporal and in October 1917 his rank was made up to full corporal. In May 1918 he was promoted to sergeant. Three months later he was attached to the 2nd Battalion, Auckland Light Infantry Regiment of the 1st New Zealand Infantry Brigade, for preliminary infantry training prior to applying for a commission with the engineers.

Forsyth first met his wife, Mary, in Glasgow in 1916 when he was addressing a Christian association meeting while on leave. After his death she worked as a missionary and later lived in Belfast. She remarried but never had any children. On her death a nephew in Scotland inherited her first husband's decorations and decided to sell them. In November 1981 Forsyth's VC was offered for sale at Sotheby's, together with his other medals: 1914–15 Star, BWM and VM, and his Anzac plaque for Gallipoli. The expected price was £9,000–£10,000 and the decorations were purchased for £9,500 in 1982 by a Melbourne dealer who offered them for resale shortly afterwards in Australia. They are now part of the collection of Lord Ashcroft in the Imperial War Museum.

In 1921 Samuel Forsyth as well as Richard Travis VC were the subjects of Richard Wallwork who was commissioned to produce paintings of the two dead soldiers for the National Collection of War Art. The two men were also two of the New Zealand-born VC holders who were commemorated outside the Returned Servicemen's Association HQ, Dunedin, New Zealand in November 1921. In September 1996 the plaques were moved to a site close to Dunedin Railway Station, and in 2001 they were moved again, this time to the Dunedin Cenotaph in the Queen's Gardens. Forsyth was also commemorated with a tablet at the Sailors' Friend Society Institute in Wellington.

D.L. MacIntyre

Henin and Fontaine-lès-Croisilles, France, 24–27 August

To the north of Bapaume and as part of the attacks on the Hindenburg Line, the two City of Glasgow Battalions of the 1/5th and 1/6th Highland Light Infantry respectively successfully captured Henin and the lower slopes of Henin Hill by 9 a.m. on 24 August. The two battalions were part of the 157th Infantry Brigade of the 52nd Lowland Division. Two battalions of the 156th Infantry Bde then came up on their left; 1/7th Royal Scots and 1/7th Scottish Rifles. The two brigades were now opposite the main Hindenburg positions. Moving uphill at Henin Hill the 157th Brigade ran into British artillery, which was concentrating on the Hindenburg Line. Owing to communications being down this problem was not finally sorted out until mid-afternoon and the two Highland Light Infantry battalions pushed on uphill under a light barrage but were repelled by machine gun and trench mortar fire.

During the action at Henin, T/Lt David MacIntyre of the Argyll and Sutherland Highlanders who was attached to the 1/6th Battalion Highland Light Infantry, won the first part of his VC. The second part was won at Fontaine-lès-Croisilles. The award was gazetted on 26 October 1918 and tells the story of his gallantry as follows:

> For most conspicuous bravery in attack when, acting as Adjutant of his battalion, he was constantly in evidence in the firing line, and by his coolness under most heavy shell and machine gun fire inspired the confidence of all ranks. Three days later he was in command of the firing line during an attack, and showed throughout most courageous and skilful leading in face of heavy machine gun fire. When barbed wire was encountered, he personally reconnoitred it before leading his men forward.

> On one occasion, when extra strong entanglements were reached, he organised and took forward a party of men, under heavy machine gun fire and supervised the making of gaps. Later, when the greater part of our line was definitely held up, Lieut. MacIntyre rallied a small party, pushed forward through the enemy barrage in pursuit of an enemy machine gun detachment, and ran them to earth in a 'pill-box', a short distance ahead, killing three and capturing an officer, ten other ranks, and five machine guns. In this redoubt he and his party raided three 'pill-boxes' and disposed of the occupants, thus enabling the battalion to capture the redoubt. When the battalion was ordered to take up a defensive position, Lieut. MacIntyre, after he had been relieved of command of the firing line, reconnoitred the right flank, which was exposed. When doing this an enemy machine gun opened fire close to him. Without any hesitation he rushed it single-handed, put the team to flight, and brought in the gun. On returning to the redoubt he continued to show splendid spirit while supervising consolidation. The success of the advance was largely due to Lieut. MacIintyre's fine leadership and initiative, and his gallantry and leading was an inspiring example to all.

After he was wounded at Mœuvres near Cambrai on 27 September 1918, MacIntyre was invalided home.

David Lowe MacIntyre was born at the Free Church Manse in Portnahaven, Islay, Argyll on 18 June 1895, the second son of a clergyman, the Revd Archibald Stewart MacIntyre, of 25 Downie Terrace, Corstorphine Road, Edinburgh, and his wife Elizabeth (*née* Lowe). The Revd MacIntyre was a minister in the United Free Church. His son David attended the village school before moving on to George Watson's College in Edinburgh, then becoming a student of art at Edinburgh University. He became a member of the University OTC in 1914.

On 6 May 1915, at the age of 19, he was gazetted to the 13th (Reserve) Battalion, Argyll and Sutherland Highlanders. He embarked for the Middle East and then Mudros from Southampton on 17 February 1916 and was attached to a battalion of another Scottish regiment, the 1/6th Battalion Highland Light Infantry (City of Glasgow) (157 Brigade, 52 Division). On 17 March he sailed to Egypt and was appointed temporary lieutenant on 1 July and to temporary captain on 31 October.

During the war MacIntyre served in Palestine and Syria until 2 April 1918, and at the beginning of November 1917 his battalion had been involved in fighting the Turks in the third and last Battle of Gaza. His battalion arrived in France on 10 April 1918 and became part of the Third Army. Macintyre served in France from 10 April to 27 September. He had been adjutant of the 6th HLI since June. After he had won his VC he was wounded at Mœuvres and sent home to a hospital in Wandsworth. He attended an investiture in the Ballroom of Buckingham Palace on 13 December 1918 and was one of nine men to be awarded the VC at the ceremony.

MacIntyre had two brothers, who served in the Scottish Horse and Black Watch respectively. After David was discharged from the Argyll and Sutherland Highlanders in 1919 he made his home in Middlesex. In acknowledgement of his winning the VC MacIntyre was presented with an illuminated address and gold watch by the people of Corstorphine, then in Midlothian. On 19 March 1919 the Glasgow Islay Association also made a presentation to him. This time the gifts included a smoker's stand, a siver inkstand and a wallet containing £131. David MacIntyre attended the VC Garden Party at Buckingham Palace on 26 June 1920 and was a member of the Honour Guard for the Unknown Warrior on 11 November.

Also in 1920 he joined the Civil Service and entered the Office of Works in London. In 1929, nine years later, in Crown Court Church, London, MacIntyre married Elspeth Moir Forsyth on 20 February. The couple's first home was in Northwood, Middlesex. Also in 1929 Macintyre attended the House of Lords Dinner on 9 November.

It was at the family home in Northwood that the couple had their two children: a daughter, Marion, born in 1929 and a son, David, born in 1932. In 1936 Macintyre was made the principal in charge of the Scottish Branch. On the outbreak of war in 1939 he was seconded to London, only returning to Edinburgh in 1943, while the rest of his family remained in Scotland.

In 1943, having returned to Edinburgh, MacIntyre was presented with a second gold watch in recognition of his service in the Home Guard in London. After the Second World War was over he attended the Victory Parade in London on 8 June 1946 and, on 30 June, took part in a parade at King's Park, Edinburgh. This parade was arranged by the Scottish section of the British Legion and was to commemorate the twenty-fifth anniversary of the setting up of the Legion in Scotland. It was attended by the King and Queen together with their two daughters, Princess Elizabeth and Princess Margaret. Ten thousand members of the Legion from all parts of Scotland took part in the march past, and about 100,000 people attended overall. The service was conducted by the Very Revd Charles L. Warr, assisted by the King's Assistant Chaplain-General. Queen Elizabeth II was presented with bouquets from three daughters of soldiers who were taking part in the events, who included the daughter of Capt. D.L. MacIntyre. Before leaving, the royal party spoke to the eight holders of the VC who attended. Three of them – David MacIntyre, David Hunter and Adam Archibald – had won their VCs in the last period of the First World War. The royal party were also introduced to Gen. Sir Ian Hamilton, who had been commander-in-chief at Gallipoli. A few weeks later, on 28 August, MacIntyre assisted the Duke of Buccleuch when the two men opened a museum at Melrose Abbey.

MacIntyre had been made Under-Secretary Ministry of Works in Edinburgh and in this capacity attended various functions connected with the two world wars. In 1956 he took part in the parade in the VC Centenary Parade in Hyde Park. In 1959 in his 65th year, Macintyre retired as Under-Secretary Ministry of Works (Scotland). During his time in the Civil Service his name was associated with many important projects including the reconstruction of the bombed House of Commons and the restructuring of the Scottish Naval and Military Museum in Edinburgh.

David MacIntyre's home address was 39 Buckingham Terrace, Edinburgh, and on 31 July 1967 he died in the Civil Service nursing home, also in Edinburgh. After a service of remembrance in Corstorphine Parish Church on 3 August he was cremated at Warriston Crematorium, Edinburgh and his ashes scattered in the garden of remembrance. MacIntyre's VC is on display in the National War Memorial of Scotland in Edinburgh Castle. His other decorations were the BWM, VM and Coronation Medals for 1937 and 1953. In the New Year's Honours list of 1949 he was appointed Companion of the Order of the Bath (Civil Division).

The MacIntyre children and other members of the family followed the wishes of Elspeth after her death in 1996 when they presented his decorations to the then United Services Museum in Edinburgh Castle at a special luncheon on 23 November 1998. The name of the museum was later changed to the National War Museum of Scotland. Finally a Smith and Wesson .455 revolver belonging to David MacIntyre was presented to the Argyll and Sutherland Highlanders in Stirling Castle.

H.J. Colley

Martinpuich, France, 25 August

In positions between the towns of Bapaume and Albert in the Department of the Somme, the 10th (S) Lancashire Fusiliers (52nd Brigade, 17th Division) received orders at 1.30 a.m. on 25 August 1918 to advance eastwards, with the village of Martinpuich as their first objective. The 12th (S) Manchester Battalion of the same brigade was to pass to the south and join up with the Lancashire Fusiliers to the north on the far side and the village was then to be 'mopped up'.

It soon became obvious that Martinpuich was much more strongly defended than had been first thought. In addition, the enemy artillery caught the advancing troops as they began to move off at zero hour, which was 4 a.m. Despite this, the village was eventually captured although the enemy artillery prevented the 52nd Infantry Brigade remaining there. When the attacking troops had reached a hill about half a mile east of the village, a large body of the enemy – estimated to be about three companies – was seen moving down the forward slope of the next ridge, obviously about to make a counter-attack. The 10th Lancashire Fusiliers quickly took up positions in some nearby trenches, and the enemy was upon them at about 4.15 p.m. By good fortune four machine guns belonging to the 17th Machine Gun Battalion happened suddenly to become available at this point and with their use the counter-attack was brought to a halt, thus preventing the enemy from recapturing the village. Part of B Company of the 10th Lancashire Fusiliers suffered heavy casualties, which was when Acting Sgt H. Colley gained his VC when seeing the company's difficulties. He rushed forward to assist two forward platoons and succeeded in rallying the men and forming a defensive flank in the trench. The trench was shared with the enemy and eventually the group drove the attackers off. Only three men of the garrison were left unwounded and tragically Colley died of stomach wounds that same night. The 52nd Brigade advance beyond Martinpuich was stopped mainly as a result of machine-gun fire coming from the direction of High Wood to the south-east. Colley's posthumous VC was gazetted on 22 October 1918 as follows:

> On 25 Aug., in front of Martinpuich, shortly after its capture, a very strong counter-attack was delivered by the enemy. Sergt. Colley's company was holding an advanced position, with two platoons in advance and two in support. The forward platoons were ordered to hold on at all costs. This N.C.O. rushed forward without orders to help the two forward platoons. He rallied the men, and threatened to shoot anyone who went back. The enemy were advancing quickly, and had already obtained a footing in this trench. Sergt. Colley then formed a defensive flank and held it. Out of the two platoons only three men remained unwounded, and he himself was dangerously wounded in the stomach. It was entirely due to Sergt. Colley's action that the enemy were prevented from breaking through, and were eventually driven off. His courage and tenacity saved a very critical situation.

Colley was buried at Mailly Wood Cemetery, Plot II, Row Q, Grave 4.

Lieutenant Colonel Ronald Cotton wrote to Colley's parents five days before the citation was published. There is no record of Colley's VC having been presented at Buckingham Palace, but it might have been posted to his younger brother, Albert, as he was next of kin. If it ever was formally presented, the ceremony would probably have been carried out in February 1919 and given to John Colley. Albert had served with the Royal Warwickshire Regiment, being permanently injured and discharged when buried by a shell and gassed at Messines in June 1917.

Harold John Colley, the son of John Colley, a pattern maker, and his wife Hannah Elizabeth (*née* Hadley), was born on 26 May 1894 at No. 60 Winson Street, Dudley Road, Smethwick, Birmingham. He attended Dudley Road Council School which still exists as a building. The family consisted of two boys and three girls, and moved to Smethwick when Harold was about 10 years old. John Colley worked at Tangyes Ltd, Cornwall Works, and later at Henry Pooley's in Brook Street. After Harold left school he worked first for a jeweller, then as a silver spinner at J & R Griffin Ltd, Link Works, Soho Hill.

As an active parishioner, he was a member of the Bearwood Road Baptist Church and took a full part in the church's activities, including the position of wicket-keeper in the Mission Cricket Eleven. He was also a gymnast of note and a keen cyclist. The Baptist church has been demolished and replaced by a new building but the original church hall still remains. In the 1911 census Harold is listed together with one younger brother and older three sisters.

A few weeks after the war began, Colley enlisted on 1 September 1914 from the family home at No. 74 Cheshire Road, Smethwick, as a private with the Duke of Cornwall's Light Infantry, where his number was 5615. He was first a cyclist, but later a despatch rider, working in that capacity when he went to France in the early part of 1915. He took part in the main battles over the following two years and in the spring of 1917 a gallant deed was recognised by Colley's commanding officer when he was awarded a Certifcate of Meritorious Service 'in recognition of conspicuous gallantry and devotion to duty in going forward under heavy trench mortar and machine-gun fire, and digging out two men who had been buried by a trench mortar bomb'.

After being wounded in this action on 30 March he returned to England for treatment for a few weeks, and on returning to France was transferred to the 10th Lancashire Fusiliers. By now he was a lance corporal with the new number of 40684.

Colley won the MM on 4 June 1918, gazetted on 10 November, when the enemy began a bombardment on the front of the 52nd Brigade to the south of Beaumont Hamel. The main part of the attack that followed was against the 10th Lancs. Fusiliers, commanded by Lt Col R.E. Cotton, 7th Yorkshire Regiment. The barrage lifted to the support line at 2.40 a.m. and small parties of Germans followed it: they had been using formerly-used trenches to break into the battalion's front line on a frontage of several hundred yards, managing to overwhelm the left flank. To the right, however, the enemy met vigorous Lewis-gun fire. Lance Corporal Harold Colley, together with two men, bombed along the trench, successfully pushing out the invaders after about ten minutes. Five of the enemy were killed and eight captured, with the remainder being driven off.

News reached the family home that Colley had been awarded the VC before the news of his death from wounds and Colley's quartermaster wrote to his parents along the following lines: 'He had won the respect and esteem of all who knew him – and more particularly of the C.S.M. and myself, who worked with him in and out of the line. It has been a blow to lose such a man. He will be greatly missed, both for his cheerfulness and manliness and his devotion to duty.'

Colley's colonel paid the following tribute:

> It will be some slight consolation to you to know that your gallant son has won the Victoria Cross for his splendid action on 25th August, which resulted in his death. He held a most important trench during the German counter-attack until there were only three men left that had not been either killed or wounded. He saved a very critical situation, and it was with the greatest pleasure that I have heard that he has gained the highest award. You must indeed be proud of him. The battalion which I have the honour to command is filled with pride that one of their comrades has been awarded the highest decoration for valour and added one more V.C. to the number already gained by the Regiment. The Lancashire Fusiliers have to their credit more V.C.s than any other Regiment in the British Army – and a proud record it is. Our sympathy with you in your loss is very real, and we all regret that such a gallant man died from his wounds in the hour of victory.

After the war, on 22 February 1919, John Colley was presented with an illuminated copy of the Birmingham City Council's resolution of congratulations. In 1920 an annual cycle race was set up with a cup presented each year, to perpetuate Harold Colley's memory. A Colley trophy, presented by a nephew, was given, to be awarded in races arranged by the Vintage Motorcycle Club in Birmingham. On 4 June 1925 John attended the opening of the Hall of Memory in Birmingham and on 18 April 1926 he and his wife Hannah were invited to unveil Smethwick's War Memorial where their son's name is listed. On 13 June 1923 the couple met the Prince of Wales when he visited the Smethwick Council House.

Harold's name was included in a plaque set up in the war memorial hut at his church. When the hut was knocked down in 1964 to make room for a new church on the same site, the plaque was placed in the church porch entrance. Another plaque, in bronze, was set up at the entrance to Smethwick Council House on the high street. His name is also included in the Book of Remembrance which can be found inside the entrance to the local library. At the time of writing, it is possible that a road named after Harold will be part of a new housing development on the site of the former Cape Hill Brewery in the town.

Colley's decorations which, apart from the VC and MM, include the 1914–15 Star, BWM and VM have been in the care of the Fusiliers' Lancashire Museum in Bury since 4 November 1989.

B.S. Gordon

Near Maricourt, France, 26–27 August

On 26 August 1918 the Maricourt plateau, between the Bray–Montauban gulley and the Somme, was still in German hands. The plan for the following day was for the 58th (London) Division to drive the enemy out of Maricourt and for the 41st Australian Battalion to capture the Somme River bend at Fargny Mill, to the south of the plateau.

During the period 26–27 August, L/Cpl B.S. Gordon, 41st Battalion (Queensland) AIF (11th Brigade, 3rd Australian Division) gained a VC during the fighting at Fargny Wood, close to the mill itself. On the left of the 41st Battalion, the 43rd was being troubled by machine guns operating in Maricourt Valley, and in the evening the 41st Battalion was ordered to relieve it. Later these instructions were altered and the 41st was then ordered to pass through the positions of the 43rd and to move out to Fargny Wood and Fargny Mill, positions to the north of the Frise bend, on the north bank of the Somme River. The operation began at 11 p.m. and by 2.50 a.m. the battalion had reached its objectives, sending up flares to denote their arrival.

At 4.55 a.m. the battalion was ordered to attack a second time, this time with the 58th Division. Their mission was to capture a system of trenches to the east of Maricourt. After they fought through Spur Wood the left company reached a bank to the south of Fargny Wood and a quarry to the east of it. The company then moved past the Fargny Mill riverbend to the small cliff or bluff named the Chapeau de Gendarme, which is on the edge of the road to the village of Curlu. After a creeping barrage, a German machine gun position to the right was dealt with by L/Cpl Gordon and by 6 a.m. C Company reached its objective when B Company passed through its lines. The opposition encountered was then dealt with by the two companies. It was at this point that L/Cpl Gordon of C Company played a significant role in the proceedings, by capturing a machine gun and killing its gunner. B Company then used its own machine guns and mortars to approach the objective. Gordon repeatedly went into Fargny Wood, finally accounting for more than sixty German prisoners. By 8.05 a.m. on 27 August, the 41st Battalion had advanced over a thousand yards before consolidating. The remainder of the day was spent in a precarious position, with the Somme River at their backs and the enemy in front of them at the adjacent Fargny Wood and Maricourt Spur. The battalion was later relieved by the 34th Battalion during the night.

Gordon was awarded the VC for his extreme gallantry which was gazetted on 26 December 1918 as follows:

> For most conspicuous bravery and devotion to duty on 26–27 Aug. 1918, east of Bray. He led his section through heavy shell fire to the objective, which he consolidated. Single-handed he attacked an enemy machine gun which was enfilading his company, killed the man on the gun and captured the post, which contained one officer and ten men. He then cleared up a trench, capturing twenty-nine prisoners and two machine guns. In clearing up further trenches he captured twenty-two prisoners, including one officer, and three machine guns. Practically unaided he captured, in the course of these operations, two officers and sixty-one other ranks, together with six machine guns, and displayed throughout a wonderful example of fearless initiative.

Bernard Sidney Gordon was born on 16 August 1891 in Launceston, Tasmania, the son of Charles Gordon a cabman and later hotel owner and his wife Mary (*née* Reynolds). Bernard was educated at Deloraine and Devonport before becoming a cooper's machinist at Beaconsfield. He later had a job in Townsville, Queensland, where he dealt with re-mounts due to be sent to India. He enlisted from Townsville on 27 September 1915. He married later in the year on 29 December when on home leave in Launceston. His wife was Evelyn Catherine Lonegerin and the couple were to have six children. Bernard embarked for active service in May 1916 and served in France and Belgium between 1917 and 1918 all the time with the 41st Battalion, and he was first wounded in Belgium on 5 October 1917. He was promoted to lance corporal in June 1918 and on 8 August, the first day of the Battle of Amiens, won a MM near Hamel, while he had taken on an enemy machine-gun position and captured it. He also dealt with a sniper who had been giving trouble.

After winning his VC, Gordon was wounded a second time on 1 September, when the 41st Battalion was advancing on Mont St Quentin, to the north of Péronne. He was evacuated to England three days later.

In January 1919 Gordon returned to Australia and was discharged in Queensland in April. He then ran a grocer's shop in Crayfield. After a few years he moved to the mainland, to take up dairy farming at Lincolnfield near Beaudésert in Queensland. He was to farm for the next forty-three years. He married a second time – Caroline Edith Manley (*née* Victorsen), a widow in Brisbane on 15 September 1938 – and they had two sons and one daughter. At this time his main recreations were horse-racing and boxing. He was a very popular man with a good sense of humour.

Although his main military service was during the First World War, Gordon also served for a time in Queensland during the Second World War, when he was a member of the 2/31st Battalion (Kennedy Regiment).

In June 1956 he was a member of the Australian contingent to London, attending Hyde Park VC Ceremonies when approximately 300 VC holders took part out of the 400 still living. A picture of Mr and Mrs Gordon appeared in the journal *Overseas,* in which the couple are featured shaking hands with Lady Gowrie, widow of the ex-Governor General of Australia. When it was opened in January 1960 a soldier's club was named after Bernard Gordon at 101st Wireless Regimental HQ, Cabarlah, near Toowoomba in Queensland.

Gordon's home address was Lincolnfield, 3 Mile Road, Beaudésert, Queensland and in the early 1960s he and his wife sold their dairy farming business interests and moved to Torquay where the couple purchased a block of flats and a group of cottages, which provided them with an income. Their own address was Bay Home, 35 Esplanade.

On 19 October 1963 Bernard Gordon died at his home in Torquay at the age of 72 and was cremated at Mount Thompson Crematorium and his ashes interred in Pinaroo Lawn Cemetery in Albany, where there is also a plaque to his memory.

He was survived by his second wife Caroline, four sons, four daughters, and two stepsons. His decorations were held by the family who offered them for sale at Bonhams & Goodman in Sydney on 28 November 2006. The hammer price of A$480,000 (£160,356) was reached when they were purchased on behalf of Kerry Stokes, a media mogul who later donated them to the Australian War Memorial in Canberra. Apart from the VC and MM, the medals consisted of the BWM, VM and Coronation Medals for 1937 and 1953. Kerry Stokes had already purchased the decorations of Capt. Alfred John Shout earlier in the year.

Gordon's name is one of ninety-six Australian VCs won which are commemorated in Victoria Cross Park Memorial in Canberra and dedicated in July 2000, a hundred years after Australia won its first VC. The same ninety-six names are also commemorated in the Victoria Cross Memorial in the Queen Victoria Building in Sydney.

R.S. Judson

Near Bapaume, France, 26 August

On 26 August 1918 the 63rd (Royal Naval) Division planned to capture the village of Thilloy before advancing to the south-east of Bapaume. The New Zealand Division was to capture Bapaume itself as well as the high ground to the east of the town. The 5th Division was to co-operate on the left and move towards Beugnâtre. Zero hour was 6.30 a.m. To the south of Bapaume, the New Zealand 1st Brigade and the 63rd (RND) was unable to make much progess against very strong German defences. The right-hand battalion, the 2nd Wellingtons, tried to advance in daylight but made little progress.

In the evening the New Zealanders tried again, but still enemy machine-gun fire was too strong for them. At this point a company of the 1st Auckland Regiment moved forward to assist them, and a bombing section under Sgt R.S. Judson succeeded in passing through the strong line and ran forward under very heavy fire to capture a machine gun in a German-held sap. Leaving his men to consolidate, Judson moved forward a further 200yds on his own up a sap, to bomb two machine-gun crews in front of him. Standing on a parapet, he ordered them to surrender, before jumping down to kill two men and capture the two machine guns.

This prompt and gallant action allowed the New Zealanders to advance still further. However, a light artillery barrage failed to destroy the enemy machine-gun posts in the Thilloy area and as a result the division was unable to make any further progress. Clearly, the Thilloy area had been heavily reinforced by the enemy and in addition New Zealand patrols were being harassed by machine guns from the direction of Bapaume. This led to the withdrawal of advance posts and prevented any renewal of an attack. Despite Judson's exploits, bombing alone was not the answer. During the night the 1st Auckland replaced the 2nd Wellingtons in the line, becoming responsible for the whole of the 1st Brigade front. Judson gained a VC for his gallantry, which was gazetted on 30 October 1918 as follows:

> For most conspicuous bravery and devotion to duty when, in an attack on enemy positions, he led a small bombing party under heavy fire and captured an enemy machine gun. He then proceeded up the sap alone, bombing three machine gun crews before him. Jumping out of the trench, he ran ahead of the enemy. Then, standing on the parapet, he ordered the party, consisting of two officers and ten men, to surrender. They instantly fired on him, but he threw a bomb and jumped amongst them, killed two and put the rest to flight, and so captured two machine guns. This prompt and gallant action not only saved many lives, but also enabled the advance to be continued unopposed.

Judson was presented with his VC at Buckingham Palace on 26 February 1919.

Reginald Stanley Judson was a son of Edgar William Judson, a farmer, and Emma Frances (*née* Holmden) and born in Wharehine, Northland, New Zealand on 29 September 1881. On leaving school in Port Albert Reginald became an engineer and boilermaker in an Auckland foundry. His home address was 20 Dedwood Terace, Ponsonby, Auckland and he married Ethel May Grice at Wareretu, Northland on 19 April 1905. The couple were to have three sons and one daughter.

Information in his attestation papers describe him as being 5ft 7½in, slightly built, with brown hair, a fair complexion and blue eyes, weighing 147lb. At the time of enlisting, on 19 October 1915, in the New Zealand Expeditionary Force, he joined part of the 9th Reinforcements as a rifleman in the 3rd (New Zealand) Rifle Brigade, where his regimental number was 24/1699. In January 1916 he sailed for Egypt and soon after arrival transferred to the 1st Battalion Auckland Infantry Regiment. In April he left for France and Flanders, but was seriously wounded in the abdomen during the Battle of the Somme on 15 September 1916 and evacuated to the United Kingdom for hospital treatment. This was followed by convalescence and later training duties and he was then put in charge of a RE Depot in Codford between September 1917 and April 1918. After twenty months off from active service he returned to France in May, where he rejoined the 1st Battalion, Auckland Regiment, and was promoted to sergeant. Following this, he won the DCM, MM, as well as the VC, all within the five-week period from July to August 1918.

On 24–25 July Judson won his DCM for his actions near Hébuterne 'showing conspicuous determination in the attack', and also for his role at Rossignol Wood, in which he helped reorganise a post from which the New Zealanders had been forced out by superior numbers. The citation was as follows:

> ... for conspicuous gallantry and devotion to duty during an attack on the enemy positions. He led a patrol along a sap leading to the enemy. This patrol forced the enemy to retreat before their bombs for a distance of 600 yards and so enabled the troops to hold the captured trench. He was indefatigable in organizing the trench during the next 24 hours under heavy bomb and machine gun fire and personally bombed the enemy out of an angle in the sap where they were collecting. The work of this NCO throughout was splendid and his courage and enthusiasm inspired all near him.

A few weeks later Judson won his MM, on 16 August, north of Puiseux-au-Mont, for leading a section against enemy machine-gun positions without loss to his men. The haul was one officer, sixteen men and two guns.

In 1972 a letter from a former army colleague of Judson's was published in *Review*, headed 'Stan Judson's Exploit':

> I was in charge of a Lewis gun section on the left flank of the NZ Division. We did not advance very far before the German machine guns opened up on us. We had a few casualties including two liaison men from an English Division. However a few of us crouched in a shell-hole about five feet deep.
>
> The enemy bullets kicked the dust of the rim of the shell-hole. I did something then that I was not proud of. I placed the gun on top of the shell-hole keeping my head down out of danger, and pulled the trigger. Although I was shooting blind the German guns were silenced so I was able to put my head up and fire in their direction, keeping them quiet which I thought would be only temporary.
>
> However in the meantime Stan Judson was running across open flat ground till he reached the German trenches and immediately tossed in Mills Bombs.
>
> The grenades had the immediate effect of making the Germans jump out of their trenches and surrender. We took them forward to the sunken road which was our objective.

> Whilst going forward with the prisoners we were annoyed by a lone sniper trying to pick us off. A short burst into a tiny wood by our Lewis gun silenced him.
>
> The following day Judson came around to thank me for giving him covering fire. Needless to say I did not tell him that the first blast was blind shooting.
>
> He also said that he inspected the tiny wood and found a Spandau with the water jacket full of holes and several soldiers dead.
>
> He also picked up a tiny pistol which was very ornate and fitted into the palm of his hand. He seemed very proud of it, though usually not given much to souverniring.

The writer also described Judson as a kind and gentle person who was 'transformed' when going into action.

After the war Judson joined the New Zealand Staff Corps and was commissioned on 14 February 1919 after being attached to first an Officer's Cadet Battalion at Trinity College Cambridge and later to one in Aldershot. He had a short spell in the New Zealand Hospital in Walton-on-Thames in May, then embarked for New Zealand on 9 June, but was struck off the strength on 31 October 1919. He and his wife Ethel divorced in 1920 and Reginald remarried, a war widow, Kate Marion Lewis, a draper, on 27 March 1928. The couple were to have one daughter. After the war Reginald had joined the Permanent Staff Corps of the New Zealand Military Forces and from 1920 to 1929 was stationed in Auckland and New Plymouth and in this period was promoted to lieutenant.

In Judson's service file there is a medical report dated 2 July 1924, in which he is described as suffering from what amounted to total nervous exhaustion. In addition, he had a heart condition which might have been connected with him being exposed to Thosgine gas in September 1918. In October 1929 he was made the adjutant to the Taranaki Regiment, and was also appointed Area Officer at New Plymouth. On 21 April of the same year he attended the presentation service for the awarding of new colours to the Auckland Regiment by the governor-general, Sir Charles Fergusson. In March 1936 Captain Judson applied for an extension of four months' service on the New Zealand Staff Corps, to increase his pension once he reached the age of fifty-five. In his letter of application he revealed that:

> The engineering trade was my occupation before the War. But owing to the presence of eight pieces of shrapnel near the heart,

> which were left in an abdominal wound received in the 1916 Somme Battle, and also the effects of poison gas, it may not be possible for me to take up such heavy work again ...

Judson continued his army service after his fifty-fifth birthday in 1936 and continued serving with the Permanent Staff Corps of the New Zealand Military Forces until January 1938 when he was placed on the Retired List of Officers with the rank of captain. During the period 1938–39 he was secretary to the principal of Mount Albert Grammar School. However, he was soon back in service as the Second World War broke out in September 1939 and he then served with the New Zealand temporary staff duty on the commencement of the Second World War as an adjutant of a home defence unit guarding vital positions. By the end of the war he had become major and in September 1946 was placed on the Retired List of Officers.

After leaving the army he returned to civilian life as a farmer at Doubtless Bay, Mangonui, Northland. He had always taken an active role in local politics and for ten years served as a member of the Auckland City Council. He was also a member of the Auckland Fire Board and of the Auckland Drainage Board for ten years. In addition, he was a member of the Auckland Transport Board for nine years and had been a JP and coroner.

Judson attended various VC Commemorative functions, including the New Zealand VC Dinner in Wellington on 9 November 1929. In 1940 he was in command of a group of ex-servicemen at Auckland Town Hall when Major General Freyberg VC was given a civic welcome on 2 January.

His home address in 1963 was 29 Speight Road, Kohimarama, Auckland. Despite still suffering from war wounds, he lived on to his ninetieth year and died in Jane Cavenis Private Hospital, Mount Eden, Auckland, on 26 August 1972, leaving a widow, two sons and two daughters. His funeral was held in a chapel before burial at Waikumete Lawn Cemetery, Soldiers Block M, Section 13, Plot 69. He is commemorated at the HQ, Dunedin, RSA, New Zealand. His decorations, in addition to the VC, DCM and MM already mentioned, were the Military Medal, 1914–15 Star, BWM, VM, War Medal 1939–45 Star and New Zealand War Service Medal, two Coronation Medals for 1937 and 1953 and the New Zealand Long & Efficient Service Medal. They are held at the Queen Elizabeth II Army Museum, Walouru. On 2 December 2007 his VC was one of nine stolen from the museum but after a reward was offered the medals were returned.

C.S. RUTHERFORD

Monchy, France, 26 August

On 26 August 1918 the 2nd and 3rd Divisions of the Canadian Corps began an attack which straddled the Arras–Cambrai road. The latter town was 20 miles away and the essential village for the Canadians to capture was Monchy-le-Preux 2½ miles away. It was during the fighting for possession of this village that Lt C.S. Rutherford of the 5th Canadian Mounted Rifles Battalion, Quebec Regiment (8th Brigade, 3rd Canadian Division) won his VC in what became known as the Battle of the Scarpe. The Canadian Mounted Rifles (CMR) had been converted to infantry and provided four infantry battalions for the Canadian Corps. All four of them – 1st, 2nd, 4th and 5th – formed the 8th Infantry Brigade of the 3rd Canadian Division. Rutherford's VC was gazetted on 15 November 1918, when he was on leave in Scotland, as follows:

> For most conspicuous bravery, initiative and devotion to duty. When in command of an assaulting party, Lieut. Rutherford found himself a considerable distance ahead of his men, and at the same moment observed a fully-armed strong enemy party outside a 'pill-box' ahead of him. He beckoned to them with his revolver to come to him; in return, they waved to him to come to them. This he boldly did, and informed them that they were prisoners. This fact, an enemy officer disputed, and invited Lieut. Rutherford to enter the 'pill-box', an invitation he discreetly declined. By masterful bluff, however, he persuaded the enemy that they were surrounded, and the whole party of forty-five, including two officers and three machine guns surrendered to him. Subsequently he induced the enemy officer to stop the fire of an enemy machine gun close by, and Lieut. Rutherford took

> advantage of the opportunity to hasten the advance of his men to his support. Lieut. Rutherford then observed that the right assaulting party was held up by heavy machine gun fire from another 'pill-box'. Indicating an objective to the remainder of his party, he attacked the 'pill-box' with a Lewis gun section, and captured a further thirty-five prisoners with machine guns, thus enabling the party to continue their advance. The bold and gallant action of this officer contributed very materially to the capture of the main objective, and was a wonderful inspiration to all ranks in pressing home the attack on a very strong position.

At the time of the Armistice on 11 November 1918 Rutherford was on leave in Scotland and it appears that he was only informed of his VC when he bumped into his commanding officer in London, Col George Pearkes, who told him the good news. He remained in London until the investiture at Buckingham Palace on 23 November 1918 when he received his VC from the King. He left for France and remained there until March 1919.

Charles Smith Rutherford was born on 9 January 1892 at a farm in Haldimand Township near Colborne, Ontario. He was the son of John T. and Mabella Rutherford. Charles attended Dudley Public School before taking up work on the family farm.

On 2 March 1916 he enlisted in a reserved battalion to the 3rd Battalion (Queen's Own Rifles) of Canada as a private in Toronto and he trained at Valcartier Camp, and after a short spell with the 2nd Quebec Regiment he was transferred to the 5th Canadian Mounted Rifles with whom he took part in the Ypres and Somme battles. He was subsequently wounded in Regina Trench near Courcelette, during the Somme battle of 1916 and convalesced in England, but returned to France in time to take part in the assault on Vimy Ridge in April 1917. Two months later he was wounded again, at Arvillers, near Amiens when helping to hold the line prior to it being handed over to the French Army.

Rutherford was a sergeant at the time of the Passchendaele campaign in 1917 when he won the MM and was one of thirteen members of the 5th CMR who captured two farms named Vapour and Source on the left of the Canadian advance. The small group then proceeded to hold on to these two farms despite repeated counter-attacks. It was for his gallantry on that occasion that Capt. George Pearkes, his company commander, won his VC on 30–31 October.

After an officer's course in Bexhill-on-Sea, Rutherford was commissioned in April 1918 and when back in France was put in charge of No. 9 Platoon and won the MC on 8 August 1918, the German Army's 'Black Day'. On this pivotal day Rutherford led his platoon in an advance to Arvillers in front of Amiens, from which the enemy had very recently withdrawn. The village was then handed over to French troops whose objective it was, but who had been delayed in their advance. Nearly three weeks later Rutherford won his VC at a time when the Allies were beginning to have the mighty German Army on the run.

After the war Rutherford returned to a hero's welcome at Ottawa Central Station. He resumed farming and worked in Colbourne as such for the next eighteen years. In 1921 he married Helen Haig from Baltimore who was a graduate of the University of Toronto and a trained dietician. The couple were to have four children, one son and three daughters. In the early 1930s Rutherford was a charter member of Lt Charles Rutherford VC Branch in Colborne, and was later made the branch president. He had also served as the clerk-treasurer of Halimand.

On Christmas Eve 1935 Rutherford accepted the post of sergeant-at-arms of the Ontario Legislature, when he took over from another holder of the VC, Capt. Walter Rayfield, who won his VC east of Arras between 2 and 4 September 1918. Rayfield had recently been appointed the Deputy Governor of Don Jail, Toronto. For his new position Rutherford wore a uniform consisting of flowing robes, a tricorn hat and a sword.

In 1939 Rutherford became postmaster of Colborne and was one of the VC holders introduced to King George VI and Queen Elizabeth during their tour of Canada. When the Second World War broke out he enlisted in Ottawa, becoming a member of the Veterans' Guard of Canada when his duties included supervising German prisoners in prisoner-of-war camps. For a year he later served in the Bahamas as part of the guard to the Duke of Windsor when the latter was Governor of Bahamas. Rutherford was promoted to captain in 1943 and in 1944 he was transferred to the Royal Military College in Kingston.

When the war ended in April 1945 Rutherford finished his service in July with the rank of captain and returned to his job at Colborne Post Office until 1955. Later, he and his wife opened a dry goods store in Keswick, north of Toronto, until their retirement in 1960, during which time they moved to Coburg in 1973. Six years later the couple returned to Haldimand Township and to Colborne in August 1979 when they were given a public welcome home complete with motor motorcade.

At this point, the couple lived with Dora Grant, one of their daughters. Helen died the following year.

During the last years of his life Rutherford became quite a celebrity as one of a dwindling group of VC survivors from the First World War, and on occasions he discussed how his three main gallantry medals were won. In an interview with a Toronto newspaper when he was quite elderly he talked of the time that he won his MM at Passchendaele at the end of October 1917:

> George (Pearkes) – he was a captain then – was leading us. I was a sergeant. We were digging in when I looked up. I saw 100 Germans coming towards us. We were only a handful but we started shooting and they disappeared.
>
> George got the VC that day for getting us to the top of that ridge. I guess we'd never have got there if he hadn't been along ... I got the MM that day too.

After the war the two Canadian winners of the VC from the same regiment met up in London, and Rutherford recalled that Pearkes congratulated him for winning the VC. However, Rutherford spoke of other things he had experienced in the war, and of the first time in the trenches on the Somme he said: '... all the men around me were killed'. His second experience was as bad, when: 'I carried a dead comrade through a four-foot tunnel that had a foot of water in it. The hardest thing I had to do.'

Of becoming an officer, which he did in April 1918, Rutherford said:

> The government gave us money to buy our uniforms. But we had to have a revolver, a compass and field glasses. I managed to get a revolver from someone who had no more use for it. And I used it until the end of the war. We captured two towns, first Arvillers, the German division headquarters where I managed to get a paymaster and a lot of German money. The only other things they left behind were a box of pigeons and 300 new machine guns. Then we captured Bouchoir and that was as far as we could go.

However, it seems unlikely that the Germans left as many as 300 machine guns behind and perhaps Rutherford's memory was at fault on this occasion.

That day (8 August 1918) Lt Rutherford won the MC and during the next few days the Canadian Corps moved to the Arras sector in preparation for an attack against the village of Monchy-le-Preux.

On 26 August he and his men began to move forward for an attack in the pouring rain in the middle of the night: 'Three miles up we ran into four field guns. We captured about 20 men who came out of their dugout and surrendered. Then we went on to Monchy.' At one point Rutherford became separated from his men: 'I was gone about 10 minutes. When I came back I couldn't see my men. I thought they'd gone into the town as the barrage lifted. So I ran as hard as I could to catch up with them.' But his men had gone into some woods:

> When I was within a 100 yards of the town all I could see were Germans. So I decided to go and do the best that I could with them. All I had was my loaded revolver. I walked up to the Germans and demanded they surrender. They were my prisoners. One German who spoke English said 'no prisoners ... No you prisoner.' They asked me to go to their dugout but I wouldn't.
>
> He (the German) went in and when he came out, he gave an order for the others to drop their rifles. They did. Boy, was I in a fix! I didn't know what to do next.
>
> Then one of their machine guns opened fire on A company. I said 'your machine gun is firing at my men.' I was afraid that my men might start firing back. So I said 'you go and stop your machine gun and I'll stop my mine ...'
>
> I ran back. When I was out of sight of the Germans I took my hat off and waved my men to come on. They were soon there and I sent two men back with 40 prisoners. Then we went over to the other machine gun and got 30 prisoners here.
>
> The records show that the 3rd Canadian Divison took Monchy-le-Preux that day. I was in the 3rd Canadian Division.

At the time of this interview, which was about 1983, Pearkes would have been 95 and Rutherford would have been about four years younger, and readers should take Rutherford's age into account. The two men were the oldest winners of the VC from the First World War to be still living in Canada, Rutherford living at this time on his daughter's farm to the north of Colborne, Ontario, and Pearkes in Victoria, British Columbia.

During his final two years Rutherford lived at the Rideau Veteran's Home in Ottawa where at the age of 97 he died on 11 June 1989, the very last of the 633 men to win the VC in the First World War. Three days later he was given a full military funeral at Colbourne United Church, which was attended by a sixty-member guard of honour from 1st Canadian Signal Regiment of Kingston, Ontario. Also in attendance at the Union Cemetery in Colborne was Christine Stewart MP and Fred Tilston, a VC holder from the Second World War.

Rutherford was survived by his son and three daughters, and thirteen grandchildren. He earned thirteen medals and, according to his granddaughter Mary Ellen Cain, kept his VC in a sock drawer. Apart from the VC, MC and MM, they included from the First World War the BWM and VM. From the Second World War he was awarded the 1939–45 Star, Defence Medal (1939–45), Canadian Volunteer Service Medal (1939–45) and War Medal (1939–45). His other decorations included Coronation Medals for 1937 and 1953, the Queen Elizabeth II Silver Jubilee Medal (1977) and the Canadian Centennial Medal (1967).

After his death his obituaries were fulsome and *The Times* wrote the following of his career:

> Few exploits in the annals of the Victoria Cross equal the extraordinary courage which gained Rutherford his award. Indeed his three major medals, achieved in a single year of fighting, attest to phenomenal bravery over months of unremitting combat, which saw the Allies pass from deep despondency, through acute crisis, to the verge of complete victory.

Rutherford's decorations are privately owned and he is commemorated by having a mountain named after him in Jasper National Park, Alberta. He is also remembered in the Royal Canadian Military Institute in Toronto where his service revolver, which he used during the war, is kept. As we have seen the Legion Branch 187 in King Street, Colborne is named after him.

H. Weale

Near Longueval, France, 26 August

On the evening of 25 August 1918 the 113th Brigade, 38th (Welsh) Division was given orders to advance at 4 a.m. the next day on the village of Longueval, to the north-east of Albert, with the intention of pushing the enemy out of High Wood in front of the accompaning 114th Brigade. The 13th Royal Welch Fusiliers (RWF) led the advance, with the 16th and 14th RWF in support. As the 13th Battalion was badly cut up during the fighting, it wasn't long before the supporting battalions joined in the fray. The advance moved from the west towards Longueval but heavy machine-gun fire from Montauban and the left of High Wood took its toll. As a consequence the 13th Battalion came to a standstill and B Company of the 14th Battalion moved forward on its left flank and into Bazentin le Grand village, where, at about 9 a.m., it managed to push the enemy out of Bazentin le Grand and follow it towards the Longueval–Contalmaison road. However, they themselves were then pushed back to the village. C Company was ordered to clear the enemy from the left flank, assisted by a battalion of the South Wales Borderers who moved up on the left of the 113th Brigade.

By now the time was about 10 a.m. and the 17th RWF Battalion was then ordered to move eastwards to the north of Bazentin le Petit Wood. They were instructed to avoid High Wood if possible as it was thought to be still strongly held. The battalion, moving in artillery formation, was very fortunate as it found the wood virtually empty. At the same time the 13th and 16th RWF Battalions were at a standstill and the 14th moved forward on the left of the 113th Brigade. They found themselves on the site of the old windmill at Bazentin and moved forward towards a central ridge from the north-west. The battalion managed to turn the enemy flank, succeeding in the capture of a hundred prisoners and

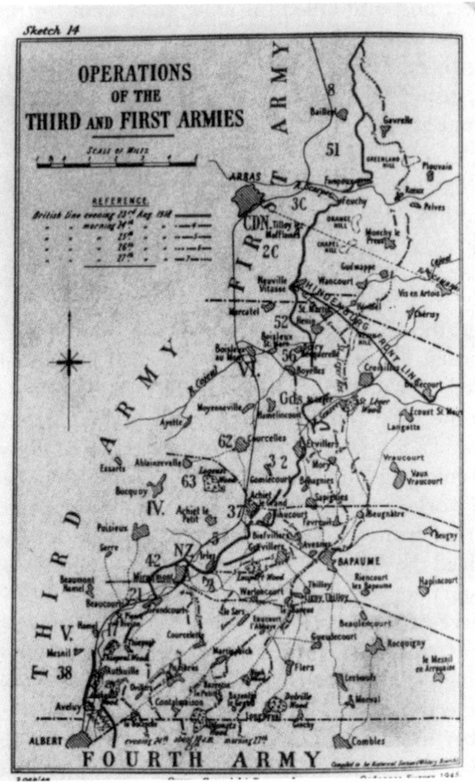

eight machine guns. It was during this part of the fighting that Lance Corporal Henry Weale (14th RWF) won his VC.

The 14th Battalion, which had done well in the fighting, now found itself isolated in a position about a thousand yards in front of the 113th Brigade with its flanks in the air. Not surprisingly, they were counter-attacked, and soon after 5 p.m. were forced to retreat to a point about 500yds to the east of Bazentin le Grand.

Weale's VC was gazetted on 15 November 1918 as follows:

> For most conspicuous bravery and initiative in attack. The adjacent battalion having been held up by enemy machine guns, L.-Corpl. Weale was ordered to deal with the hostile posts. When his Lewis gun failed him, on his own initiative he rushed

> the nearest post and killed the crew, then went for the others, the crews of which fled on his approach, this gallant N.C.O. pursuing them. His very dashing deed cleared the way for the advance, inspired his comrades, and resulted in the capture of all the machine guns.

Weale was decorated with his VC in the Ballroom of Buckingham Palace on 1 March 1919.

Henry Weale, the son of John and Sarah Weale (*née* Hughes), was born in Nine Houses, Shotton, Flintshire, Wales, on 2 October 1897. His family moved later to 33 Brook Road. His father worked as a general labourer in the John Summer's Steelworks and Henry was educated at St Ethelwald's School, Shotton. In the brief period between leaving school and enlisting with the 5th RWF (TF) in November 1911, the young man worked as a packer at the John Summer's Steelworks. He was discharged from the Territorial Force on 7 September 1913 and next day joined the 3rd RWF (Special Reserve), where he was allocated the regimental number of 5046.

Weale served overseas from 1 November to 10 December 1914, when he was wounded. He then returned to the United Kingdom before serving from 16 March 1915 to 1 October 1915, when he was wounded a second time. His third period of active service was from 14 September to 16 January 1917, when he was gassed. He served a fourth spell abroad from 22 August 1917 for only six days before being wounded again. He was promoted to lance corporal, unpaid, on 8 December.

After the war ended Weale was transferred to the reserve on 16 April 1919 and on 8 September he was discharged. Nearly eighteen months later he re-enlisted, on 7 February 1921, this time with the 5th RWF (TF). He served in Ireland in 1921 and was made a sergeant on 8 July. A few months later, on 6 February 1922, he was discharged and this time enlisted in Section D Army Reserve on 12 July. Four years later he was discharged again and thirteen years later, on 25 August 1939, he re-enlisted as a member of the National Defence Corps. He was transferred to the RWF and was sent to Dover and later Salisbury where he became an airfield guard. On 29 January 1941 he was found to be no longer fit for active service and was discharged for the very last time. He was 43 years of age. It would appear that in the 1920s when in the emloyment of the Courtaulds factory in Flint, that he suffered an industrial accident to his legs when some acid spilt onto them. Thus already handicapped by shrapnel still present in his neck, and also still suffering from the effects of frostbite, Weale was to find employment very difficult for the rest of his life.

During his life Weale attended various VC functions, including the June 1920 Garden Party at Buckingham Palace, the House of Lords Dinner in November 1929, the Victory Parade in June 1946 and the June 1956 Hyde Park VC Centenary. He married Susannah Harrison, daughter of George Harrison, at St Ethelward's Church in Shotton on 16 June 1919 and the couple lived in Rhyl, Wales, and had four sons and one daughter. Henry Weale had several jobs after he left the army, including returning as a packer to Summer's Steelworks, building work, and finally took up road-making.

Henry Weale died in Rhyl on 13 January 1959 at the home of one of his sons and after a service in St Thomas's Church in Rhyl he was buried in Maes Hyfryd Cemetery, Grange Road, Rhyl, the local cemetery. The grave reference is 4829. He was 62 years of age and Susannah, his wife, lived on until 1988. His name is commemorated by Weale Court, Hightown, Wrexham; Harry Weale Hall at Queensferry TA Centre, Clywd and finally with a memorial garden unveiled in Shotton, his home town in October 2010. His VC is in the collection of the Royal Welch Fusiliers in Caenarfon Castle and his other decorations included the 1914 Star, BWM, VM, Defence Medal (1939–45), War Medal (1939–45) and Coronation Medals for 1937 and 1953. His pocketwatch was added to the collection in February 2012. He had received it from his work colleagues at John Summers & Son in 1918.

W.H. CLARK-KENNEDY

The Fresnes–Rouvroy Line, France, 27–28 August

Lieutenant Colonel William Clark-Kennedy gained the VC between 27 and 28 August 1918, on the second day of the Battle of the Scarpe in the renewed Arras offensive, and it was gazetted on 14 December 1918. The citation explains how Clark-Kennedy won his VC:

For most conspicuous bravery, initiative and skilful leading on the 27 and 28 August 1918, when in command of his battalion. On the 27th he led his battalion with great bravery and skill from Crow and Aigrette trenches in front of Wancourt to the attack on the Fresnes–Rouvroy line. From the outset the brigade, of which the 24th Battn. was a central unit, came under very heavy shell and machine gun fire, suffering many casualties, especially amongst leaders. Units became partially disorganised, and the advance was checked. Appreciating the vital importance to the brigade front of a lead by the centre, and undismayed by annihilating fire, Lieut.-Colonel Clark-Kennedy, by sheer personality and initiative, inspired his men and led them forward. On several occasions he set an outstanding example by leading parties straight at the machine gun nests which were holding up the advance and overcame these obstacles. By controlling the direction of neighbouring units and collecting men who had lost their leaders, he rendered valuable services in strengthening the line, and enabled the whole brigade to move forward. By the afternoon, very largely due to the determined leadership of this officer and disregard for his own life, his battalion, despite heavy losses, had made good the maze of trenches west

> of Cherisy and Cherisy Village, had crossed the Sensée River bed, and had occupied Occident Trench in front of the heavy wire of the Fresnes-Rouvroy line; under continuous fire he then went up and down his line until far into the night, improving the position, giving wonderful encouragement to his men, and sent back very clear reports. On the next day he again showed valorous leadership in the attack on the Fresnes-Rouvroy line and Upton Wood. Though severely wounded soon after the start, he refused aid, and dragged himself to a shell hole, from which he could observe. Realizing his exhausted troops could advance no further, he established a strong line of defence, and thereby prevented the loss of most important ground. Despite intense pain and serious loss of blood, he refused to be evacuated for over five hours, by which time he had established the line in a position from which it was possible for the relieving troops to continue the advance. It is impossible to overestimate the results achieved by the valour and leadership of this officer.

Clark-Kennedy was presented with his VC, CMG and bar to his DSO in the Ballroom of Buckingham Palace on 1 March 1919 by the King.

William Hew Clark-Kennedy was the son of Capt. A.V.M. Clark-Kennedy and the Hon. Mrs Clark-Kennedy, and was born in Dunskey, Wigtownshire, Scotland, on 3 March 1879. His parents rented a house there, although the family home was actually at Knockgray, Carsphairn, Galloway, and included a house and farms together with shooting and fishing. William's father, who died in 1894, served in the Coldstream Guards and his mother died on the eve of the Second World War in 1939. William was educated at St Andrew's College, Southborough, Kent, and Westminster School, and in 1897 joined the Standard Life Assurance Company in London.

On the outbreak of the South African war he became a trooper as a member of the yeomanry regiment 'Paget's Horse', and served with distinction in the yeomanry in the Boer War 1900–01. During this time he was mentioned in despatches and also received the Queen's Medal with four clasps. In 1903 he emigrated to Canada when still on the staff of the Standard Life Assurance Company and later became assistant manager for Canada. He joined the Canadian Militia and subsequently joined the Royal Highlanders of Canada as a Reserve Officer. He married Kate (*née* Redford) of Montreal on 5 September 1914, a month after the war broke out, when he was still in a training camp in Quebec City.

Clark-Kennedy left Canada with the First Canadian contingent as a company commander of the 13th Battalion Royal Highlanders of Canada. At the time of the Second Battle of Ypres in April 1915 he was reported killed, and very nearly was. He was knocked over three times by shells, the third time being completely buried and left unconscious, the men on either side of him being killed. However, eventually he managed to dig himself out, although the enemy was close by. For his role in the Ypres battle he was awarded the French Croix de Guerre with Palm.

On 14 January his first DSO was gazetted for service in the Battle of Festubert in May 1915 and he was promoted to major at the same time. He held the rank of brigade major in 1916 and in the following year was promoted to lieutenant colonel. He left the Royal Highlanders in order to command the 24th Battalion Victoria Rifles, with whom he gained his VC. Just over three years later Clark-Kennedy was created a Companion of the Order of St Michael and St George, and later awarded a bar to his DSO which was gazetted on 11 January 1919 for activities on 8 August 1918 during the advance on the Somme. The citation was as follows:

> For great gallantry in action during which the battalion under his command reached the objective allotted to it. On several occasions, at great risk, he personally directed the capture of strong points obstinately defended by the enemy. The success which his battalion obtained in these attacks was due in no small degree to the example, courage and resourcefulness of its commander.

Clark-Kennedy was mentioned in despatches four times and after the war was appointed brevet lieutenant colonel, Corps Reserve, Canadian Militia. He was proficient at sports and especially keen on fishing and in addition was a first-rate shot. In November 1929 he travelled to London for the House of Lords VC Dinner. He later became manager of the Standard Life Assurance Company in Canada. He also became a director of the Guardian Insurance Company of Canada in 1927, and in 1943 became its chairman. He was also chairman of the advisory board of the Guardian-Caledonian group of insurance companies.

In November 1945 Clark-Kenedy retired from the Standard Life Assurance after fifty years' service. In June 1956 he attended the VC/GC Centenary Review. He later resided in Montreal, where he died on

25 October 1961, and was buried in Montreal Royal Cemetery three days later in Pine Hill Section of the Reford family plot, lot 258.

His numerous decorations, which are in private hands, include the CMG, DSO & Bar, Order of St Michael & St George, the 1914–15 Star, BWM, VM, two Coronation Medals for 1937 and 1953, Efficiency Decoration (ED) and Croix de Guerre (France). He was survived by two sons, both of whom became lieutenant colonels.

On 13 October 2006, in the 150th anniversary year of the Victoria Cross, Clark-Kennedy's name, together with the names of nine other winners of the VC, were commemorated with a sculpture in Tunbridge Wells set up in the Victoria Cross Grove in Dunorlan Park. The grove was originally planted in 1995.

C.H. SEWELL

North-East of Bapaume, France, 29 August

Lieutenant Cecil Sewell's VC action took place on 29 August between the villages of Favreuil and Frémicourt, north-east of Bapaume, in a fork made by the original Bapaime to Arras and Bapaume to Cambrai roads. Five days earlier, on 24 August, the number of tanks ready for action from the 1st, 3rd and 4th Brigades numbered fifty-three and on the following day about forty-two of these were in action on the IV and VI Corps fronts. Bapaume had been evacuated by the enemy and on 29 August a tank action took place which has gone down in the annals of the Tank Corps and also brought a posthumous VC to Lt Cecil Sewell of the Royal West Kent Regiment who was attached to the 3rd (Light) Battalion Tank Corps when in charge of a tank section of Whippet tanks. These light tanks weighed 14 tons, had a crew of three and were equipped with four Hotchkiss Mark 1 machine guns.

During an Allied advance, enemy machine-gun posts and infantry and their shell fire disputed any move forward, so in order to clear a way forward a group of four Whippet tanks were sent on ahead. Lieutenant Sewell's CO, Lt Col Walker Bell, described in a report what happened in this minor engagement in which only the four Whippet tanks took part:

> ... At about 2.00 p.m. on the afternoon of August 29, Whippets of the 3rd (Light) Tank Battalion reached the quarry at map reference H14 d43 [near the Monument Commémoratif, south-west of Favreuil]. Acting under instructions received from the New Zealand Division, one section of Whippets under Lt. Sewell was ordered to clear up the situation on the front of the 3rd New Zealand Rifle Brigade before Frémicourt and the

Bapaume–Cambrai road, where the infantry were reported to be held up by machine gun fire.

On reaching the railway line in advance of our infantry, enemy batteries and machine guns opened heavy fire on the section. In manoeuvring to avoid the fire and to retain formation, Car No. A. 233 [Caesar II] , commanded by Lieutenant O.L. Rees-Williams, side-slipped in a deep shell crater and turned completely upside down, catching fire at the same time.

Lt. Sewell in the leading Whippet, on seeing the plight of Lt. Rees-Williams' car, immediately got out of his own Whippet and went to the rescue. Unaided with a shovel he dug an entrance to the door of the cab, which was firmly jammed and embedded in the side of the shell hole; forced the door open and liberated the crew. Although the crew had, in the meantime, succeeded in extinguishing the fire, had it not been for Lt Sewell's prompt and gallant action, the imprisoned crew might have been burnt to death, as they were helpless to extricate themselves without outside assistance.

During the whole of this time Whippets were being heavily shelled and the ground swept by machine gun fire at close range. On endeavouring to return to his own car, Lt. Sewell was unfortunately hit several times, his body being subsequently found lying beside that of his driver, Gunner Knox, W., also dead, just outside the tank [*Cherubim II*], which at that time was within short range of several machine guns and infantry gun-pits.

Lt. O.L. Rees-Williams states in his report: I would like to emphasize the gallant way in which Lt. Sewell came to our assistance, although enemy machine gunners swept the ground. Had it not been for his assistance I, and my crew, would have been unable to get out.

Sewell's posthumous VC was gazetted on 30 October 1918 as follows:

When in command of a section of Whippet light tanks in action this officer displayed most conspicuous bravery and initiative in getting out of his own tank and crossing open ground under heavy shell and under machine gun fire to rescue the crew of another Whippet of his section which had side-slipped into a large shell hole, overturned, and taken fire. The door of his tank having become jammed against the side of their shell hole, Lieut. Sewell, by his own unaided efforts, dug away the entrance to the door and released the crew.

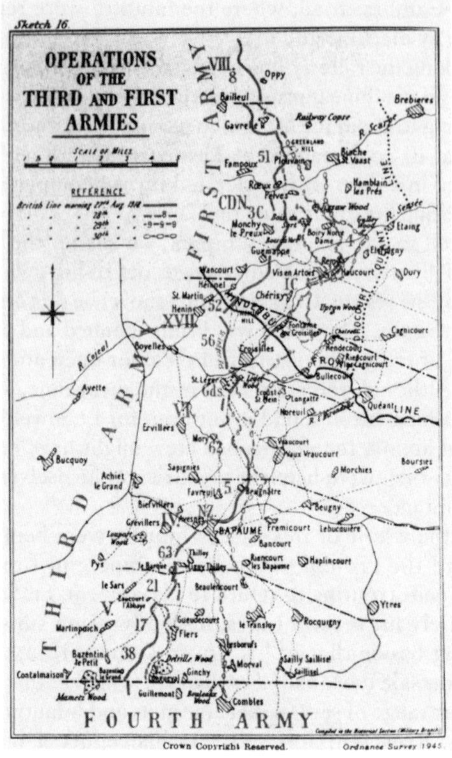

Cecil Sewell and Pte W. Knox, another member of his crew to die on 29 August, were buried side by side and in 1920 they were reinterred in Vaulx Hill Cemetery, 4 miles north-east of Bapaume, in Plot I, Row D, Graves 3 and 2 respectively. Sewell's elder brother, Herbert Victor, who was killed on 13 November 1916, is commemorated on Cecil's headstone as well as on the Thiepval Memorial to the Missing.

Cecil's posthumous VC was presented to his parents in the Ballroom of Buckingham Palace on 13 December 1918.

Cecil Harold Sewell was the son of Harry Bolton Sewell, then a clerk but later a qualified barrister and Mary Ann Sewell (*née* Kemp). He was born at 26 Crooms Hill, Greenwich, London, on 27 January 1895.

Mary Ann was to die in 1928 and Harry in 1941. Cecil had four sisters and four brothers, with Harry Kemp being the eldest, and together with Cecil, he and Herbert Victor were also to die in the war. Cecil attended Dulwich College 1907–1912 where his portrait hangs in the library, and then moved on to London University where he studied law.

His legal studies were cut short by the outbreak of war in August 1914 and in November he enlisted in the 1st (Public Schools) Battalion of The Royal Fusiliers (City of London Regiment). He carried out his early training at Clipstone Camp close to Mansfield. After five months his battalion was incorporated into the 98th Infantry Brigade which became part of the 33rd Division which was a new number for the planned 40th Division. The divison began to assemble at Clipstone on 1 July but was not to cross to France until 14 November.

In France Sewell was trained as a machine gunner but he was earmarked for a commission and sent home for training. He was commissioned into the 3rd Reserve Battalion of the Queen's Own (Royal West Kent Regiment) in August and returned to France in the following month where he transferred to the 1st Battalion. Seemingly a bit bored with his life in the trenches and on seeing a tank, the new Allied weapon, Sewell decided to apply for a transfer to the recently formed Tank Corps (July 1917) and became a member of C Battalion and was allocated to a tank named *Cherubim w*hich was equipped with four machine guns.

On 20 November 1917, the first day of the Battle of Cambrai, Sewell's tank had only moved 2 miles before it received a direct hit and burst into flames. However, he and his crew managed to escape without any serious damage. By August 1918 the 14-ton light tank called the Whippet had been introduced into the Tank Corps and Sewell's, under the command of Lt Col Walker Bell, was suitably named *Cherubim II*.

Sewell's name is one of seven holders of the VC on the Dulwich College War Memorial in South London. He is also commemorated at the family memorial at Charlton Cemetery, Woolwich, reference Section C, Grave 355 where Harry Kemp Sewell is also remembered, having died during the war as well. There is also a Toc H lamp in his name at Bovington Garrison Church. His VC and 1914–15 Star, BWM and VM, are in the collection of the Tank Museum in Bovington together with a plaque and an example of the Whippet tank with the markings of Sewell's vehicle in which he went into action. Sewell's deed has also written up in the *Victor* comic of 30 March 1968.

G. CARTWRIGHT

Near Mont St Quentin, France, 31 August

The 33rd Australian Battalion (9th Brigade, 3rd Division) was involved in the Battle of Amiens on 8 August when it helped to capture the strongly garrisoned Accroche Wood, and later it took part in the Battle of Albert. Three weeks later, on 31 August, the battalion was involved in the fight for Mont St Quentin, the key to the enemy-held town of Péronne. The 9th as well as the 10th Brigades were instructed to capture the high ground west of the Bouchavesnes–Péronne road. Under what was described as a thin barrage they advanced at 5.45 a.m. And in spite of enemy machine-gun fire from Road Wood, the Australians reached the crest of the ridge by using old trenches. They were, however, unable to make further progress, but did succeed in capturing several field guns. Later on, during a German counter-attack, the 10th Brigade was slightly driven back. The magazine *This England* has run a series called 'English Heroes', and in the winter issue of 1979 it published an article on George Cartwright VC. In the section describing the action when he gained the VC the magazine had this to say:

> It was on the morning of 31 August at a place called Road Wood near the Mont St Quentin–Bouchavesnes road, as they poised to make the attack on Mont St Quentin, that George Cartwright displayed the extreme courage and quick thinking which were to place him in the pages of history.
>
> The wood was heavily defended by a large number of enemy troops and well-sited machine guns. These were proving very dangerous to the attacking Australians who, despite all efforts, were finding it impossible to dislodge them. Heavy losses were

being suffered as they slowly advanced but the way was barred by enfilading fire from the edge of the wood, the machine guns mowing everything down before them.

Cartwright stood up and advanced through this devastating attack. Firing his rifle from the shoulder he killed three of the gun section and then rushed forward and threw a grenade at the post. After the subsequent explosion he charged and captured the gun and eight or nine prisoners! His battalion had been observing this extraordinary scene but now they stood up and cheered him before renewing their attack with vigour and fresh impetus.

Cartwright's commanding officer, Lt Col L.J. Morshead described the event:

> A most determined resistance was offered by the enemy at the outset in Road Wood – which was very strongly garrisoned, and which literally swarmed with machine guns.
>
> There was a gap of 500 metres between the 58th Division, on our left, and us.
>
> The whole line advanced unflinchingly, although suffering heavy casualties.
>
> Owing to our losses, and to a gap between C and D Companies, B Company in suppport, wheeled to the right, made good the gap, and went forward as our assault company.
>
> At 6.20 a.m. the Battalion was held up by exceedingly heavy machine gun fire enfilading us from the edge of the wood.
>
> Pte. George Cartwight, in the face of the most withering fire, stood up and advanced, firing his rifle from the shoulder.
>
> He killed three of the machine gun team. Rushing forward, he then threw a bomb at the post, and, on its explosion, he charged.
>
> Eight prisoners, and the gun were captured by Pte. Cartwright.
>
> At this the whole Battalion stood up, vociferously cheered him and renewed the attack with the greatest vigour and determination.
>
> The fighting in Road Wood was very bitter.
>
> We were greatly outnumbered, and the enemy fought well, especially his machine gunners.
>
> It was only by individual men and small parties working forward, and attacking the rear of enemy posts, that success was attained.
>
> Once the enemy thought he was surrounded, or cut off, he surrendered.

> Luckily he did not realise our few numbers.
>
> To have cleared such strong-hold as Road Wood, with so few men, seems incredible.
>
> Two days later we actually counted 120 dead Germans in Road Wood.

Cartwright was congratulated by the top brass including Generals Birdwood and Rawlinson. His VC was gazetted on 14 December 1918 as follows:

> For most conspicuous bravery and devotion to duty on the morning of the 31st August 1918, during the attack on Road Wood – south-west of Bouchavesnes, near Péronne. When two companies were held up by machine gun fire from the south-western edge of the wood, without hesitation Private Cartwright moved against the gun in a most deliberate manner under intense fire. He shot three of the team, and, having bombed the post, captured the gun and nine enemy. This gallant deed had a most inspiring effect on the whole line, which immediately rushed forward. Throughout the operation Private Cartwight displayed wonderful dash, grim determination and courage of the highest order.

Cartwright survived the August offensive without injury, but on the last day of September, during the fighting for the Hindenburg Line, he was wounded in his head and left arm seriously enough to put him out of action for the rest of the war. He was sent to hospital in England for treatment and was not discharged until January 1919. Two months later he was presented with his VC by the King in the Ballroom of Buckingham Palace on 8 March 1919, and was then repatriated to Australia where he was discharged from the army on 1 July in Sydney, New South Wales.

George Cartwight was a son of William Edward Cartright and his wife Elizabeth (*née* Stracey) and was born in South Kensington, on 9 December 1894. The family lived in Camberwell, South London, and his father was a coach trimmer and George went to school locally. The family address was No. 6 Newcham Road, Camberwell. On leaving school he migrated to Australia in his teens, working as a labourer on a sheep farm in the Elsmore District of New South Wales until the end of 1915. He then enlisted on 9 December in the AIF at Inverell, New South Wales, and was given the service number of 726. Two months later he was sent to the newly formed 33rd Battalion (9th Brigade), part of the new 3rd Australian Division, and in Sydney on 4 May 1916 embarked for England on the troopship *Marathon*. The battalion docked at Devonport and trained at Larkhill Camp on Salisbury Plain before leaving for France in early November 1916. He joined his battalion in the line to the south of Armentières, close to Rue du Bois in December. In June 1917, prior to the Battle of Messines Ridge, he was wounded and absent from his unit for a month.

In April 1918 Cartwright suffered badly during a large-scale gas attack in the Villers-Brettoneux area, but two months later was able to rejoin his battalion, remaining with it until the end of the war. On his return home he received a hero's welcome at Inverell when he was given a 'magnificent reception by an attendance of over 4000 people at the Town Hall, and presented with a gold watch and a purse of sovereigns from the citizens and a cheque of £250 from Mr. N.C. Bucknell, a well known grazier.'

On being questioned about the deed in which he gained the VC, Cartwright was very reticent. However, he did divulge the following to the press: 'We exchanged shot for shot ... but every time I pulled the trigger I think I killed one man. The other Germans started to cry, so I sent them back behind their lines.' How easy it all sounds! Private Cartwright admitted under cross-examination that he was a good shot and had been a sniper.

Cartwright was in hospital when he heard that he had been awarded the VC. 'The matron came to me one morning and told me it was in the paper,' he said. 'She was quite annoyed because I had not said anything about being recommended.' In 1920 Cartwright was one of ten holders of the VC on parade at a reception for the Prince of Wales during his empire tour. Still working in Sydney he married Elsie Broker at St Stephen's Anglican Church in Chatswood. The couple were to have two children but later divorced.

Later, he worked as a storeman in a tobacco factory, but didn't lose his connection with the army and joined the 3rd Battalion (Werriwa Regiment) and became a sergeant. In 1932 he was still linked with the 3rd Battalion which led to the formation of the 4th/3rd Battalion (Australian Rifles). On 25 February he was promoted to warrant officer. Four years later, when the 3rd Battalion was reactivated as a separate unit, Cartwright continued to serve as a member of the 4th Battalion. In October 1939 he was made a temporary captain and from March 1940 until September 1943 he was seconded for duty with the Reception Training Depot, Eastern Command. By now he was a full captain and later served with the 112th Convalescent Depot. For two years from September 1943 until 1945 he served as second-in-command of the 28th Infantry Training Battalion. After being transferred to the Australian Army Amenities Service he was demobilised in May 1946. Having left the army he got a job as an assistant cashier and married Evelyn Mary Short on 4 September 1948 in the Congregational Church in Pitt Street, Sydney. The couple lived in Epping, New South Wales.

In April 1955, at Victoria Barracks, Sydney Cartwright was awarded the Efficiency Decoration for his CMF (Citizen Military Forces) service. He attended several VC functions, including the centenary in London in June 1956 when he was part of the Australian contingent.

Survived by his second wife and a son from his first marriage, Cartwright died at his home in Epping, Lidcombe, New South Wales, on 2 February 1978 and was cremated at Northern Suburbs Crematorium, Sydney. A remembrance plaque was later displayed on the War Graves Wall, 46, Row B in the Rookwood Cemetery Garden of Remembrance. Cartwright was keen to have his VC returned to the country of his birth and his widow presented it to the Imperial War Muesum in London on 12 May 1978, when she flew from Australia in order to hand over the decoration in person. One of the conditions that she stipulated in connection with the gift was that the VC should never be separated from Cartwright's other medals or ever be returned to Australia. No explanation is given in the files as to why this stipulation was made. Apart from his VC and Efficiency Decoration mentioned above, the medals include the BWM, VM, War Medal (1939–45), Australian Service Medal (1939–45), two Coronation Medals for 1937 and 1953, and the Queen Elizabeth ll Silver Jubilee Medal (1977). Cartwright's identity tags are also part of the museum collection.

Cartwright is also commemorated in the Australian War Memorial, Canberra, which also houses the actual enemy gun that he captured during his VC action. He is also remembered in the Victoria Cross Park Memorial, also in Canberra, and in Sydney in the Victoria Cross Memorial in the Queen Victoria building.

J.P. Huffam

South-East of Monchy-le-Preux, France, 31 August

On 31 August 1918 2/Lt James Huffam of the 5th Battalion Duke of Wellington's (West Riding Regiment) 12th Brigade, 4th Division, attached to the 2nd Battalion, gained the VC for his actions at Saint Servin's Farm south-east of Monchy-le-Preux, near Arras. His VC was gazetted on 26 December 1918 and tells the story as follows:

> For most conspicuous bravery and devotion to duty on 31st Aug. 1918. With three men he rushed an enemy machine gun post and put it out of action. His post was then heavily attacked, and he withdrew fighting, carrying back a wounded comrade. Again, in the night of 31 Aug. 1918, at Saint Servin's Farm, accompanied by two men only, he rushed an enemy machine gun, capturing eight prisoners and enabling the advance to continue. Throughout the whole fighting from 29 Aug. to 1 Sept. 1918, he showed the utmost gallantry.

Huffam was presented with his VC in the Ballroom of Buckingham Palace on 12 April 1919, and was the first man from Berwick to win the VC. Back home in the same year, the citizens of Berwick and district presented him with a gold watch and a cheque in recognition of the honour that he had brought to the town.

James Palmer Huffam was one of six children, of Edward Valentine and Dorothy Huffam, and was born in Dunblane, Perthshire, on 31 March 1897. After leaving school in Berwick-upon-Tweed he joined the army on 21 February 1915 as a private in the 2/7th Battalion, Northumberland Fusiliers (T/F), and volunteered to go to France, which he did on 6 June. He served in France as a member of the 1/7th Northumberland Fusiliers (T/F) and was made a corporal in September, then sergeant in the following May. Two of his brothers were also serving, with his elder a member of the same battalion. In August 1917 James was offered a commission and returned to England, where he joined the OTC at Oxford, being commissioned as a second lieutenant in the 5th Duke of Wellington's Regiment on 30 January 1918.

After the war James remained in the army and was made a full lieutenant on 30 January 1921. He had been awarded a three-year reserve commission and served in the Indian Army with the 1/9th Gurkha Rifles. Many of these reserve commissions were awarded as a consequence of the number of officers in the Indian Army who were due for leave after having had none during the war years. Huffam, who obviously decided to remain in the army for a period of time after his original short service commission, later served with the Royal West African Frontier Force (Sierra Leone Battalion) from 30 November 1927. He was made a captain on 2 June 1928 and returned to the Duke of Wellington's.

In July 1929 he attended the Royal West African Frontier Force Dinner at the Savoy Hotel, London 1935. In the same year he married a lady with the same surname as his, Constance Marian Huffam, at St Paul's Anglican Cathedral, Malta, on 23 April. Huffam returned to India and was still there just prior to the outbreak of the Second World War, when he retired as major in August 1938.

During the Second World War Huffam rejoined the army on 1 December 1939 and was posted to the BEF in France during the period 1939–1940. He became DAPM at Dieppe in April 1940 before being evacuated with the BEF in the following month. He was mentioned in despatches (*London Gazette* (*LG*) 20 December 1940) and in November 1940 became officer commanding L Traffic Control Group, Southern Command, Winchester. This post was changed a year later to being DAPM Eastern Command. In April 1942 he was made APM 153 HQ Provost Company (Dunstable) and finally APM HQ Division (Tenby) in January 1945. He retired from the army again in August of the same year.

In June 1956 Huffam attended VC Centenary Review and was also present at the VC and GC Dinners on 24 July 1958 and 7 July 1960 respectively.

On 16 February 1968 Huffam collapsed while playing a round of golf at Stanmore Golf Club in Middlesex and later died at Edgware General Hospital, Burnt Oak, Middlesex. He was cremated at Golders Green Crematorium on 21 February 1968 and his ashes were scattered in the Garden of Remembrance. In his will he left £1,554 net (£1,645) gross and his decorations remain in private hands. Apart from the VC, they include the 1914–15 Star, BWM, VM, 1939–45 Star, Defence Medal (1939–45), War Medal (1939–45) and Coronation Medals for 1937 and 1953.

On 7 April 2013 a plaque was unveiled in Golders Green cemetery to the memory of holders of the VC whose ashes are buried there. The plaque is set in a wall within the war memorial and pool. One of the men whose names is commemorated on the plaque is James Palmer Huffam.

A.D. LOWERSON

North of Péronne, France, 1 September

When, at the end of August, the German Army was still occupying the town of Péronne, the Australians planned to send two infantry brigades to capture the high ground both to the south of the town and the high ground to the north, including the Mont St Quentin Heights, a mile to the north. This, so it was thought, would force an early enemy exit from Péronne. The 2nd Australian Division was chosen to stage the attack on the northern Heights using the 23rd and 24th (Victoria) Battalions of the 6th Brigade.

The division began the attack on the village from the north of the town of Péronne on the morning of 31 August and the immediate plan was for the advance to move in a north-easterly direction and for the remaining section of the town to be attacked the following day. The main thrust would be by the 23rd and 24th Battalions and the 23rd was to be supported by the 21st (Victoria) Battalion of the same brigade. Sergeant Lowerson was a member of the 21st Battalion (Victoria) also of the 6th Brigade and he was to win the VC after his battalion was called upon to reinforce the 23rd. He was to be one of six Australians to be awarded the VC in connection with the above actions and the capture of the village of Mont St Quentin was a triumph of arms.

Initially, the attacking Australians met with strong resistance but a heavy barrage was brought down on the village which then enabled the advance to continue. By then the supporting 21st Battalion had become part of the attacking force and the village fell to the 23rd and 21st Battalions at around 4 p.m. However, the enemy had put up strong resistance in trenches to the west of it, which the Australians took three hours to overcome.

Lowerson's company had advanced through the eastern side of the village and suffered from very heavy machine-gun and sniper fire.

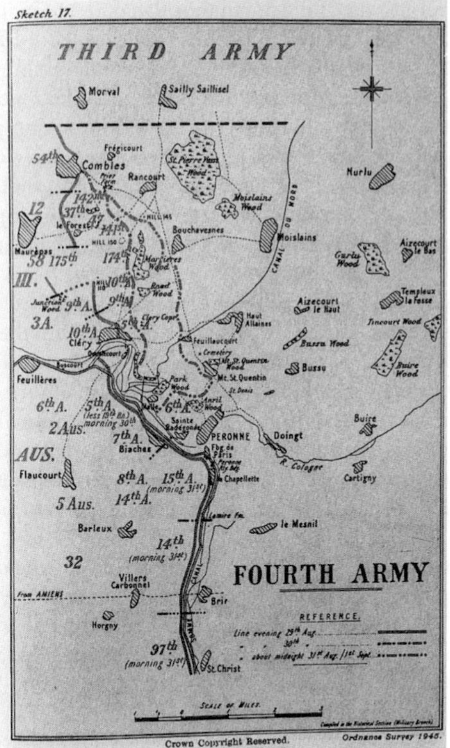

Several strong points were duly dealt with, but the troops on the left were held up at the lip of a large crater, from behind which stick bombs were being thrown. In addition, enemy machine-gun fire sprayed the area. One Australian rush failed to capture the crater and Lowerson – realising its importance – urged a group of seven men to take the crater which, according to German records, was the headquarters of the 1/96th Infantry Regiment, together with its reserve company. Lowerson gained the VC for this gallant and important action which included the capture of thirty Germans and a dozen of their machine guns. The decoration was gazetted as follows on 14 December 1918:

> For most conspicuous bravery and tactical skill, on the 1st Sept. 1918, during the attack on Mont St. Quentin, north of Péronne when very strong opposition was met with early in the attack,

> and every foot of ground was stubbornly contested by the enemy. Regardless of heavy enemy machine gun fire, Sergt. Lowerson moved about fearlessly directing his men, encouraging them to still greater effort, and finally led them onto the objective. On reaching the objective he saw that the left attacking party was held up by an enemy strong post heavily manned with twelve machine guns. Under the heaviest sniping and machine gun fire, Sergt. Lowerson rallied seven men as a storming party, and directing them to attack the flanks of the post, rushed the strong point, and by effective bombing captured it, together with twelve machine guns, and thirty prisoners. Though severely wounded in the right thigh, he refused to leave the front line until the prisoners had been disposed of and the organization and consolidation of the post had been thoroughly completed. Throughout a week of operations, his leadership and example had a continual influence on the men serving under him, whilst his prompt and effective action at a critical juncture allowed the forward movement to be carried on without delay, thus ensuring the success of the attack.

After being wounded a third time, in the thigh, Lowerson refused to leave the battalion until he was evacuated. However, he was back with his unit on 17 September to take part in the last Australian action of the war, at Montbrehain on 5 October, when he was wounded a fourth time.

He was presented with his VC by the King in the Ballroom of Buckingham Palace on 1 March 1919.

Albert (Alby) David Lowerson was a son and sixth child of English-born Henry Lowerson, an engine driver turned farmer, and his wife Mary Jane Lowerson (*née* McMaster). Albert was born at Myrtleford, Bogong, Victoria, on 2 August 1896.

Myrtleford was a small town and its main crops were hops and tobacco, and it was also the centre of a large dairy-farming area. Before the war Lowerson had been dredging for gold at Adelong, New South Wales.

At the age of 19 Lowerson enlisted in the AIF on 16 July 1915 and was given the service number of 2358. Following this, he was allotted to the 5th Reinforcements of the 21st Battalion, which embarked in September 1915. Four months later he joined the 21st Battalion on 7 January 1916 and sailed with it to France in March. At first the battalion spent some time in the Armentières sector area, but then moved southwards to the Somme and took part in the battle for Pozières in the late July–early August period and two weeks later in the front line close to Mouquet Farm, where Lowerson was wounded on 26 August and left his battalion for a month. On 1 November he was promoted to corporal and on 11 April 1917 he was made a temporary sergeant. He was wounded again in the Second Battle of Bullecourt on 3 May 1917, this time being out of action for six months, and when he returned on 1 November his rank as sergeant was confirmed. Just prior to gaining the VC on 1 September, Lowerson distinguished himself at Virgin Wood on 27 August and also at Herbécourt the following day.

After the Armistice he embarked for Australia on 1 April 1919, disembarking in Melbourne on 16 May, and was discharged on 8 July. He took up farming, concentrating on dairy and tobacco yields, but kept a link with his VC action by naming his farm St Quentin. On 1 February 1930 Lowerson married Edith Larkins at St Patrick's Cathedral in Melbourne.

After the Second World War began, Lowerson re-enlisted on 5 July 1940 and, although he was not passed fit for overseas service, he was deemed fit enough for home service. As a sergeant, he then taught at various training units, until discharged in 1944.

Lowerson did not live long after the Second World War ended, as he died of leukaemia on 15 December 1945 in his home town. He was given a military funeral and a Methodist service. Australian soldiers led the procession to the cemetery and also provided a guard of honour. One of the coffin bearers was Capt. A.C. Borella VC who lived in Victoria and had gained the VC in July 1918 during the struggle for Villers-Brettoneux. Lowerson was survived by Edith, his wife, and a daughter. In 1956 Edith attended the VC/GC centenary celebrations in London.

In September 1949 a memorial headstone was erected on Lowerson's grave by local residents from his home and was unveiled by Lt Col W. Joynt VC at a ceremony which was also attended by Capt. A.C. Borella VC.

Lowerson was also remembered in a number of other ways, including the naming of a swimming pool, which was opened by William Joynt VC at Myrtleford on 19 November 1966. He was also commemorated by a fountain, which was a gift from members of the former 21st Battalion and unveiled by the Battalion Association's President, Mr C. Falkiner. The opening ceremonies were attended by about 600 people and in his opening speech Joynt said this of Sergeant Lowerson: '... he had been an excellent soldier and the action in which he won his VC was one of the most decisive of the war and helped bring the war to an end two months later.' The ceremonies were followed by an adjournment to the local Returned Soldiers' League Hall which was followed by a lunch at a local hotel. Twenty-seven members of the Battalion Association attended the ceremony, and in later years battalion survivors made an annual pilgrimage to Lowerson's grave at the old Mytleford Cemetery, a tradition which was carried on for many years.

Lowerson's decorations are in the collection of the Australian War Memorial and, apart from the VC, include the 1914–15 Star, BWM, VM and for service in the Second World War the War Medal (1939–45), Australia Service Medal 1939–45 and also a King George VI Coronation Medal for 1937. His name is also remembered in Lowerson Place in Canberra and he is also commemorated in the Victoria Cross Park Memorial in Canberra and lastly in Sydney in the Victoria Cross Memorial in the Queen Victoria building.

R. Mactier

Mont St Quentin, France, 1 September

Private Robert (Bob) Mactier was a member of the 23rd Battalion (Victoria) (6th Brigade, 2nd Division) and gained the VC in the same action that Sgt A. Lowerson of the 21st Battalion won his, as well as Lieutenant Towner. The 23rd Battalion was part of an assault on Mont St Quentin in the early morning of 1 September. In order to keep the number of casualties as low as possible in the preliminary assault, the company commander who was to lead the 23rd from Florina Trench, Lt F.J. Jenkins, decided to seek an alternative approach. He discovered the possibility of making a detour using a position named Kholm Trench, which would allow the company to reach its allotted positions. However, by the time this route was discovered there were only twenty minutes left before zero hour.

The battalion was then replaced in Florina Trench by the 14th Brigade (5th Division) and after moving out of the position they turned left to cross the Péronne road which cut the northern end of Florina Trench. Having crossed this road to resume the advance, the head of the column found itself held up by a machine gun protected by a barbed-wire barricade. Other similar posts could be seen further on. An initial attack, under the leadership of Cpl R. Finlay who was killed, failed. This was when Pte Mactier, a company runner, was ordered by Lt Jenkins to investigate the situation. Gathering up a supply of bombs, and armed with a revolver, Mactier rushed forward, summed up the situation and took on the barricade single-handed. The citation for his posthumous VC 'for the greatest bravery' was gazetted on 14 December 1918 and tells the story of Mactier's gallantry:

> For most conspicuous bravery and devotion to duty on the morning of 1st Sept. 1918, during the attack on the village of

> Mont St. Quentin. Prior to the advance of the battalion, it was necessary to clear up several enemy strong points close to our line. This the bombing patrols sent forward failed to effect, and the battalion was unable to move. Private Mactier single-handed, and in daylight, thereupon jumped out of the trench, rushed past the block, closed with and killed the machine gun garrison of eight men with his revolver and bombs, and threw the enemy machine gun over the parapet. Then, rushing forward about 20 yards, he jumped into another strong point held by a garrison of six men, who immediately surrendered. Continuing to the next block through the trench, he disposed of an enemy machine gun which had been enfilading our flank advancing troops, and was then killed by another machine gun at close range. It was entirely due to this exceptional valour and determination of Private Mactier that the battalion was able to move to its 'jumping-off' trench and carry out the successful operation of capturing the village of Mont. St. Quentin a few hours later.

Mactier was initially buried close by, but later his body was moved to Hem Farm Cemetery, Hem-Monacu, Plot II, Row J, Grave 3. 2/Lt G.E. Cates is also buried there. Mactier's VC was presented to his father, Mr Robert Mactier, by His Excellency Sir Ronald Munro-Ferguson, who was Governor-General of Australia, at a ceremony at Melbourne Town Hall on 13 June 1919.

Robert Mactier was a member of a Presbyterian family, the son of a farmer, Scottish-born Robert and Christina (*née* Ross) Mactier, born on 17 May 1890 at Tatura, Victoria. He was the seventh of ten children and was educated at the state school, Tatura. Later he worked on his father's farms and became an all-round sportsman who had an 'irrepressible sense of humour'. He enlisted on 1 March 1917, and was given the service number of 6931, and on 11 May left for England. After training as part of the 19th Reinforcements he joined the 23rd Battalion in Belgium on 23 November and was posted to B Company as a scout. In April 1918 Mactier fought in the Somme close to Albert, during which time he was gassed. In the following month he became a scout at company headquarters. In July he was involved in the brilliant operation of the capture of Hamel and in the third week of August wrote home stating that 'Victory was in sight' and 'the war will be over by next spring'.

A radio series on the winners of the VC in the period 1936–37 described Mactier, who never married, as follows: 'Bob Mactier was typical of his kind, the countryman who became a soldier ... a healthy man ... well behaved ... quiet and unassuming; he had nothing spectacular in his make-up.' In 1956 two of Mactier's sisters represented the family, travelling to London for the VC/GC Centenary commemorations.

The action by the 2nd Australian Division in the period 31 August–2 September to capture the heavily fortified position of Mont St Quentin to the north of the town of Péronne was commemorated after the war by the Australians, who paid for a monument to honour their fallen comrades. The design of the monument depicted an Australian soldier about to bayonet a German eagle. Not surprisingly the advancing Germans in the Second World War took exception to this design and promptly destroyed the monument down to its pedestal. The monument was one of the few that they damaged.

Two years after the Second World War ended, veterans of the 2nd Division urged the Australian Government to obtain funds to place a replacement memorial on the former site. In the autumn of 1971 their dream was realised when the new 10ft high bronze of a Digger was shipped from Melbourne and sent to Péronne. It was designed by a British immigrant to Australia, Mr Stanley Hammond. It was dedicated at a ceremony that took place on 2 September at a time when the many Australian veterans who were present were in their seventies.

Mactier's deed was written up in the *Victor* comic issue of 10 February 1968. His name is commemorated in a soldier's club at Watsonia Barracks in Melbourne, where there is also a bronze bust of him designed by Wallace Anderson. The club was officially opened by the Minister for the Army in May 1960. Another reminder of him is the naming of Mactier Place in Canberra.

In 1983 his family presented his decorations to the Australian War Memorial in Canberra and apart from the VC they included the BWM and VM.

In addition to his decorations and commemoration at the Australian War Memorial in Canberra he is also remembered in the Victoria Cross Park Memorial in the same city and in Sydney with the Victoria Cross Memorial in the Queen Victoria building.

In his home town of Tatura in Victoria, a park is named after him and a plaque in the garden was unveiled in 1 September 1998, eighty years to the day from when he won his posthumous VC. At the time of writing there are plans to erect a statue of him in the park. Robert and his parents also have a stained glass window in St Andrew's Church in Tatura dedicated to them.

E.T. Towner

Mont St Quentin and Péronne, France, 1 September

Lieutenant Edgar Towner was one of six members of the Australian Forces to win a VC in the fighting for possession of Mont St Quentin as well as Péronne during the period 31 August–1 September 1918. On 1 September he was in charge of Number 3 Section of 7th Machine Gun Company, attached to the 24th Battalion (6th Brigade, 2nd Division) in an attack against the village of Mont St Quentin to the north of Péronne. The village overlooked Péronne together with the River Somme which ran through it.

The MGC section was positioned on the right flank of the 24th Battalion where it joined up with the 23rd Battalion's left flank. This flank had as its principle objective the summit of Mont St Quentin and it was hoped that the village of Feuillaucourt to the north-west could also be mopped up during the advance. The Australians were then to push on to the Péronne road to complete their objectives.

The ground was open and uphill and the only protection for the Australians was a sunken road which ran below and parallel to the Mont itself. The German defence was made up of strong points with machine guns and riflemen. An Allied artillery barrage began at 6 a.m. But as it was raining visibility was difficult. Almost at once the Australians began to suffer casualties, but despite this, they succeeded in taking the left-hand village of Feuillaucourt. About half an hour later, with C Company in the lead, they encountered strong enemy forces, resulting in a withdrawal to the part of the sunken road where it joined the Péronne road. Such was the intensity of the German defence and fire that the whole of the Australian attack was held up. The Germans were also preparing a counter-attack, but it was at this point that Lt Towner took a hand. Although there is no surviving account of what happened in his own words, there is an account noted down in 1941 by a Lt F. Clune who had recently met Towner and had encouraged him to talk about how he won his VC. However, it does not add to the very detailed account of his gallantry as set out in the official citation published in the *London Gazette* of 14 December 1918:

> For most conspicuous bravery, initiative and devotion to duty on 1 Sept. 1918, in the attack on Mont St. Quentin, near Péronne, when in charge of four Vickers guns. During the early stages of the advance he located and captured, single-handed, an enemy machine gun which was causing casualties, and turning it on the enemy inflicted severe loses. Subsequently, by the skilful tactical handling of his guns, he cut off and captured twenty-five of the enemy. Later, by fearless reconnaissance under heavy fire, and by the energy, foresight and promptitude with which he brought fire to bear on various enemy groups, he gave valuable support to the infantry advance. Again, when short of ammunition, he secured an enemy machine gun, which he mounted and fired in full view of the enemy, causing the enemy to retire further, and enabling our infantry to advance. Under intense fire, although wounded, he maintained the fire of this gun at a very critical period. During the following night he steadied and gave valuable support to a small detached post, and by his coolness and cheerfulness inspired the men in great degree. Throughout the night he kept close watch by personal reconnaissance on the enemy movements, and was evacuated exhausted thirty hours after being wounded. The valour and resourcefulness of Lieut. Towner undoubtedly saved a very critical situation, and contributed largely to the success of the attack.

Despite the great difficultes in dislodging a very determined enemy from the summit, the Australians nevertheless achieved it in a comparatively short space of time and by 8.20 a.m. the town of Péronne had also fallen. It was one of the dominion's finest actions of the war.

Lieutenant Towner was presented with his VC and MC in the Ballroom of Buckingham Palace on 10 April 1919 together with Cpl Arthur Hall.

Edgar Thomas Towner, the son of Edgar Thomas Towner and his second wife Greta (*née* Herley), was born at his father's home, a grazing property in Glencoe Station, in the Barcoo district of north-west Queensland, on 19 April 1890. The Barcoo district was made famous by A.B. 'Banjo' Paterson with his poem 'Bush Christening'.

As the family lived in a fairly remote area, Towner was initially educated at home by his mother who spoke several European languages. Her son continued his education at the Blackall State School and later in Rockhampton. Edgar then worked with his father until he decided to enlist in Blackall on 4 January 1915. His service number was 1067 and he left Brisbane for the Middle East in June with the 7th Reinforcements to the 25th Battalion. He never served in Gallipoli, remaining in Egypt. On 1 February 1916 he was promoted to sergeant and the 25th left Alexandria in March, bound for Marseilles for service in Belgium and France. Four months later Towner took part in the Battle of Pozières in July. He was commissioned four months later on 18 November and posted from the 25th battalion to the 2nd Machine Gun Battalion, becoming a full lieutenant on 24 February 1917. During this period he was allotted to the 7th Machine Company (3 November 1916) and was for a brief time responsible for the battalion transport company. He was twice mentioned in despatches on 9 April 1917 and won his MC in early 1918 when serving south of Morlancourt and Albert. The citation was published on 24 September as follows:

> For most conspicuous gallantry and devotion to duty, one of the first to reach the objective, he got his guns into action very quickly, thereby greatly assisting the right company in consolidating. He also brought a captured machine gun into action. When one of the infantry posts was badly blown in he went out at great risk and helped to re-organise it.

He had been mentioned in despatches a second time on 7 April 1918. When in command of a machine-gun section on 10–11 June 1918 he took part in a daylight raid in order to re-establish a post which was in danger of being captured in which he again displayed considerable gallantry and skill.

Five weeks after the capture of Mont St Quentin, Lt Towner was admitted to the Red Cross Hospital in Rouen where he was treated for a gunshot wound to the scalp. This was followed by three weeks' sick leave in England and he returned to his unit on 19 October.

After the war, Towner left England on 30 April 1919 to return to Australia, arriving in Sydney on 14 June 1919. He was demobilised on

16 August when his name was transferred to the Reserve of Officers with the rank of lieutenant. He returned to his home in Valpaiso but didn't have enough money to spend on stocking it and he therefore sold the property three years later and took up odd jobs. In 1925 he went into partnership on the Kaloola Station close to Longreach. He later bought out his partner and took up a second one with the Russleigh Pastoral Company at Isisford, before becoming a director of the Bursleigh Pastoral Company.

Two years before the Second World War broke out Towner rejoined the Australian Army as a captain on 8 August 1937, and was sent to the 2/26th Battalion. After a period as company commander he was made second-in-command of the battalion, the CO being Lt Col H.W. Murray, VC. At the age of 52 Towner, now a major, retired from the army because of ill health, on 21 February 1942, and returned to his property at Kaloola.

Edgar Towner was a versatile man – a soldier, sheep farmer and businessman, who also had a deep interest in history and geography. Apparently he was especially interested in researching the life of Sir Thomas Mitchell, the first man to discover the Barcoo River where Towner's father was one of the earliest settlers. Towner was also a fellow of the Royal Geographical Society of Australia and of the Royal Historical Society of New South Wales. In 1946 he persuaded the government to issue a postage stamp commemorating the centenary of Mitchell's discoveries in central Queensland, and in 1956 he was awarded the Dr Thomson Foundation Gold Medal for his geographical work. During his lifetime Towner became possibly one of the most financially successful holders of the VC won in the First World War and by his death had amassed an 80,000-acre farm with 25,000 sheep in central Queensland.

Towner, who was a big and imposing man, never married and was always a bit of a 'loner'. He died at Longreach Base Hospital on 18 August 1972 and his military funeral took place on 21 August, with the town of Longreach coming to a standstill as hundreds of mourners lined the street to pay their respects. His coffin was placed on a gun carriage and a firing party, chosen from members of the 2nd Battalion, the Royal Australian Infantry, took an active part. The funeral service was held in a packed St Andrew's Church and was conducted by Brother Francis. After the coffin was taken out to the gun carriage, the procession marched slowly to the Longreach Town Cemetery. In addition, 150 soldiers participated, and they slow marched, preceding the flower-strewn gun carriage. Towner's decorations were borne by a Maj. Gunder who walked behind the carriage. A tribute of poppies was made by members of the Returned Soldiers' League who later cast them into the grave as they slowly filed past. After the playing of the Last Post the firing party fired three volleys and thus the service officially ended.

Towner's VC and medals are privately held and in addition to his VC, MC and other decorations he is commemorated in a number of ways, firstly in Canberra in the Australian War Memorial in Canberra and with Towner Place being named after him. Towards the end of 1983 there was a furore in the Australian press because Towner's VC was being put up for sale by its then owner, a Dr W.A. 'Bill' Land in Spink's, Sydney, at the Wentworth Hotel. It was considered that such important medals of extreme gallantry belonged to the Australian War Memorial and should never be in private hands as part of some private collection. Land had purchased the VC in the early 1970s from a dealer who had bought it from a member of the Towner family after Towner died in 1972. The Australian War Museum indicated that it would not bid for the medal and indeed its director, Air Vice-Marshal James Fleming, said that it was most unfortunate the medal had been offered for sale in the first place. Gallantry awards should not be put up for monetary gain. The expected sale price for Towner's group of nine medals was AU$30,000. Apart from the three already mentioned, they included the 1914–15 Star, BWM, VM (plus MiD Oak Leaf), War Medal (1939–45), and Coronation Medals for 1937 and 1953. At the last moment the medals were withdrawn from the sale and had been refused an export licence. However, according to the Australian press, they were sold in Brisbane about fifteen years later at the end of 1998 for AU$160,000.

As stated above, Towner is commemorated in the Australian War Memorial in Canberra and with the Victoria Cross Park Memorial in the same city. He is also remembered in the Victoria Cross Memorial in the Queen Victoria building, Sydney.

In recent years his home town of Blackall have done him proud having raised AU$80,000 in order to commission a statue of their 'local hero' in the town. The sculptor was William Eicholz and the statue was installed on a sandstone plinth. A plaque on the statue describes it as 'Towner's Call' and portrays the hero hatless. It was dedicated in on 24 April 2009, ninety-one years after his death.

W.M. CURREY

Péronne, France, 1 September

On 1 September 1918, two Australians from the 54th Battalion AIF (14th Brigade, 5th Division) gained the VC in the fighting for Mont St Quentin and Péronne and a third, Pte William Currey, also won the same award as a member of the 53rd Battalion of the same brigade and division. Initially the two battalions were to advance together to clear the ground around Anvil Wood, north-west of the town's outskirts and the ramparts of Péronne. They were then to consolidate and join up with the 23rd Battalion, AIF (6th Brigade, 2nd Division). From this new line, the 56th Battalion was then to capture the ground beyond.

From the outset, the battle was bitterly contested and the 53rd Battalion lost many casualties in the opening stages. The right-hand portion of the battalion duly entered Anvil Wood and the north-west part of the town. During the fighting Pte Currey dealt with the crew of a German field-gun which was firing at point-blank range and causing heavy casualties. After which the battalion companies were able to proceed into the wood itself where they captured many prisoners, as well as two more field-guns and two machine guns. However, the situation to the north of the wood was less satisfactory and two companies were decimated by machine-gun fire from Mont St Quentin. Fortunately two men managed to capture an enemy field-gun and to turn it against the enemy.

As the 53rd Battalion emerged from Anvil Wood it came under extremely heavy fire and took up positions near the town cemetery which bordered the eastern side of the wood. To the north, Mont St Quentin was still in German hands and the position of the battalion was quite dangerous. At this point Currey captured a machine-gun post by himself. This was at about 4.30 p.m. Half an hour later the unit was ordered to continue its advance, this time in full view of the enemy, and it came under withering fire.

Most of the battalion was unable to move forward and thus remained on the old cemetery line. At about 3 a.m. on 2 September, Currey volunteered to find an isolated small party under Lt W. Waite, which was in a forward position, and inform them of orders to withdraw. Currey moved forward into No-Man's-Land towards Waite, then stood up and yelled as loud as he could, 'Waitsy get in!' Not suprisingly, German gunners turned their attention in the direction of Currey's voice, but both he and Waite's party managed to return safely and the role of the battalion in the battle for Péronne then ended. It had cost 252 casualties, but the enemy casualties were just as heavy, and at least 200 were taken prisoner. With the assistance of the artillery and other battalions the capture of Péronne was completed by 10 a.m. on 2 September. Towards the end of the month, on 29 September, the 5th and 3rd Australian Divisions linked up with American troops and together broke through the enemy defences guarding the St Quentin Canal. Three days later Currey and the 53rd Battalion were withdrawn from the line and took no active part in the remainder of the war.

Private Currey's VC was gazetted on 14 December 1918:

> For most conspicuous bravery and daring in the attack on Péronne on the morning of 1 Sept. 1918. When the battalion was suffering heavy casualties from a 77mm. field-gun at very close range, Private Currey, without hesitation, rushed forward under intense machine gun fire and succeeded in capturing the gun single-handed after killing the entire crew. Later, when the advance of the left flank was checked by an enemy strong point, Private Currey crept around the flank and engaged the post with a Lewis gun. Finally, he rushed the post single-handed, causing many casualties. It was entirely owing to his gallant conduct that the situation was relieved and the advance enabled to continue. Subsequently he volunteered to carry orders for the withdrawal of an isolated company, and this he succeeded in doing despite shell and rifle fire, returning later with valuable information. Throughout the operations his striking example of coolness, determination and utter disregard of danger had a most inspiring effect on his comrades, and his gallant work contributed largely to the success of the operations.

He was presented with his VC by the Rt Hon., Sir Robert Crauford Munro-Ferguson, PC GCMC, Governor General of Australia, on

7 October 1919 at the Victoria Barracks, Sydney. He was discharged from the army during the same year.

William (Bill) Matthew Currey, the son of William Robert Currey and Mary Ellen (*née* Lang), was born in Wallsend, near Newcastle, New South Wales, on 19 September 1895. William senior was a labourer and later a miner. After school at the Dudley and Plattsburg public schools, his son moved to 'Tasma', 160 Francis Street, Leichhardt, Sydney, where he completed his education at the local public school before taking up a job as an electrician. For eighteen months prior to the war he served in the militia and then six months with the 31st Infantry Regiment at Haberfield. In the summer of 1914 he quickly applied to serve with the AIF. He appears to have lied about his age, but this was discovered and he was discharged. For almost a whole year he served as part of the guard at a German internment camp in Holsworthy. However, in 1916, before his twenty-first birthday, his parents gave permission for him to enlist once more, which he did in Sydney, but this time he was turned down on medical grounds. Following surgery for varicoceles, he was finally given his wish and accepted for military service with the AIF on 9 October 1916 at Victoria Barracks in Leichhardt, and allocated the service number of 1584A. He was posted to the 4th Light Trench Mortar Battery as a reinforcement, and went overseas on 9 November 1916 on board HMAT *Benella*, arriving at Devonport on 9 January 1917. On 6 February he was transferred to the 53rd Battalion and later in the year he fought at Polygon Wood, France, before returning to the Somme. In February 1918 he was granted three weeks' leave in England, returning to his brigade in March which was in positions to the north of Villers-Bretonneux. From 9 August to 3 August he attended the 14th Infantry Brigade School prior to his VC action to the north of Péronne.

After the war, Currey returned on board the *Orsova*, disembarking at Sydney on 3 March 1919, and was discharged as unfit for general service on 2 April. On leaving the army he initially found suitable employment hard to come by, and for a time he worked as a storeman in the NSW government railways. Together with thirteen other holders of the VC he was a guest on Armistice Day at the Hotel Australia as guests of the Hon. Hugh Donald McIntosh MC. At around this time Curey took an interest in politics, becoming a member of the Australian Labor Party. He married Emmie Davies, daughter of Mr C.F. Davies, on 10 April 1920, with George Cartwright VC and Wally Brown VC to act as best man and groomsman respectively. He finally found a job as an electrician with the New South Wales State Railways. On Armistice Day 1929 he was one of the fourteen VC-holding guests at a luncheon at Government House in Sydney given by the governor of New South Wales, Sir Dudley de Chair, and his wife.

In 1930–32 he was a member of the 45th Battalion as part of the citizen forces and was later promoted to warrant officer. Between 1940 and 1941 he was with the Australian Instructional Corps.

During an interview with an Australian journalist at the outbreak of the Second World War, Currey declared very strongly that he did not agree with conscription. He also advised Australians against getting involved in this war without an assurance that victory would mean a new world order: 'We were duped last time and fought to obtain something, which we were promised, but never got.' He served briefly with the Army Instructional Corps before becoming a member of the New South Wales parliament, representing Kogarah from 1941, and was also the Assembly's first VC holder. He had acquired a useful knowledge of social and economic problems. He was to make many friends in the Labor Party and throughout his life was a keen supporter of the causes espoused by ex-servicemen. Also in 1941 a memorial library was installed at Dudley, paid for by the parents and citizens of the town, to commemorate two former pupils and VC holders, William Currey and Clarence Jeffries, who also hailed from Wallsend and who had won his VC at Passchendaele in October 1917. At an election in May 1944 he achieved a greater majority of support and won his seat again in May 1947.

In the summer of 1947 Currey became ill, and in April 1948 collapsed in Parliament House. Doctors ordered him to have a complete rest, but he died from heart failure only a few days later in Sydney on 30 April 1948. During the war Currey had been gassed twice and also buried by explosions, and it is possible that these experiences contributed to his early death at the age of 52. On his death he left a widow, two married daughters as well as a granddaughter.

He was cremated at Woronora Crematorium, Sydney, where his ashes were interred. Four holders of the VC attended his funeral. Currey's name is commemorated by a plaque in Rookwood Cemetery Garden of Remembrance. He is also commemorated on the war memorial at Leichardt Park, Sydney, New South Wales, and at a memorial park in Abermain in the same state, which is named after him. A plaque to his memory was attached to the Balmain War Memorial on 11 November 2001. In 1956 a plaque to his memory was erected in Speaker's Square in the NSW legislative assembly but, owing to building alterations, it was taken down in 1970 and subsequently mislaid. In the same year a service of rededication was held at Dudley Public School, at the Jeffries-Currey Memorial Library on 1 May 1976. The same two men who attended this school are also remembereed on a memorial wall in Sandgate General Cemetery in Newcastle, which was unveiled on 16 April 2000.

William Currey's VC was the first to be presented to the Australian War Memorial after the opening of the Hall of Valour in 1981, a move made by his daughter, Mrs J.E. Luton. His other decorations were the BWM, VM and the 1937 Coronation Medal. In addition, Currey's portrait was painted for the Australian War memorial by Sir John Longstaff. He is also commemorated in the Australian War Memorial, Canberra, the Victoria Cross Park Memorial, also in Canberra, and in Sydney in the Victoria Cross Memorial in the Queen Victoria building.

On 11 November 2008, ninety years after the end of the First World War, the plaque previously erected in Speaker's Square was rededicated, having been 'lost' in the bowels of the NSW Legislature for thirty-two years.

A.H. Buckley

Péronne, France, 1–2 September

Alexander Buckley won a VC as a temporary corporal on 1–2 September 1918 at Péronne. He was a member of the 54th Battalion AIF (14th Brigade, 5th Australian Division) as was Cpl Arthur Hall, another Australian soldier who gained the same honour on the same day. Private William Currey of the 54th's sister battalion, the 53rd, was the third man to win a VC during the same actions.

On 1 September the 54th Battalion, the right-hand battalion of the Australian 14th Brigade, advanced as part of an attack on the north-western outskirts of Péronne. The objective was to clear the territory between the town itself and the heights and village of Mont St Quentin to the north as far as the banks of the River Somme which ran through the south-west part of the town.

The battalion found itself facing a dense barbed-wire front before reaching the first enemy trench, but the Australians were in no mood to be deterred by such an obstacle. They simply charged the obstruction and 'blazed away' with Lewis-gun fire at the enemy, which was only 30yds away. Others ripped up the wire picquets in order to crawl under the barbed wire. This was enough for the German defenders who soon fled from their positions.

However, on the right of the second line a hostile machine gun did pose a major hazard to the advancing Australians. Accompanied by the two NCOs, Cpl A.C. Hall and T/Cpl A. Buckley stalked the crew of the enemy machine gunners and managed to rush the post and in the process capture it together with twenty-two prisoners.

Soon the enemy retreated into the town, entering it by crossing the Cléry roadbridge over the castle moat. Although they promptly destroyed the bridge behind them, to the right was a small wooden footbridge which four Australians began to cross, only to be met by heavy machine-gun fire from the battlements of the old castle. While Lt D. McArthur was examining the footbridge, together with Buckley and two colleagues, they were killed by machine-gun fire, and at 6.45 Lt J. Adams sent word that his company had been stopped. However, the enemy made a crucial blunder by not adequately defending the destroyed Cléry roadbridge. This enabled the Australians to set up a plank bridge under the line of the broken bridge, which allowed them direct access to the town. Within twenty minutes the Germans in the vicinity surrendered and eventually after a lot of mopping up, Australian troops managed to re-capture the town.

Buckley's posthumous decoration was gazetted on 14 December 1918 as follows:

> For most conspicuous bravery and self-sacrifice at Péronne during the operations on 1–2 Sept. 1918. After passing the first objective his half-company and part of the company on the flank were held up by an enemy machine gun nest. With one man he rushed the post, shooting four of the occupants and taking 22 prisoners. Later on, reaching a moat, it was found that another machine gun nest commanded the only available foot-bridge. Whilst this was being engaged from a flank, Corpl. Buckley endeavoured to cross the bridge and rush the post, but was killed in the attempt. Throughout the advance he had displayed great initiative, resource and courage, and by his effort to save his comrades from casualties, he set up a fine example of self-sacrificing devotion to duty.

Alexander Henry Buckley was born in Warren, New South Wales, on 22 July 1891. He was the fourth child of James Buckley and his wife Julia (*née* Falkanhagan), both of whom came from Victoria. Alexander was educated at home by his parents, and later took up farming with his father on Homebush, a property close to Gulargambone.

At the age of 23, on 3 February 1915, Buckley enlisted in the AIF at Dubbo, New South Wales, and was allocated the service number of 1876. Service records described him as well built, more than 6ft tall.

He embarked for England on 23 June 1916, arriving in August. He was a member of the 3rd Reinforcements to the 54th Battalion, having joined it in France at Flers on the Somme in November 1916. A few months later, in the spring of 1917, he fought with the 54th in the

Arras battles at Bullecourt and later in the year served at Polygon Wood and Broodseinde. In November 1917 he was promoted to temporary corporal. In April 1918 he moved to the Villers-Brettoneux area and in August took part in the Battle of Amiens.

After his death Buckley was buried in Péronne Communal Cemetery Extension, Plot II, Row C, Grave 32. This cemetery is adjacent to the town cemetery and contains the graves of at least 500 Australians. Although the town cemetery is on the same site as it was over ninety years ago, it is now surrounded by houses and allotments. Lieutenant D. McArthur, killed at the same time, was buried 5 miles to the west of the town in Herbécourt British Cemetery, Grave C 16.

Alexander Buckley is commemorated at VC corner in the Australian War Memorial, where his decorations are on display. Apart from a posthumous VC, they are the BWM and VM. He is also commemorated in the Victoria Cross Park Memorial, also in Canberra, and in Sydney in the Victoria Cross Memorial in the Queen Victoria building.

Street in Moreuil marking the action of 8 August. (Courtesy of Peter Batchelor)

Hangard Wood Cemetery. (Courtesy of Peter Batchelor)

Hatchet Wood. (Courtesy of Peter Batchelor)

Plaque to F.G. Coppins, Chapel of the Chimes Crematorium. (Courtesy of Donald C. Jennings)

R. Spall recorded on the Vimy Memorial. (Courtesy of Donald C. Jennings)

Quinton Cemetery, Birmingham where G. Onions is buried. (Courtesy of Donald C. Jennings)

W.D. Joynt's medals. (Courtesy of Paul Street)

Plaque at Brighton Lawn Cemetery, Melbourne for W.D. Joynt. (Courtesy of Paul Street)

C.S. Rutherford in later life.

L.D. McCarthy.

A drawing of H. Weale.

The grave of C.S. Rutherford at Union Cemetery, Colborne, Ontario, Canada. (Courtesy of Donald C. Jennings)

W.H. Clark-Kennedy's grave. (Courtesy of Donald C. Jennings)

Cartoon cover depicting Mactier's winning action. (Courtesy of D.C. Thomson & Co. Ltd)

The memorial at Mont St Quentin. (Courtesy of Peter Batchelor)

The plaque for B.S. Hutcheson. (Courtesy of Donald C. Jennings)

The grave of C.W. Peck, Fraser Cemetery, Vancouver. (Courtesy of Donald C. Jennings)

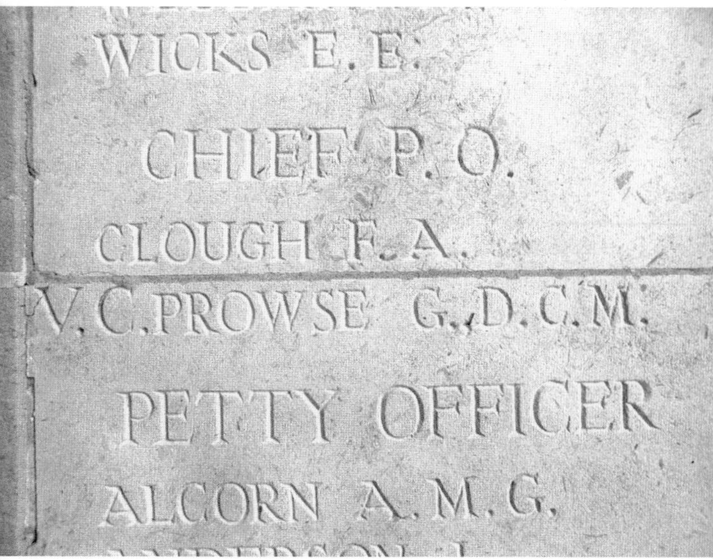

The commemoration of G. Prowse at Vis-en-Artois. (Courtesy of Peter Batchelor)

*Sgt L. Calvert with family and members of the Calvert Testimonial Committee, Conisborough Station. (*Mexborough & Swinton Times, *19 April 1919)*

*Sgt L. Calvert (far right, front) outside the Mansion House, Doncaster. (*Mexborough & Swinton Times, *1920s)*

A.C. Hall

North-West of Péronne, France, 1 September

On 1 September 1918 Cpl Arthur Hall won the VC to the north-west of Péronne when he was working with T/Cpl Alexander Buckley, both men being membersof the 54th Battalion (AIF) 14th Brigade, 5th Division. The battalion was the right battalion of the Brigade advance to the north-west of the town, and was to move into the town if it was strongly opposed.

The battalion advanced in the small hours from the direction of Halle to the north-east in drizzling rain and under heavy fire. Corporal Hall won his VC during the advance when he captured two enemy machine guns together with fifteen prisoners. He later found himself close to the site of a bridge (Cléry) over the grassy ramparts that ran close to the castle's moat at the same time that the enemy was attempting to destroy it. He reported that there was no sign of any organised resistance, although when part of his unit was crossing the footbridge over the 6ft deep moat, it came under heavy fire when Alexander Buckley was one of those men killed. Hall's message led to the erection of a new crossing made from planks that stretched over the moat and debris, positioned under the site of the original bridge.

A large party of the enemy then began to fire from the castle battlements but a burst of Lewis-gun fire caused most of the Germans to surrender, while the remainder were captured from the rear.

Hall's 54th Battalion subsequently entered Péronne where it began to clear the town of the enemy. This was no easy task and they suffered casualties from machine guns which were often placed on the rooftops of the narrow streets. However, despite this, the battalion managed to mop up the enemy positions and reach the town centre. During these operations Hall was heavily involved in organising and leading assault parties. The battalion extended its frontage to the left of the town, while the enemy artillery carried out desultory irregular shelling. It was during the following day that Hall rescued a colleague under heavy fire, which was another one of the actions for which he was awarded the VC.

Reading the various accounts of how Péronne fell to the AIF at the beginnning of September 1918, it seems to have been carried out with a combination of Australian courage and an unusual lack of adequate defensive preparation on the enemy's part. In addition the defenders seemed to have been all too ready to give themselves to the tough dominion troops.

Hall's VC was gazetted on 14 December 1918 as follows:

> For most conspicuous bravery, brilliant leadership and devotion to duty during operations at Péronne on 1 and 2 Sept. 1918. During the attack on the 1st Sept. a machine gun post was checking the advance. Single-handed, he rushed the position, shot four of the occupants and captured nine others and two machine guns. Then crossing the objective with a small party, he afforded excellent cover in support to the remainder of the company. Continuously in advance of the main party, he located enemy posts of resistance and personally led parties to the assault. In this way he captured many small parties of prisoners and machine guns. On the morning of the 2nd Sept. during a very heavy barrage, he carried to safety a comrade who had been dangerously wounded and was urgently in need of medical attention, and immediately returned to his post. The energy and personal courage of this gallant non-commissioned officer contributed largely to the success of the operations, throughout which he showed utter disregard of danger and inspired confidence in all.

Hall was decorated at Buckingham Palace with his VC on 10 April 1919 in the same investiture as Lieutenant Edgar Towner was also awarded his VC.

Arthur Charles Hall, the eldest son of Charles and Emma Jane Hall (*née* King), was born at Granville, New South Wales, on 11 August 1896. He attended school at All Saints College in Bathurst and later became an overseer on his father's farm station in the period 1909–12. When he enlisted on 3 April 1916 at Dubbo, his height was noted as

5ft 10½in. He was allocated the service number of 2631. Six months later he embarked for England from Sydney on 7 October and his ship reached Plymouth six weeks later on 21 November. He was one of the 6th Reinforcements for the 54th Battalion.

Hall was well qualified for the army as he had not only spent two years' service in the Senior Cadets but he was also an expert rifle shot, the result of culling kangaroos. After training in England he was sent to the 5th Australian Divisional Base in Étaples. He was made an acting corporal on Christmas Eve and joined the 54th Battalion in Montauban, France, on 8 February 1917. The battalion had been raised a year before, in Egypt, on 1 February 1916.

On 30 March 1917 Hall was seriously wounded in the leg and on the folowing day he was sent to the 9th CCS and later to the 12th General Hospital in Rouen. He returned to his unit three weeks later. In May 1917 he took part in the second battle for Bullecourt and later fought in September at Polygon Wood.

On 12 June, Hall was made a lance corporal prior to becoming a full corporal on 4 October. In January 1918 he reported sick and was sent to the 3rd Canadian CCS and then to England where he spent some time in Exeter War Hospital. He was allocated two weeks' leave and returned to his battalion France on 2 June.

In late July he was sent to Boulogne for raiding training and his battalion moved back to the Somme battlefield to take part in the fighting at Villers-Bretonneux in April. In July the battalion was at Morlancourt and in early August it took part in the great Allied offensive. After the fall of Péronne and the capture of Mont St Quentin, the last major batle of the war in which the 54th Battalion took an active role, was between 29 September and 2 October. In early October Hall was one of those men transferred to the 56th Battalion of the 14th Brigade when the 54th and 56th were amalgamated.

Hall was informed that he had won the VC on 8 December, which was six days before it was officially announced. After a spell of leave he returned to France on 8–9 January 1919 and was promoted to temporary sergeant on 6 March. Already having had some leave linked with him attending an investiture at Buckingham Palace, a visit that didn't materialise, he had a few more days off beginning on 2 April before finally attending his investiture on the 10th.

He arrived back in Australia on 26 June 1919 and was discharged from the Australian Army in Sydney on 3 August. He then took up sheep farming at the Glenelg and Willeroon stations in Nyngan, New South Wales. These two stations were previously owned by his father where we have seen that he had been overseer before enlisting.

Hall bought a property called Gundooee, Coolabah, in New South Wales. Eight years later he married Catherine Jessie Hemington Harris, daughter of H. Harris, and the wedding took place on 26 April 1927 at the Union Church, Lahey's Creek. The couple were to have one daughter and three sons: Helen, George, Dennis and Charles.

During the Second World War, Hall was mobilised on 6 January 1942 and was later commissioned and served with the 7th Garrison Battalion. He finally left the army and his name was placed on the Retired List on 16 November 1943. At the end of hostilities he returned to sheep farming and also built up a fine herd of Poll Devon cattle. He took part in local activities and was for twenty years the president of the Nyngan Picnic Race Club, as well as being a founder member and participant of the Collabah District Rifle Club. He was also a member of the Nyngan District Historical Society. Ten years later he was invited to attend a VC dinner in Sydney but was unable to attend, though he did manage to travel as a member of the Australian contingent to Britain for the VC centenary in June 1956. He had already been introduced to Queen Elizabeth II and Prince Philip at the Anzac Memorial in Hyde Park, Sydney on 5 February 1954. Other VC holders present included; Lt J. Maxwell, Lt P. Storkey and Private William Jackson.

Arthur Hall died in Nyngan District Hospital on 25 February 1978 and was buried in the small St Matthew's Anglian Churchyard, West Bogan, Coolabah, New South Wales. The church had been built from timber cut from Hall's own property. He was survived by his wife and their four children. In his will he left AU$160,191 and donated his VC to the Australian War Memorial in Canberra. His other decorations were the BWM and VM from the First World War and from the Second World War they included the War Medal (1939–1945) and Australian Service Medal (1939–45). In addition he was awarded Coronation Medals for 1937 and 1953 and the Queen Elizabeth II Silver Jubilee (1977). He is remembered at the Victoria Cross Park Memorial, also in Canberra, and in Sydney in the Victoria Cross Memorial in the Queen Victoria building. The Nygan War Memorial also includes his name.

On 8 December 2011, in the presence of the Governor of New South Wales, the Coolabah to Brewarrina main road was renamed the Arthur Hall VC Way.

J.G. Grant

East of Bancourt, near Bapaume, France, 1 September

During the Second Battle of Bapaume (31 August–3 September 1918) when the New Zealand Division was part of IV Corps of the Allied Third Army, east of Bancourt, an NCO member of their 1st NZ Brigade won the VC for conspicuous bravery.

On 1 September the plan was for the 1st and 3rd New Zealand Brigades to continue to take part in the Allied advance with 1st Brigade on the right of the 42nd Division, which was holding the village of Riencourt to the south-east of Bapaume. Close to the village was the crest of a hill that would provide greater observation, which had been lost on 30 August, and it was now desirable for it to be retaken. On the left of the New Zealand Brigade was the 5th Division. Assisted by artillery the operation began successfully between 4.30 a.m. and 5.30 a.m. when seventy members of the 23rd (Saxon) Division were quickly taken prisoner. The section of the crest allocated to the New Zealand Rifles and the 1st Battalion Wellington Regiment (1st NZ Brigade) was not to be a straightforward task, but one of their NCOs, Sergeant John Grant, in charge of a platoon, did sterling and gallant work when accompanied by Lance Corporal C.T. Hill in making a breakthrough after dealing with five enemy machine guns. After the objective was re-taken it was intended to push patrols forward easterly as far as the Haplincourt road, but intense German machine-gun fire prevented this. However, on the following day, further progress was made by the brigade with the assistance of tanks and artillery.

For his gallantry in the capture of the crest Sgt Grant gained the VC, which was gazetted on 27 November 1918 as follows:

> For most conspicuous bravery and devotion to duty near Bancourt on the 1st September 1918, when sergeant in command of a platoon forming part of the leading waves of the battalion attacking the high ground to the east of Bancourt. On reaching the crest, it was found that a line of five enemy machine gun posts offered a serious obstacle to further advance. Under point-blank fire, however, the company advanced against these posts. When about twenty yards from the posts, Sergt. Grant, closely followed by a comrade, rushed forward ahead of his platoon, and with great dash and bravery entered the centre post, demoralizing the garrison and enabling the men of his platoon to mop up the position. In the same manner he then rushed the post on the left, and the remaining posts were quickly occupied and cleared by his company. Throughout the whole operation on this and the two previous days, Sergt. Grant displayed coolness, determination and valour of the highest order, and set a splendid example to all.

For his part in the action L/Cpl Hill was awarded a DCM. A couple of months later Grant was wounded at the beginning of November and was invalided back to England, later being presented with his VC by the King in the Ballroom of Buckingham Palace on 26 February 1919.

John Gildray Grant, of Scottish descent, was born at Hawera, New Zealand, on 26 August 1889. After a primary school education he became a self-employed builder and contractor. His next-of-kin was his mother, Jane Grant of Princess Street, Hawera. When he was 25 years old he enlisted on 14 June 1915 and was allocated the service number of 10/2580. In his service papers he is described as being 5ft ½in, with a fresh complexion, dark brown hair and blue eyes. He embarked for Egypt with the 7th Reinforcements in October as a private in the Wellington Regiment. He was then posted to the 1st Battalion at Ismailia and in April left for France. He was made a corporal in June 1917 and six months later was promoted to sergeant. After winning his VC he was sent to OCTU in Cambridge in October, joining the No. 5 Officer Cadet Battalion in Trinity College. He was commissioned in February 1919. He returned to New Zealand in October and, after being demobilised in January 1920, served in the Territorial Force for the next ten years until retirement. He resettled in Hawera, Wellington.

In 1929 Grant attended the VC Dinner on 9 November in London. Six years later in 1935 some concern was expressed in Northern Military Command in Auckland when they learnt from an article in the *Star* newspaper, dated 27 April 1934, about a holder of the VC who needed relief support. It was 'a reflection on the Government that such a man should be allowed to remain unemployed'. However, a memorandum from the Colonel Commanding Northern Command of the New Zealand Defence Forces replied to an enquiry about Grant from General HQ New Zealand Military Forces as follows:

> re: V.C. on Relief.
>
> With reference to your memorandum D. 48/61 dated 3rd May, as far as I have been able to find out, the contents of your letter are substantially correct.
>
> I am given to understand that one J.G. Grant, V.C. is working at a relief camp at Paeroa Race Course. I understand that efforts are being made at Paeroa, by the Mayor, to get Grant employment.
>
> As far as I can find out Grant has on several occasions been provided with permanent employment, but is alleged to be unable to hold it, owing to his erratic habits. It appears that he [is] extremely unreliable, and it is to this factor alone that he owes his present position.
>
> I understand that he is identical with the J.G. Grant, formerly Lieutenant with the Wellington Regiment of N.Z.E.F.

In June 1956 Grant was a member of the ANZAC contingent to London for the VC Centenary celebrations and, despite suffering from poor health, he insisted on attending a VC reunion in London in July 1968. He was unable to travel in a RAF plane to London and the New Zealand Public opened a subscription appeal which raised money to pay for his flight in a civilian aircraft, accompanied by two nurses. With hindsight it would appear that John Grant was a clear case of undiagnosed post-traumatic stress disorder or PTSD.

Two years later Grant died, on 25 November 1970, at the Roskill Masonic Village in Auckland at the age of 81, and was buried in the Golders Cemetery, Waikumete, Block M, Section 9, Plot 95. He had been a Mason for six years.

In his commemoration there is a plaque to his memory at Waikumete Memorial Park and he is also commemorated at the HQ, Dunedin RSA (Returned Services Association). A street in Hawera is also named Grant VC Avenue. His decorations are displayed alternately in

Pure Arik (Taranaki Museum), New Plymouth, Taranaki and the Army Museum at Waiouru. They include the VC, 1914–15 Star, BWM, VM and Coronation Medals for 1937 and 1953. Grant's VC was one of nine New Zealand VCs stolen but later recovered after a reward was offered.

C.J.P. NUNNEY

Near Vis-en-Artois, France, 1–2 September

Private Claude (Red) Nunney of the 38th Battalion Eastern Ontario Regiment (Ottawa) (12th Canadian Brigade) 4th Canadian Division won what was to be a postumous VC south-east of Arras. The objective was to attack the Drocourt-Quéant Line, an action which had been delayed. On 1 September the 38th Battalion positions were close to the village of Vis-en-Artois prior to the previously delayed but eventually successful Canadian capture of the line.

Private Nunney was one of seven men serving in the Canadian Expeditionary Force to be awarded Britain's highest military honour in connection with the capture of this very important enemy defence line, which was a very strongly held backbone of the German resistance. Together with a support line it boasted a very sopisticated system of interlocking trench systems as well as tunnels, concrete shelters, machine-gun posts and in addition a dense mass of barbed wire. It even boasted a light railway system. The Buissy Switch linked the line with the Hindenburg support system. The lines joined on the forward slope of a position known as Mont Dury between the village of that name and the Arras–Cambrai road and the support line was on the reverse slope. The switch line ran in front of Buissy and Villers-lès-Cagnicourt in a south-easterly direction. The Canadian plan was to use the 4th and 1st Divisions to attack the section of the line closest to the Cambrai road and to then roll up the German defences to the north and south. Six companies of Mark V tanks were also to be used. The British 57th (West Lancashire) Division was to the right of the Canadians.

On 1 September the Canadian positions recently captured by them were then subjected to a heavy enemy artillery barrage. The *Official History* noted the following of the actions on 2 September:

> When at 5 a.m. the 72nd, 38th and 85th Battalions of the 12th Canadian Brigade advanced, each on a five-hundred yard front, the twenty-two tanks allotted to this brigade had not arrived, and some opposition was experienced from enemy outposts, some of which were so close to the jumping-off line as to be untouched by the barrage. Then, aided by the tanks, the D-Q front and support systems were taken without difficulty; in places the Germans fought stoutly and three tanks were lost, whilst in others they were eager to surrender ...

Nunney's VC was gazetted on 14 December 1918 as follows:

> For most conspicuous bravery during the operations against the Drocourt–Quéant line on 1 and 2 Sept. 1918. On 1 Sept., when his battalion was in the vicinity of Vis-en-Artois, preparatory to the advance, the enemy laid down a heavy barrage and counter-attacked. Private Nunnery, who was at this time at company headquarters, immediately on his own initiative proceeded through the barrage to the company outpost lines, going from post to post and encouraged the men by his own fearless example. The enemy were repulsed and a critical situation was saved. During the attack on 2 Sept. his dash continually placed him in advance of his companions, and his fearless example undoubtedly helped greatly to carry the company forward to its objectives. He displayed throughout the highest degree of valour until severely wounded.

Private Nunney died of his wounds sixteen days later at Vis-en-Artois CCS on 18 September and was buried 12 miles east of St Pol at Aubigny Communal Cemetery Extension, Plot IV, Row B, Grave 39. His brother Alfred, who was a member of the 80th Battalion, had been killed in action a few weeks before, on 10 August 1918.

Claude Joseph Patrick Nunney was born in Hastings on 24 December 1892 although many accounts of his life say he was born in Dublin, a fiction which probably came from Nunney himself. There is no question of him being Irish though, and he inherited an Irish temperament from his Irish mother whose maiden name was Sargent. Details about his childhood are very sketchy, although it is known that when he was about 13 years of age he and several of his siblings were packed off to Canada when his family was very poor and it was thought the children would have a better chance in life if they emigrated to Canada. At first in 1905 Claude, whose real name was Stephen Sargent Claude Joseph Patrick Nunney, was placed in an orphanage, at St George's House in Ontario. However, a certain Dr D.D. McDonald took an interest in the boy and Claude was subsequently moved to live with McDonald's mother who lived in the community of Pine Hill in nearby Glengarry County in Lancaster Township. At this point Claude attended Separate School No. 9 in the township. It was in this way that Claude became a Canadian citizen.

In 1912, after the death of his foster mother, Nunney joined the 59th Stormont and Glengarry Regiment, which was a non-government militia unit. He later enlisted in the 38th Eastern Ontario Regiment (Ottawa) Battalion on 8 March 1915 at Alexandria, Ontario. His battalion left for Bermuda in August 1915 where it relieved the Royal Canadian Regiment and, after a few months, moved to England in May 1916. Three months later the 38th Battalion left for France as part of the 4th Canadian Division in August 1916, and took part in the Battle of the Somme. A few months later Nunney won the DCM during the Canadian capture of at Vimy Ridge in April 1917. The citation published in the *London Gazette* was as follows:

> For most conspicuous gallantry and devotion to duty. Although wounded in two places, and his section wiped out, he continued to advance carrying his gun and ammunition, and alone stopping an attack by over 20 enemy. He continued on duty for three days, showing exceptional fearlessness and doing magnificent work. He also won the MM at Gouy Souvins on 17 September 1917.

A document from the collection of a Miss H. Menzies, daughter of Sgt A. Menzies (who used to be Nunney's sergeant), includes some pithy comments about Nunney's Irish character, although the wording is not always consistently accurate:

> He did some excellent work in France under me, but owing to his Irish temperamant, generaly caused trouble when fighting under others.
>
> As a sergeant in D. Company, whilst on duty in the front line, he lost his temper and threw the Company Sergeant Major down the steps to a dugout, breaking his arm and causing other minor injuries.
>
> Sentenced to five years detention, but whilst under guard in the horse lines a British plane crashed and immediately went into

flames. Red broke through his guard, entered the burning plane and brought out the pilot. He was severely burnt, and evacuated to Étaples Military Hospital. Whilst there the Germans made a very heavy air-raid on the whole area, causing great damage. Red dashed out of bed and for hours kept bringing in wounded.

Sentence suspended on the recommendations of British H.Q. and Red rejoined the Battalion. Previously he had been awarded certain decorations.

At the battle of Amiens, 1917 [*sic* 1918], the Battalion made great progress (I was not there, being in hospital in London). When stiff resistance on the third day of the battle was encounterted. Red, as private Nunney, dashed ahead through the barrage and killed or wounded the crews of three enemy machine gun posts.

The following day Red, now once again a platoon sergeant, was in charge of a platoon in an advanced position. The enemy attacked and Red stood up in front of his men in the open shouting 'Come on Boys, let them have it'.

Red was shot through the throat, died shortly afterwards, the platoon, now very much below strength, held off the attack …

In 1962, forty-four years after his death, a plaque to commemorate Nunney's memory was erected at the Glengarry Municipal Building by the Glengarry Historical Society in conjunction with the Claude Nunney Memorial Branch. It was unveiled on 22 August by William H. Proctor, a former member of the 38th Battalion, at the municipal building, County Roads 18 and 26, North Lancaster. It was one of several erected by the Department of Travel and Publicity on the advice of the Archaeological and Historic Sites Board of Ontario. The dedication part of the service, which was attended by local dignitaries, was conducted by Monsignor E.J. Macdonald, Vicar-General of the Diocese of Alexandria, who had served in the First World War and had won the MC.

The text of the plaque in front of the local branch of the Royal Canadian Legion which is named after him reads as follows:

Claude J.P. Nunney, V. C. 1892–1918

Born in Hastings, Nunney was brought up in Lancaster Township, Glengarry. He enlisted in the 38th Battalion, CEF, in 1915 and in 1916

was sent to France where he won the Military Medal and Distinguished Conduct Medal. On 1 September 1918 his unit was heavily counter-attacked near Vis-en-Artois. On his own initiative Private Nunney went through the German barrage to the forward posts, where, by his fearless example, he encouraged his companions to repulse the enemy. During the Canadian attack on the following day, he was continually in the forefront, and 'displayed throughout the highest degree of valour'. Severely wounded, he died on 18 September, and was awarded the Victoria Cross posthumously.

There is also a plaque on Main Street, Lancaster, Ontario to the First World War dead from Glegarry in 1921, set up in the grounds of the library by the Red Cross Society of Glengarry. The names of the fallen listed include that of Claude Nunney. Another memory of him is with the naming of an air cadet squadron, the 253 The Claude Nunney VC Squadron.

Nunney's posthumous VC, DCM, MM and service medals the BWM and VM are in the collection of the Cornwall Armoury in Ontario.

A. Evans

South-West of Étaing, France, 2 September

Lance Sergeant Walter Simpson, also known as Arthur Evans, of the 6th (S) Lincolnshire Battalion (33rd Brigade, 11th Division) gained the VC on 2 September 1918, to the south-west of Étaing 17 kilometres to the east of Arras. He was involved in a daring patrol sent out to reconnoitre and to gain touch with a neighbouring division on the west bank of the River Sensée. The very detailed citation for Simpson's VC was gazetted on 30 October 1918 as follows and his name was changed to Evans in the issue of the *London Gazette* of 31 March 1919:

> For most conspicuous bravery and initiative when with a daylight patrol sent out to reconnoitre and to gain touch with a neighbouring division. When on the west bank of a river an enemy machine gun post was sighted on the east bank. The river being too deep to force, Sergt. Simpson volunteered to swim across, and having done so, crept up alone in rear of the machine gun post. He shot the sentry and also a second enemy who ran out; he then turned back and caused four to surrender. A crossing over the river was subsequently found, and the officer and one man of his patrol joined him, and reconnaissance was continued along the river bank. After proceeding some distance machine gun and rifle fire was opened on the patrol, and the officer was wounded. In spite of the fact that no cover was available, Sergt. Simpson succeeded in covering the withdrawal of the wounded officer under most dangerous and difficult conditions, and under heavy fire. The success of the patrol, which cleared up a machine gun post on the flank of the attacking troops of a neighbouring division and obtained an identification, was greatly due the very gallant conduct of Sergt. Simpson.

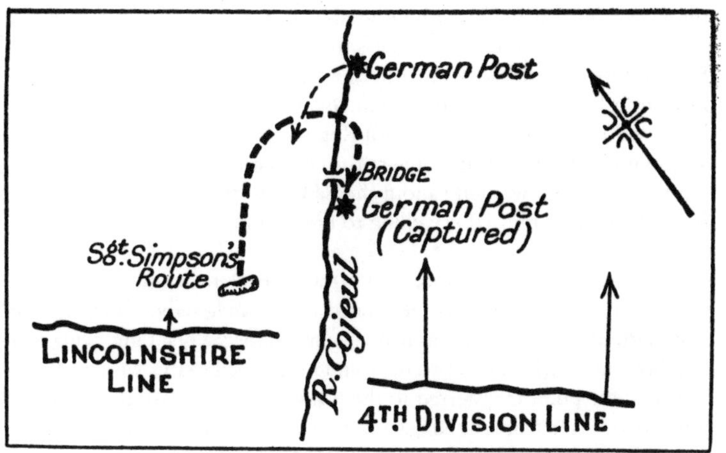

SERGEANT SIMPSON WINS V.C.

Simpson was decorated with his VC at Vincent Barracks, Valenciennes on 6 December 1918 by the King during a visit the monarch was making to his victorious army in France after the guns had fallen silent on 11 November.

Arthur Evans was the son of Robert Evans and Eleanor Ann Evans (*née* McCann). His father was a timekeeper in a local engineering works and his son was born at No. 33 Caradoc Road, Seaforth, Litherland, Liverpool on 8 April 1891. After leaving St Thomas's School the young man worked for a short time in a Liverpool office until he decided to quit because the job did not suit him. From then onwards he seems to have lived a very colourful life for much of the next twenty years.

Initially he joined the Royal Navy as a stoker, but after an accident in which his ribs were damaged he was invalided out. He then decided to join the Merchant Navy and joined a ship's crew bound for America. Once in the States he jumped ship, and some accounts indicate that he was in charge of a large party of native labour which was working on the Panama Canal. After this third job he took some time off to explore parts of South America together with a couple of friends, an Australian and a Scotsman, during which he suffered from fever, possibly malaria. Tiring of South America, he then travelled to Cuba and then on to the USA. On this occasion he joined a four-masted ship which took a year to reach England, having sailed via Australia. Once back in England he joined his stepbrother and sister in their family home in Bolton in Lancashire. Finding that this homely life did not suit him, he joined the 1st King's Liverpool Regiment in May 1914 and it was at about this time that for some reason he changed his name to Walter Simpson. He had wanted to join the RFC, but this was not to be, and instead he found himself travelling to France only a few weeks after the war had begun.

In August 1914 Simpson took part in the Mons Retreat and was in action in the Ypres Salient. He was mentioned in despatches and also fought at Festubert. In May 1915 he was badly wounded for the first time, being sent to a hospital in Manchester to recover. He returned to the Western Front and at some point transferred to the 6th Lincolnshire Battalion, having possibly deserted from the King's Liverpool Regiment after they arrived in France from the Middle East in July 1916. In October 1917 Simpson was seriously wounded again and was also gassed.

Returning to England once more, he was sent to a hospital in Bath to recuperate. After his discharge from the hospital he spent some time back at the family home in Bolton before being sent to Ireland, although there are no details of what he got up to there and by the spring of 1918, he was back in France.

After winning his VC in early September Simpson sent the revolver, which he stated that he had used with good effect in his VC action, to his sister with a note. 'The carrier and "it" swam the river. Its internals are getting a little rusty but perhaps Jack [his brother] will oil it. Don't be afraid of it – I've extracted all its teeth!'

Simpson won a DCM after his VC, which was gazetted on 2 December 1918 as follows:

> For great courage and initiative near Cambrai. He was in charge of a platoon acting as a fighting patrol on the night of 6/7th October 1918, with instructions to clear the country north of the Château of Aubencheu-au-Bac to the Canal-de-la-Sensée. A strong enemy post was encountered. He promptly rushed the post killing ten, wounding several, and taking one prisoner. The prisoner secured afforded most valuable information. He has shown excellent leadership and the utmost disregard of all danger.

While manning a machine gun, shortly after this incident Simpson was buried alive and thought to be killed. However, despite having lost consciousness, he didn't die as fortunately his face had been exposed to the air.

The archival sources which contain information on Simpson's life often include facts which are totally inconsistent or downright preposterous. This confusion particularly applied to his life prior to the war. On being discharged from the army on 19 November 1921 he changed his name back to Arthur Evans and one version of what he did after leaving the army is as follows:

> Simpson re-joined the Army and spent five more years with the Lincolnshire Regiment in India. Then on 1 July 1925 he travelled to New Zealand and became an instructor in the Defence Department, a position that he held for about three years as a voluntary soldier. In 1928 he emigrated to Australia with his wife.

A second version states:

> After leaving the Army Evans went to America again and returned to England in 1924 when he married a Miss H. M. Whittaker [Ellen Maud Whitaker] of Woodside Wimbledon on 9 April. At the time of the British Empire Exhibition at Wembley in the summer of 1924, Simpson was employed as a messenger for Lloyds Branch and stole £500 from a bank safe. At Wealdstone Police Court he was bound over and his exemplary war record was taken into account together with the crime being a first offence. His address at the time was given as being a house in Wimbledon. It was at this time that he and his wife decided to emigrate and make a new life in New Zealand before moving to Australia four years later.

The truth is probably a mixture of both accounts, but it is highly unlikely that he ever returned to America. Once the couple reached Australia in 1928 they made a home in Sydney, New South Wales. Evans then served as a voluntary soldier with the Australian Tank Corps in October 1932 and later became a sergeant. He attended the VC Dinner in 1929 for holders of the VC in Sydney. After serving with the Australian Tank Corps for two and a half years, Evans' health broke down and he was no longer able to carry out his duties as a sergeant. After a long illness, he died in the Prince of Wales Hospital, Randwick, on 1 November 1936, as a direct result of gas poisoning in the Great War. He had been a patient in the hospital for ten months, while his wife stayed in a room there to be within call. Because illness officially 'had not previously been caused by his war service', this would have barred him from entering the Repatriation Hospital, but Lord Gowrie VC, Governor-General of Australia, arranged that Simpson should indeed qualify for treatment in the hospital.

Arthur Evans was cremated at the North Suburbs Crematorium, Sydney, and was then given a very impressive military funeral, with thousands of people lining the streets of Sydney to pay their respects. His coffin was drawn on a gun carriage, preceded by the band of the Royal Australian Artillery, and after a train journey to Rookwood the band continued to accompany the procession. At the cemetery, members of the Australian Tank Corps fired volleys over the grave with revolvers. No fewer than seven holders of the VC attended the funeral and soon afterwards they launched an appeal for assistant funds for Ellen, Evans's widow, and 3-year-old son, Arthur George.

In 1936 the Australian Government decided that his ashes should be returned to the country of his birth and decided they could be taken to London by members of the group of Australian VC winners invited to the the Coronation of King George VI in London. Arthur Sullivan VC (a former great mate of Evans), General C.J. Powter and Trumpeter C.R. White were the men chosen for this honour.

The last named had sounded the Last Post at Rookwood Cemetery and Evans's ashes were placed in a casket which was then interned with the remains of his stepbrother John on 29 March 1937 in Park Cemetery, Lytham-St-Annes. At the service of reburial a firing party from the Loyal Regiment (North Lancashire) fired over the grave and the Last Post and Reveille were both sounded.

About ten days later a tragedy occurred after Arthur Sullivan's return to London. On his way to Wellington Barracks, where he was quartered, he stopped on the pavement of Birdcage Walk to sign autographs. At some point he slipped and fell, knocking his head against the kerb, then almost immediately was run over by a cyclist. He died soon after being admitted to hospital. Sullivan, who had won his VC in the North Russian Campaign, was in his turn given a full military funeral in London before his ashes were returned to Sydney for a second military funeral service in July. A bronze plaque was placed on the railings of Birdcage Walk by the spot where he fell.

A former member of the Parachute Regiment who discovered the Evans family grave in the early 1990s decided to do something about its run-down state and in due time the Royal Anglian Regiment took charge, arranging for the grave to be cleaned up and for stones to be placed along its sides. The grave was re-dedicated at a special service in April or May 1992.

As well as the VC and DCM, Evans's decorations, which are in private hands, included the 1914–15 Star & Clasp, BWM, VM and MiD Oakleaf. Apart from his headstone, he also has a street named after him in Canberra, Evans Crescent.

Arthur Evans, who was small of stature, was described as being a loyal subject of the King. However, it is clear from the above portrait that he was a bit of a mystery man, and the reason for his name change is unknown. It appears that he was a man who did not take kindly to discipline and was not frightened of leaving one service position for another. What saved him from getting into hot water with 'the authorities' was of course his war record. One wonders though whether his main motive was to be in charge of his own destiny, something that is rarely possible in times of war.

J. Harvey

North of Péronne, France, 2 September

The date of 2 September 1918 was mainly known for the breaking of the German defensive position, the Drocourt–Quéant Line, and no fewer than eleven VCs were won on this day. However, the battle front was at least 23 miles long and extended from the Scarpe to the Somme. The action in which Pte Jack Harvey (1/22nd (County of London) Battalion, (The Queen's) (TF) London Regiment (142nd Brigade, 47th Division), won his VC east of the village of Bouchavesnes to the north-east of Péronne, was during what was later to be designated as the Second Battle of Bapaume.

The 142nd Brigade moved off at 5.30 a.m. on 2 September and passed through the lines of the 141st Brigade of the same division, on the western side of St Pierre Vaast Wood. The object of the 142nd Brigade was the south-west of Vaux Wood and also Monastir Trench. During the brigade's advance over ground cut up by trenches and shell-holes, the enemy maintained a heavy barrage and offered strong opposition. It was at this point that Pte Harvey, a company cook, saved the situation by dashing forward on his own to destroy an enemy machine-gun position. Having put the gun and its team out of action Harvey moved down a trench and on reaching a dugout 'encouraged' its thirty-seven occupants to surrender. In addition he relieved them of any useful property. During the action he lost a bag of rations but was later to find a replacement. To the right, Harvey's battalion reached a trench north-east of the village of Moislains, the northern part of which had already been occupied by the 140th Brigade. Several groups of Germans were between the two brigades and began to use bombs against the 140th but eventually they were mopped up. On the left, the 1/24th Battalion cut off a large party of the enemy a little to the west of St Pierre Vaast Wood and sixty-two men were captured. The 24th was then able to proceed to the brigade objective to the south-west of Vaux Wood.

Harvey's VC was gazetted on 15 November 1918 as follows:

> For most conspicuous gallantry and disregard of personal danger on 2nd Sept. 1918 during the advance north of Péronne. The advance of his company was held up by intense machine gun fire; this man at once dashed forward a distance of fifty yards alone through our barrage and in the face of heavy enemy fire, and rushed a machine gun post, shooting two of the team and bayoneting another. He then destroyed the gun, and continued to work his way along the enemy trench, and going forward alone for about two hundred yards, single-handed rushed an enemy dug-out, which contained thirty-seven Germans, and compelled them to surrender. By these two acts of great gallantry he saved the company heavy casualties, and enabled the whole of the attacking line to advance. Throughout the entire operation he showed the most magnificent courage and determination, and by the splendid example he set to all ranks materially assisted in the success of the operation.

Harvey was presented with his VC in the Ballroom of Buckingham Palace on 8 March 1919.

Jack Harvey was born at No. 2 Curral Grove, Old Kent Road, Peckham, on 24 August 1891. He was the son of Mr and Mrs W. Harvey and his father was a yard foreman who later married a second time, to a Mrs Eastwood. The couple lived in Redhill and when his father died in about 1928 he was buried in Reigate.

Jack Harvey went to Ruby Street School, Old Kent Road, Peckham, and enlisted in Jamaica Road, Bermondsey, on 26 November 1914 as a private in the 1/22nd Battalion, London Regiment (The Queen's) (TF), his service number being 681139. He was billeted for some time in his father's home town of Redhill in Hooley Road and before going overseas he married Rose in 1915. His battalion was part of the 142nd Brigade of 47th Division, and he served in the war on the Western Front for three and a half years. The campaigns he took part in are a roll-call of the Western Front battles and included: Loos September/October 1915, High Wood September 1916, the Butte de Warlencourt October 1916, Messines Ridge June 1917, Bourlon Wood November 1917 and the

Somme again in March 1918. This was followed by the advance to victory between August and November 1918.

Two months after the war finished Harvey was discharged on 10 January 1919. He later attended a presentation in Camberwell in the same year when he was presented by the mayor, Alderman Coats, with an illuminated address together with a purse of money contributed to by members of the borough. In 1920 he attended the June VC Garden Party at Buckingham Palace.

For most of his life Harvey lived in Peckham, his birthplace, working at London Bridge for thirty-four years as a maintenance engineer at George Payne's tea and chocolate works. In June 1929 he attended the House of Lords Dinner for holders of the VC. Later, when the Second World War broke out, he and his wife moved to Merstham where he became an active and popular member of the local branch of the British Legion. The couple also had a son who was serving in the Royal Navy.

At the early age of 48, Harvey died at home in 76 Brook Road, Merstham, Surrey, on 15 August 1940, the cause of death being thrombosis of the left coronary artery. His son, J.V. Harvey, was present at his father's bedside. Jack Harvey was buried in Redstone Cemetery, Redhill, in Section C, with the grave number of 2359. This was after a full military funeral and the guard of honour lined up at the entrance to the cemetery, together with a group of members of the British Legion Branch at Merstham and other servicemen. When the cortège arrived the order was given to present arms. At the service, which was taken by the Revd A.E. Wilkinson, it emerged that he too was a member of the 47th Division as Harvey had been. A former colleague, Mr H. Russell, who had been with Harvey nearly twenty-two years before, when he won his VC, also attended.

Rose, Harvey's widow, sold her husband's VC and decorations for £60 to a Canadian collector after she remarried and it is still in private hands. His other medals are the 1914–15 Star, BWM, VM and 1937 Coronation. It would appear that the last named was missing from the group and has never been re-discovered.

An oil painting of Jack Harvey used to be with the trustees of 6th (Territorial) Battalion, Queen's Regiment, at Portsmouth Road, Kingston-upon-Thames. At one point it might have been moved to Wandsworth to the 6th (Volunteer) Battalion, The Queen's Regiment.

In March 1983 Harvey's decorations came on the market and were bought for £10,000 by a police constable, Nigel McCrery, from Nottinghamshire, who later earned his living working in television and writing. On 2 September 1984, on the sixty-sixth anniversary of Harvey's winning the VC, a service of dedication taken by the

Revd Douglas Walker, chaplain to the 5th Queen's, was held at Redstone Cemetery at the graveside of Jack Harvey. Among those present was Philip Gardner, who won his VC in Tobruk in 1941. Fifteen of Harvey's relatives also attended, together with various civic and military dignitaries. Nigel McCrery also attended together with his father. The Last Post was played at the graveside by a member of the Queen's Regiment, and because the grave had fallen into a state disrepair and was also unmarked, the Regiment paid for cleaning up the site and for erecting a new headstone. At the present time Harvey's decorations are on display in the Lord Ashcroft Gallery at the Imperial War Museum, Lord Ashcroft having purchased them privately in 2001. However, the set isn't complete as the real Coronation Medal for 1937 is still missing.

B.S. Hutcheson

East of Arras, France, 2 September

Captain B.S. Hutcheson was a Medical Officer in the Canadian Army Medical Corps and in September 1918 was attached to the 75th Battalion. 1st Central Ontario Regiment. The main action on 2 September was the Allied penetration of the German defensive position known as the Drocourt–Quéant Line, during which the Canadian Expeditionary Force distinguished itself when attacking this line together with the assistance of British Infantry Divisions on either flank. During this day Capt. Hutcheson was east of Arras and won the VC, which was gazetted on 14 December 1918 as follows:

> For most conspicuous bravery and devotion to duty on 2 Sept., when under most intense shell, machine gun and rifle fire, he went through the Quéant–Drocourt Support Line with the battalion. Without hesitation and with utter disregard of personal safety, he remained on the field until every wounded man had been attended to. He dressed the wounds of a seriously wounded officer under terrific machine gun and shell fire, and, with the assistance of prisoners and of his own men, succeeded in evacuating him to safety, despite the fact that the bearer party suffered heavy casualties.

Again using an undated letter written in answer to a enquiry from a Capt. Gwynn, Hutcheson wrote of when he won the VC as follows:

> My medical detail and I worked along the crest attending to the wounded when the battalion was held up short of its objective. The rifle, machine gun and artillery fire was intense. We got to the wounded by crawling or running in a stooping position and when

the field of fire became too hot flattened out on the ground like limpets on a rock ...

Captain Hutcheson was presented with his VC and the MC at Buckingham Palace in the Quadrangle of Buckingham Palace on 22 May 1919.

Frances Young Bellenden Seymour Hutcheson was born on 16 December 1883 at Mount Carmel, Illinois, son of Mr Hutcheson and Luella Bellenden Hutcheson. He graduated in medicine in Chicago, Illinois, at the North-Western University and later worked as a physician and surgeon at Mound City, Illinois. Having renounced his American citizenship he enlisted in the 97th Battalion on 14 December 1915 and having been commissioned as a lieutenant in the Canadian Army Medical Corps served as MO, then later served with the 75th Battalion. He had arrived in France towards the end of 1916 and he was promoted to captain a month later. He won his MC on 8 August 1918, on the first day of the August Allied offensive (gazetted 3 November 1918) and in a reply to an enquiry from a Capt. Gwynn he later wrote a graphic account of this action on which the following is based.

On the left of the Amiens–Roye road about 26km south-east of Amiens the Canadian advance passed between Beaucourt and Le Quesnel. The latter had fallen to the enemy on 27 March 1918. The Canadian advance was under observation from enemy balloons which were linked to artillery batteries and accurate pin-point shelling made the treatment of the wounded a very hazardous business. The casualties were scattered throughout the whole town of Le Quesnel and thus several searches had to be made in order to find them all. A cellar area was used by Hutcheson as a dressing station which was staffed by Hutcheson, two NCOs and two privates. A company belonging to the 4th Canadian Mounted Rifles suffered grievously from enemy shelling when passing close to a street corner and Hutcheson's team dealt with the many casualties. In spite of these setbacks the village was re-taken on the 9th by Hutcheson's 75th Canadian Infantry Battalion.

After gaining a VC in September Hutcheson was demobilised in 1919 and appointed captain in the Canadian Militia. He reclaimed his American citizenship after the war. After some time he resigned from this post and became City Health Officer in Cairo, Illinois, later marrying a Frances Young from Nova Scotia.

In 1939 he travelled from Illinois in order to be presented to King George VI and Queen Elizabeth during their visit to North America, at a reception at the British Embassy in Washington on 9 June 1939. During the proceedings he was invited to accompany the King and Queen to Arlington Cemetery to lay a wreath at the Tomb of the Unknown Soldier.

Bellenden Hutcheson died after a long illness at Cairo, Illinois, on 9 April 1954 and was buried at Rose Hill Cemetery in Mount Carmel, Section B, Lot 145, Grave C. He has a memorial in Mount Carmel Court House and his decorations are in the care of the York Armoury, Toronto, Ontario. Apart from the VC, they include the MC, BWM and VM together with Coronation Medals of 1937 and 1953.

On 12 September 2009 the successors of the 75th Battalion, namely the Toronto Scottish Regiment (Queen Elizabeth, the Queen Mother's Own) moved into a new armoury which they shared with the Toronto Police Service. It was named after Capt. Hutcheson and can be found in 70 Birmingham Street, Toronto. His decorations are in the collection of the Hodden Grey Museum in the same complex.

A.G. KNIGHT

Villers-lès-Cagnicourt, France, 2 September

A/Sgt Arthur Knight, 10th Battalion (2nd Brigade, 1st Canadian Division) won his VC as one of six members of the CEF in the fight for the Drocourt–Quéant Line on 2 September 1918, at a point just south of the Arras–Cambrai road at a village called Villers-lès-Cagnicourt, halfway between Arras and Cambrai. On the front of the 2nd Brigade the 5th Battalion engaged in hand-to-hand fighting for the jump-off line and then, aided greatly by a shrapnel barrage, the 7th Battalion passed through their lines to began the assault on their portion of the Drocourt–Quéant Line, experiencing little difficulty in taking part of the line and mopping up. At 8 a.m. the 10th Battalion took over the advance in an area which was beyond the barrage zone. Until then tanks had been in the forefront, knocking out one enemy post after another, but several of them were destroyed during the process. East of the Drocourt–Quéant Line, the German artillery slowed the 10th Battalion's advance with intense fire from machine guns and trench mortars in the Buissy Switch, east of Villers-lès-Cagnicourt. However, the 10th Battalion still managed to capture Villers-lès-Cagnicourt by late afternoon. The battalion established a line to the east of the village and, after an allied barrage targeted the enemy positions, the Canadians managed to move forward to capture the Buissy Switch just before midnight. Thus by now the 1st Canadian Division had captured two systems of the Drocourt–Quéant Line and was approaching a further objective, the Canal du Nord.

Sergeant Arthur Knight's VC was gazetted on 15 November 1918 and tells the story as follows:

> For most conspicuous bravery, initiative and devotion to duty when, after an unsuccessful attack, Sergt Knight led a bombing

> section forward, under very heavy fire of all descriptions, and engaged the enemy at close quarters. Seeing that his party continued to be held up, he dashed forward alone, bayoneting several of the enemy machine gunners and trench-mortar crews, and forcing the remainder to retire in confusion. He then brought forward a Lewis gun and directed his fire on the retreating enemy, inflicting many casualties. In the subsequent advance of his platoon in pursuit, Sergt. Knight saw a party of about thirty of the enemy go into a deep tunnel which led off the trench. He again dashed forward alone, and, having killed one officer and two N.C.O.s, captured twenty other ranks. Subsequently routed, single-handed, another enemy party which was opposing the advance of his platoon. On each occasion he displayed the greatest valour under heavy fire at very close range, and by his example of courage, gallantry and initiative was a wonderful inspiration to all. This very gallant N.C.O. was subsequently fatally wounded.

Knight, who would have been unaware of winning the VC, died of wounds the following day in a field hospital near Hendecourt-lès-Cagnicourt and was buried 10 miles south-east of Arras in the Dominion Cemetery, Plot I, Row F, Grave 15. The cemetery was begun by the Canadian Corps after the storming of the Drocourt–Quéant Line on 2 September 1918.

In the National Archives of Canada is a 'Circumstances of Death card' which goes some way into pinning down the date of Knight's death. It states: 'Killed in Action. While taking part in operations with his Company he was struck in the head by shrapnel from an enemy shell, at about 3 p.m. on 3 September 1918, when 500 or 600yds left of Buissy. He died shortly after being wounded.' This was the day after his VC action, in which he wasn't wounded, although his citation suggests that he was.

Arthur George Knight, the son of Edward Henry and Ellen Knight, was born in Haywards Heath, Sussex, on 26 June 1886. When he was still quite young his family moved to Redhill, Surrey, and their home was No. 1 Somerset Road, Meadvale, in the southern part of Redhill.

Arthur attended St John's School, Meadvale, and later Redhill Technical and Trade School where he studied carpentry. He was subsequently apprenticed to a local firm of builders, Bagaley & Sons.

In 1911 he emigrated to Saskatchewan, where he lived and worked as a carpenter. Three years later he enlisted, on 19 December 1914, and was posted to the 46th Canadian Battalion for training. His service number was 486402. Later, he sailed to England when he was transferred to the 32nd Battalion at Shorncliffe on 19 July 1915. He then travelled to France where he was a member of the 10th Canadian Battalion from 29 August. He was soon promoted to corporal and later to sergeant. He served on the Somme, at Vimy, Passchendaele and Amiens. In November 1917 he was awarded the Belgian Croix de Guerre which was gazetted on 12 July.

Three months after his death his parents were presented with their son's posthumous VC at Buckingham Palace on 19 December 1918. Later at some point, the decoration was presented to his regiment and is on display in the Glenbow Museum, Calgary. It is one of three VCs in the museum's collection and, apart from the VC and Croix de Guerre, they include the 1914–15 Star; BWM and VM. A crescent named after him also commemorates his memory and there is also a memorial plaque outside 1843 Rae Street, Regina, which was his last home. A previous house, where he used to live, 1646 Albert Street (North) has been demolished. Finally, in Canada, there is a mount in Jasper National Park, Alberta, which is named after him.

Knight was a member of the Reigate Church Lad's Brigade. In Redhill, Surrey, his name is commemorated at the top of the war memorial of St John the Evangelist Church, Redhill, where he used to sing in the church choir. Arthur Knight's name also appears on the church's draft Roll of Honour in the August and September 1919 editions, published prior to the production of the war memorial, which takes the form of a framed list on vellum which hangs within the church. A commemorative stone memorial was also erected outside the church but carried no individual names on it.

W.H. METCALF & C.W. PECK

Near Cagnicourt, France, 2 September

Two of the six members of the Canadian Expeditionary Force who gained the VC on 2 September 1918 in the attack on the Drocourt–Quéant Line were members of the same battalion, the 16th Manitoba Battalion (Canadian Scottish): the American-born L/Cpl W.H. Metcalf and the battalion commanding officer, Lt Col C.W. Peck. In the early hours of 2 September 1918 the Drocourt–Quéant Line was attacked by three battalions of the 1st Canadian Division, namely the 16th and 13th of the 3rd Brigade on the right of the attack opposite Cagnicourt, and the 7th Battalion of the 2nd Brigade to the left.

The two battalions of the 3rd Brigade had a 1,600yd front and were assisted by eight tanks. They pushed forward, up a long slope, towards the very heavily enemy-wired positions. Initially, there was little resistance and many of the enemy were quite happy to surrender. By 7.30 a.m. the 13th Battalion had already taken two trenches of the front system of the Drocourt–Quéant Line. Moving forward the battalion then took the support system as well, but murderous machine-gun fire from the right, where the British 57th (West Lancashire) Division had not yet arrived, began to strike the 16th Battalion after about 200yds and checked progress. It was during the following period that Metcalf and Peck were to earn their VCs. The history of the 16th Battalion (CEF), tells the story of what happened in considerable detail.

Men from Numbers 1 and 4 Companies had reached as far as a second of five belts of wire, when the artillery covering them suddenly ceased firing on the Drocourt–Quéant front line. Almost immediately, the enemy took advantage of the situation, setting up two or three of their machine guns from the parapet to begin firing at the Canadian attackers. The 16th Battalion was not stopped in its tracks, though, and despite the heavy fire managed to move forward in rushes. When they had reached another belt of wire – which was from 8 to 10ft wide – they were forced to take cover in shell holes, as the Germans had started bringing up more machine guns.

The battalion history quotes from a narrative compiled by a member of No. 4 Platoon of Number 1 Company, a Sgt F.E. Earwaker:

> We had been there (in a shell hole) but a short time when Lieut. Campbell-Johnson passed word along to try once more, we all got up together and didn't get more than five yards before we met up with the heaviest fire from the trench in front of us that I had ever faced. Down I went into a shell-hole; Lieut Campbell-Johnson flopped on his stomach right in the wire about twelve feet to my right.

Shortly afterwards, Campbell-Johnson was shot in the head and a Sgt Reid came back into a shell-hole, while Earwaker threw a smoke bomb. The two men felt helpless as every time they showed themselves they were shot at. They then decided to wait for a tank to assist them and soon afterwards they heard the sound of one approaching:

> Suddenly a heavy fire started from the trench in front of us. We looked up to see what it was about and there we saw the tank with Lance-Corporal Metcalf walking beside it, a little to the right in front of it, pointing with his signal flags in our direction. It was still pretty early and you could hardly recognise him except by his flags. The tank was coming on at an angle from the left flank. I saw Metcalf walking about thirty yards and then we decided it was our turn to help. We made a dash for the trench and made it before the Germans got their guns on us. When we captured the trench, we found a nest of machine guns on not more than a fifty foot frontage. Behind them was a big dug-out. The tank started to amble out in front the minute we got into the trench; about fifteen minutes later I saw it in the smoke five hundred yards in front.

Another witness, Pte J.H. Riehl, took up the story:

> When the tank came to within three hundred feet of the German wire, a heavy machine gun fire was opened upon it from the

> front trench. Corporal Metcalf jumped up from the shell-hole where he was with his flags pointing towards the enemy's trench, led the tank towards it and then along it. The enemy kept heavy machine gun fire on the tank and as it got close to the trench commenced to throw at it clusters of bombs tied together.
>
> When we afterwards got into the trench, we found seventeen German machine guns at the same place, and all of them had been well used. How Metcalfe escaped being shot to pieces has always been a wonder to me.

As a result of this defiant action the heavily wired Drocourt–Quéant Line was broken. William Metcalf's VC was gazetted on 15 November 1918 as follows:

> For most conspicuous bravery, initiative and devotion to duty in attack, when, the right flank of the battalion being held up, he realised the situation, and rushed forward under intense machine gun fire to a passing Tank on the left. With his signal flag he walked in front of the Tank, directing it along the trench in a perfect hail of bullets and bombs. The machine gun strong points were overcome, very heavy casualties were inflicted on the enemy, and a very critical situation was relieved. Later, although wounded, he continued to advance until ordered to get into a shell hole and have his wounds dressed. His valour throughout was of the highest standard.

Metcalf was presented with his VC at York Cottage, Sandringham, on 26 January 1919 when he was accompanied by Cyrus Peck, his commanding officer who was also presented with his VC.

Although the 16th Manitoba Regiment (Canadian Scottish) Battalion had broken into the front of the main Drocourt–Quéant Line, we have seen it was subsequently held up in front of the support line. It was at this point that the battalion commander, Lt Col Cyrus W. Peck, took what was to be a very active role in the battle. Despite the bursting of shells together withering machine-gun fire, he went forward to make a personal reconnaissance. As a result, he set about organising several tanks to protect his open flank before leading his battalion forward to their objective. The 16th Battalion history notes of this action that a Capt. Johnston, who was second-in-command of No. 1 Company,

found that a flanking battalion had no knowledge of any planned attack and furthermore had no intention of taking part in it. After Johnson had delivered this message to his CO there was a total silence until one of the NCOs present spoke up, saying:

> 'There's the Colonel!' All turned, and were able to distinguish the form of Colonel Peck, followed by his piper a few yards away, coming towards them. The officer commanding Number 1 told the Commanding Officer what Johnston had just reported and the Colonel replied: 'Well, it doesn't make any difference, we've got to go forward whether they do or not, that settled matters'.

A reserve battalion, the 15th, later pushed through the 16th's lines and, moving forward slowly, suffered huge casualties before reaching the Bois de Bouche which was about 3,000yds from the Buissy Switch which linked the line with the Hindenburg support system. The lines joined on the forward slope of a position known as Mont Dury between the village of that name and the Arras–Cambrai road. The support line was on the reverse slope. The switch line ran in front of Buissy and Villers-lès-Cagnicourt in a south-easterly direction.

Lieutenant Colonel Cyrus Peck's VC was gazetted on 15 November 1918 and takes up the narrative as follows:

> For most conspicuous bravery and skilful leading when in attack under intense fire. His command quickly captured the first objective, but progress to the further objective was held up by enemy machine gun fire on his right flank. The situation being critical in the extreme, Colonel Peck pushed forward, and made a personal reconnaissance under heavy machine gun fire and sniping fire across a stretch of ground which was heavily swept by fire. Having reconnoitred the position, he returned, reorganised his battalion, and, acting upon the knowledge personally gained, pushed them forward and arranged to protect his flanks. He then went out under the most intense artillery and machine gun fire, intercepted the Tanks, gave them the necessary directions, pointing out where they were to make for, and thus pave the

> way for a Canadian infantry battalion to push forward. To this battalion he subsequently gave requisite support. His magnificent display of courage and fine qualities of leadership enabled the advance to be continued, although always under heavy artillery and machine gun fire, and contributed largely to the success of the brigade attack.

Later, the general officer in command of the Canadian First Division, Sir Archibald Macdonell, described Peck's actions in the following way:

> When the advance was held up in front of the Bois de Bouche, MacPeck walked along the front of his line and the Fifteenth Battalion, cheering up the men, and constantly repeating: 'She's a bear, boys, she's a bear!'

William Henry Metcalf was an American, born at Waite Township, Walsh County, Maine, USA, on 29 January 1894. After leaving grammar school in his home town he became a barber. During a fishing trip to New Brunswick on the Miramachi River with a few friends in 1914 he learnt that war had been declared a few days earlier.

In August, having decided he wanted to enlist, he crossed the border to Canada and joined the Canadian Forces when he was given the service number of 22614. In the main sources for Metcalf's life the year of his birth is often given as 1885 and this confusion was caused by Metcalf himself who wanted to be seen as nine years older than he actually was when he joined the Canadian Forces. He did not inform his mother of this deception. His first regiment was a militia unit, the 71st Regiment at Fredericton in New Brunswick. A few weeks later, on 22 September, he joined the 12th Battalion, a regular battalion at Valcartier in Quebec. After initial training the 12th Battalion left for England on 14 October and on reaching England Metcalf was questioned on behalf of his mother by the American ambassador who asked whether he was the man that all the letters had been written about. Anyway Metcalf lied his way out of this one, convincing the ambassador that he had got the wrong man. Subsequently Metcalf joined the 18th Battalion prior to serving in France and Flanders, this time with the 16th Manitoba Regiment (Canadian Scottish) CEF (3rd Canadian Brigade, 1st Canadian Division). The Canadian Scottish wore kilts and when taking part in marches were accompanied musically by the sound of bagpipes.

The 18th Battalion took part in the 1915 Battle of Ypres, then fought on the Somme in October 1916, during which time Metcalf won the MM. He was promoted to lance corporal, but after gaining his VC in September 1918 he was wounded and had to remain in hospital for nine months. Later his bullet-ridden kit was put on display in London. Altogether he was wounded six times during the war and won a bar to his MM. At the end of hostilities he married a hospital nurse, Dorothy Winifred Holland.

In 1919 Metcalf was demobilised and apppointed an officer with the Canadian Militia, later returning to the USA with his new wife to live in New York, before moving to Eastport, Maine, where he worked as a mechanic. The couple later moved again, to South Portland.

For the remainder of his life Metcalf attended as many VC functions as possible, including the House of Lords Dinner in November 1929, his rank by that time being a captain.

In June 1953 he visited London for the Coronation of Queen Elizabeth II and in June 1956 he again travelled to London, this time to attend the ceremonies in Hyde Park for the centenary of the VC, where he was the only American-born man among the 300 VCs on parade. Three years later Metcalf attended a reception and dinner at the Royal Canadian Military Institute on 17 November 1959.

Again putting the record straight, William Metcalf died in his home in South Portland, Maine, on 9 August 1968 and not in a nursing home in Lewiston. His funeral, three days later, was attended by more than forty members of the Royal Canadian Legion, including a contingent of bagpipers. He had requested to be buried at Bayside Cemetery, Eastpoint, Maine, which overlooked a part of Canada across the St Croix River, the international boundary. He left behind him Dorothy, his wife, together with three sons and Sheila a daughter. His sons had served with the American Forces during the Second World War. Dorothy was presented with the Union Jack, which was used to cover her husband's coffin during the ceremonies as she had no wish for her husband's coffin to be draped with the new Canadian maple-leaf flag or the Stars and Stripes. Metcalf was one of six American-born men who were awarded the VC. For many years he was a member of the St Croix New Brunswick Branch of the Royal Canadian Legion.

At the beginning of 1998 the Canadian Scottish Regimental Museum in Victoria asked one of William's sons, Stanley, if they could borrow his father's VC for use in an 80th-anniversary display. Stanley asked the museum director whether he would take the whole collection. William Metcalf's VC, which was kept in a manila envelope in his son's home in Bucksport, was presented to the Canadian Scottish Regimental

Museum in Victoria, British Columbia, by Stanley, together with his father's other war memorabilia of newspaper clippings and old photographs. On 1 October 1998 an armoured car arrived at Stanley Metcalf's house on Route 1 in Bucksport to collect his father's medals and the other mementoes. Apart from the VC, the medals consist of the MM and Bar, 1914–15 Star, BWM, VM and Coronation Medals for 1937 and 1953.

The original headstone above Metcalf's grave never showed the design of the Victoria Cross and as it was getting into a poor state the Royal Canadian Legion decided to replace it with a new headstone which would also incorporate the VC design. This new stone was dedicated at a ceremony on 4 October 2012. Metcalf's grave also includes the remains of his wife Dorothy who died in 1992 and their daughter Sheila.

The Peck family migrated from New England to New Brunswick in 1763. Cyrus Wesley Peck was born in Hopewell Hill, New Brunswick, Canada, on 26 April 1871, and was educated in the local public schools. On 27 June 1887, when he was 16 years old, his family moved to New Westminster, British Columbia, in order that his father could work in the lumber business in the Fraser River port city on the lower British Columbian mainland. At the same time Cyrus took up military training and sailed to Britain, with the idea of enlisting in the British Army. However, he later changed his mind and volunteered for service in South Africa, but his application was rejected. Returning to Canada, he went to the Klondike and eventually worked in business in Prince Rupert as a salmon canner. Later, he was elected Unionist MP for Skeena.

Peck and Kate E. Chapman got married in March 1914 and in time the couple had three sons: Horace Wesley, Edward Richard and Douglas Cyrus. Peck had been a member of the militia and joined the Canadian Expeditionary Force in 1914, when he was made a captain in the 30th Battalion on 1 November. He gave his occupation as broker on his attestation papers. He was not a tall man but even so a very impressive one, being 5ft 8in tall and weighing 225lb. Peck left for France in February 1915 and was promoted to major two months later, on 25 April. In May he was transferred to the 16th Battalion. A few days later, on the 21st, he was wounded in the legs by gunshot in Festubert and on 23 May was invalided to England on the hospital ship *St Patrick*. On 5 July he returned to the 16th Battalion and became its commander a year later in November during the Battle of the Somme.

In mid-April 1917 Peck was invalided to England again, this time suffering from gastritis. In the same year, during his absence, he was re-elected to the Canadian House of Commons in what was called the Khaki Election. (He was the member for Skeena and a supporter of Sir Robert Borden's Union Government.) He returned to France on 1 June to rejoin his battalion, and his DSO was published in the Birthday Honours Award of 4 June.

London Gazette citation:

> During an attack he showed fine courage and leadship. He led his battalion, under great difficulties caused by heavy mist, to its final objective, nearly three miles. After severe fighting he personally led his men in an attack on nests of machine guns and protecting the enemy guns, which he captured. Some of the guns were of 8 in calibre.

On 10 January 1918 Peck assumed temporary command of the Canadian 3rd Infantry Brigade until 15 January, and then again between 15 February and 15 March 1918.

A month after winning his VC on 2 September Peck was gassed on 4 October, later returning to England, although he was back in Ottawa on 5 January 1919 attending to business in the House of Commons in Ottawa. A bar to his DSO was gazetted on 11 January 1919, and he received his VC at York Cottage, Sandringham, on 26 January 1919. He was with his colleague, William Metcalf, who was also presented with his VC on the same occasion.

Peck, whose nickname in the war was MacPeck, introduced to his Canadian Scottish Regiment a Highland tradition of being piped into battle. During the war his name was mentioned in despatches five times. After ending his four-year war service on 11 June 1919, he remained in contact with his military connections and in November 1921 was transferred to the Reserve of Officers with the rank of colonel. In the same year he commanded the Canadian rifle team at Bisley. In 1920 he was made commanding officer of the newly formed Canadian Scottish Regiment after the amalgamation of the 88th and 50th Battalions.

After being defeated in the federal elections in 1921, Peck went to the British Columbia legislature in 1924 as Member for the Islands when he lived in Vancouver Island for a time. His island constituency was said to be unique in Canada and no longer exists as an electoral district. The constituency was made up of 100 islands, both large and small, which were off the inner coast of Vancouver Island. In 1928 he was re-elected as Conservative in 1928. In the following year he travelled to London for the dinner given by the Prince of Wales in the House of Lords, where he was the most senior member of the Canadian VC contingent. In 1930 the Gulf Islands Ferry Company purchased a Canadian Pacific Car Ferry *Island Princess* and re-named it *Cyrus Peck*. It was in service until 1966.

Peck was appointed aide-de-camp to two governor-generals, Lords Byng and Tweedsmuir and in 1936 he was appointed to membership of the Canadian Pensions Commission, a position which he held for five years. In April 1956, on the occasion of his eighty-fifth birthday, a group of members of the Canadian Scottish Regiment paid their respects, wishing him luck for his forthcoming June trip to England when he and his wife were to attend the VC centenary commemorations in London. After their London visit, the couple stopped off in Toronto for four days to meet up with old friends from Hamilton, Toronto and other parts of Ontario, and some former comrades from the Canadian Scottish and 48th Highlanders called on the Pecks at the Royal York Hotel where they were staying. Afterwards they went on to British Columbia. In his last years Peck lived at Hopewell, Sidney, Vancouver, British Columbia, where he died in hospital on 27 September 1956, having suffered a heart attack nine days before. He was cremated, half of his ashes being interred in the family plot in Fraser Cemetery, while the other half were taken by a former colleague to be scattered at sea off the Pacific coast of Prince Rupert Sound. Peck's wife, Kate, survived him and was still alive in 1987 at the age of 101. Peck had also left three sons, although by 1987 only two of these (Joe and Ed) were still living.

During that same year the two sons presented their father's VC to the Canadian Scottish Regiment (Princess Mary's). The ceremony took place during a parade at the Bay Street Armoury, involving 150 members of the Canadian Scottish Regiment from all parts of British Columbia. Ed described his father as being 'an extremely loyal and enthusiastic Canadian'. In 1993 Peck's decorations were presented by his family to the Canadian War Museum in Ottawa and the presentation took place seventy-five years to the day when he won the VC on 2 September 1918. His name is also commemorated with a plaque which is on display in the Canadian Houses of Parliament in Ottawa. His decorations, in the Canadian War Museum in Ottawa, apart from the VC, include the DSO & Bar, 1914–15 Star, BWM, VM, and MiD with Oakleaf, the King George V Silver Jubilee and Coronation Medals for 1937 and 1953. One of his sons wrote a book on his father's life published in Canada entitled *Cyrus Peck, VC*.

G. Prowse

Pronville, France, 2 September

On 2 September 1918 – the day that the German defence line, the Drocourt–Quéant Line, was penetrated – the 63rd Royal Naval Division was involved in the attack on Pronville south of the main Arras–Cambrai road. The village was part of the Line to the south of Buissy and west of Quéant.

The 188th Brigade, who were in trenches before Hendecourt-lès-Cagnicourt, were chosen for the attack and were to pass through the lines of the 57th Division and reach the Quéant-Marquion railway between the Hindenburg Support and the Canadian Corps.The brigade was delayed mainly through artillery support being given to other divisions and they were held by the yet uncaptured enemy support lines. After artillery support had been arranged, the brigade moved as far as the Quéant–Buissy road, slightly short of their objective. The attached Drake Battalion of the 189th Brigade was then brought up on the left and by 6.15 p.m. it was approaching the village of Pronville and cleared the enemy from a long ridge in front of the 188th Brigade before crossing over the enemy-held railway line before breaking through the Hindenburg Support Line to reach the Quéant–Inchy road, the D22.

The Hood and Hawke Battalions of the 189th Brigade attacked the village of Inchy but, owing to machine-gun fire and heavy artillery shelling, were forced to fall back to the railway line which had been the day's objective. Subsequently the Drake Battalion remained isolated at Pronville, but the encirclement of Quéant and Pronville from higher ground to the north and east had begun.

CPO George Prowse of the Drake Battalion played a major part in the day's fighting and gained the VC for his gallantry at Pronville and subsequently two days later at Mœuvres. The Drake Battalion was ordered to continue in a south-easterly direction, clearing the high ground and continue towards the village of Mœuvres which was close to the Canal du Nord. The canal was drained of water. During this advance Prowse was heavily involved in the fighting and organised a small group of men to attack two enemy machine-gun posts and accounting for six enemy gunners and taking others prisoner. On 5 September the Drake Battalion returned to Quéant after they had been relieved. They left the village on the 27th during 63rd Royal Naval Division's attack on the Bapaume–Cambrai road when George Prowse was killed in action near Arleux. He had been leading his men in an attack close to a heavily defended sugar factory near Arleux. By 30 September the Drake Battalion had suffered 384 casualties and Prowse's name was one of the forty-five who were killed during this offensive. His body was not recovered, but his name is commemorated on the RNVR Panels at Vis-en-Artois.

His VC was earned by these two gallant acts and the official version was published in the *London Gazette* of 30 October 1918 as follows:

> For most conspicuous bravery and devotion to duty when, during an advance, a portion of his company became disorganised by heavy machine gun fire from an enemy strong point. Collecting what men were available, he led them with great coolness and bravery against this strong point, capturing it, together with 28 prisoners and five machine guns. Later he took a patrol forward in face of much enemy opposition and established it on important high ground. On another occasion he displayed great heroism by attacking single-handed an ammunition limber which was trying to recover ammunition, killing three men who accompanied it and capturing the limber. Two days later he rendered valuable services when covering the advance of his company with a Lewis gun section, and located later on two machine gun positions in a concrete emplacement, which were holding up the advance of the battalion on the right. With complete disregard of personal danger he rushed forward with a small party and attacked and captured these posts, killing six enemy and taking thirteen prisoners and two machine guns. He was the only survivor of the gallant party, but by this daring and heroic action he enabled the battalion on the right to push forward without further machine gun fire from the village. Throughout the whole operations his magnificent example and leadership were an inspiration to all, and his courage was superb.

His posthumous VC, which was the last one to be awarded with the blue naval ribbon, was presented to his widow at Buckingham Palace on 17 July 1919.

George Henry Prowse was born 25 miles south-east of Swansea in South Wales on 29 August 1886 at 8 Brynsion Terrace, Gilfach Goch near Llantrisant, Glamorganshire. He was the son of John and Harriett Prowse; John was employed as a colliery banksman. Prior to 1891 the family moved to Somerset where they lived in No. 24 Meadgate, Camerton. John worked in the local colliery. After leaving school at the age of 15, George, who was one of six children, took up mining, initially working at Grovesend Colliery in South Wales before he transferred to the Mountain Colliery at Gorseinon, South Wales. He lodged at various addresses, including Station Road, Grovesend, and No. 22 New Road, Grovesend. He became an accomplished footballer and used to play for Gorseinon Football Club.

George's mother Harriet died in 1912 and in the following year George married Sarah Lewis at Swansea Registry Office on 8 November. Sarah worked as a barmaid and later worked in a West Wales war factory also in Swansea.The couple lived with Sarah's parents at No. 65 Treharne Road, Landore, Swansea.

Six months after the war began the 6ft tall Prowse enlisted in the Royal Naval Volunteer Reserve in Swansea on 26 February 1915 although as a miner he would have been exempt. His service number was W (Wales) Z424.

Even by 1914 it was clear to the naval authorities that there were more naval reservists available than could be accommodated within the fleet, so Winston Churchill, the First Lord of the Admiralty, suggested that a division should be raised from these surplus men. Hence the Royal Naval Division was born, which initially consisted of two brigades of four battalions each. The battalions were named after different British admirals and it was the Drake Battalion with which Prowse was to serve. But at first he was a member of the 5th Battalion and on 18 June was sent to Blandford in Dorset with the 2nd (Reserve) Battalion. He was promoted to petty officer on 20 June and on 9 September he was then transferred to the Drake Battalion of the 1st Brigade. He served in Gallipoli, France and Flanders, distinguishing himself in battle several times. It is not clear how long he served in Gallipoli for, but possibly only three weeks. He spent some time in hospital in Malta and returned to duty on 3 December and returned to the RND in Egypt on 9 January 1916. He was then sent to Mudros in Lemnos to rejoin the Drake Battalion on 31 May, who were sent to France, arriving in Marseilles on 7 June.

By now the 63rd (Royal Naval) Divison had been placed under the control of the War Office instead of the Admiralty. The Drake was now one of four battalions making up 189th Brigade. The three brigades which made up the division now included the 190th which was made up of military battalions. The division took part in the final stages of the Battle of the Somme in November 1916. Prowse was seriously wounded by gunshot wounds to his left thigh on the 13th and after treatment in France he was transferred to Epsom War Hospital before being discharged in early 1917. After two months back at Blandford he returned to France on 28 March where he rejoined his battalion. He took part in the Battle of Arras in April and in the struggles to capture the village of Gavrelle he was again badly wounded both in his shoulder and also beneath the heart. After emergency treatment he was sent back to England and this time became a patient in the Wharncliffe War Hospital in Yorkshire on 28 April.

After convalescence and a period when he trained new recruits he returned to France, arriving back with his battalion on 8 April 1918. By the end of the month he had been promoted to Chief Petty Officer. Records show that he was granted special leave from 26 July to 9 August and conjecture would imply that all was not well with his marriage to Sarah. He appears anxious to return to France.

As well as winning a VC, he also earned the DCM which he won for action at Logeast Wood on 21 August 1918, and the citation published after his death on 16 January 1919 tells the story:

> On 21st August, 1918, at Logeast Wood, he led his men with great gallantry against a machine gun that was holding up the advance of the flank of the company, and in spite of difficulties of heavy mist, he captured it, disposing of the crew. On a subsequent occasion he held a position against repeated counter-attacks which were supported by an intense bombardment for twenty-four hours. His courage, leadership and cheerful disposition had an invaluable effect on his men.

Logeast Wood is bisected by the D7 road to the north-west of Achiet le Grand.

In one of his last letters to Sarah, George wrote: 'to know that I have been recommended for such an award is the greatest honour and you can quite imagine I must have done something very great. You say I shall not be "swanking" now, but you know there is not much swank attached to me.'

Prowse's decorations, apart from the VC and DCM, included the 1914–15 Star, BWM and VM, and were sold at Glendining's for £950 on 15 December 1966 when they were purchased by Messrs Spinks. In May 1992 they were offered for sale again, this time at Sotheby's. The lot, apart from the decorations, consisted of a portrait and his memorial plaque. At some point they were purchased by Lord Ashcroft in a private transaction and are part of his collection in the Imperial War Museum.

As well as being commemorated at Vis-en-Artois Memorial, Haucourt, close to the Arras–Cambrai road, George Prowse's name is also listed on the war memorial at Swansea and in Camerton Churchyard, Avon. In 1990 an accomodation block at HMS *Collingwood* was named after him. On 21 October 2006 a blue plaque was unveiled on the front of the house in Brynsion Terrace where George Prowse was born which has now been renumbered 33 The High Street.

The writer is very grateful to Derek Hunt and Edward Harris for their researches into George Prowse's early life.

L.C. WEATHERS

North of Péronne, France, 2 September

Temporary Corporal Weathers was a member of the 43rd Battalion (South Australia) (11th Brigade, 3rd Division) (AIF), and gained the VC on 2 September 1918, to the north of Péronne. The objective was the high ground which ran from the village of Bouchavesnes to Allaines to the north of Mont St Quentin. The Canal du Nord was close to the latter village. Weathers won the VC during an attack against a position known as Graz Trench, opposite Allaines, to the north of Scutari Trench.

The plan was to clear a small triangular section between the Australian 2nd Division, who were moving in a north-easterly direction, and the British 74th (Yeomanry) Division, who were moving eastwards. The accompanying barrage fell in front of the two divisions and the 43rd Battalion delayed their advance until it had ceased. At 5.35 a.m., with a platoon of the 41st Battalion attached, the battalion left its position in Rollins Trench, and moved across a valley reaching Scutari Trench. A machine gun was causing casualties to D Company, and Lewis guns were brought up. Once the machine gun was silenced the enemy was driven back to Fiume Trench and Scutari Trench was then cleared. A Company attacked in a south-easterly direction against Graz Trench when strong resistance was met, leading to hand-to-hand fighting. Enemy troops had got into a junction of trenches and were giving trouble to the two prongs of the 43rd Battalion's advance. It was at this point that T/Cpl Weathers rushed into the enemy position, bombed it and killed the leaders of the garrison. He then returned for more bombs and this time returned with L/Cpl H.H.H. Thompson. While the latter pinned the Germans down with Lewis gun fire, Weathers continued his deadly work by climbing up onto the parapet to bomb the German trench. With the assistance of three other men, he managed to capture

180 Germans, together with three machine guns, and then marched the group out. By 7 a.m. the fight was over and the 43rd Battalion (who were already occupying the trenches they had wished to capture) were consolidating their position by patrolling in a forward direction. The 11th Brigade captured 400 prisoners, five field guns and fifteen machine guns.

After Weathers had unknowingly earned his VC, the 43rd Battalion had a short break from the line, taking part in the Allied advance again 6–9 September. Weathers took part in his battalion's attack on the section of the Hindenburg Line between Bony and Rosnoy. There was then another period of recuperation and training and on 28 September the battalion moved up for another tour of duty, this time to attack the Beaurevoir Line. It was during this attack that Weathers was mortally

wounded and died without knowing that he had won a VC. He was killed by a shell burst north-east of Péronne on 29 September 1918 during an early morning attack which begun at 5.50 a.m. He was buried 12 miles north-east of Péronne in Unicorn Cemetery, Vendhuille, Plot III, Row C, Grave 5. He left Annie, his wife, together with two children. Their home address was Franklin Street, Fullarton Estate, South Australia.

Temporary Corporal Weathers's VC was gazetted on 26 December 1918 as follows:

> For most conspicuous bravery and devotion to duty on 2 Sept. 1918, north of Péronne, when with an advanced bombing party. The attack having been held up by a strongly held enemy trench, Corpl. Weathers went forward alone under heavy fire, and attacked the enemy with bombs. Then, returning to our lines for a further supply of bombs, he again went forward with three comrades, and attacked under very heavy fire. Regardless of personal danger, he mounted the enemy parapet and bombed the trench, and with the support of his comrades, captured 180 prisoners and three machine guns. His valour and determination resulted in the successful capture of the final objective, and saved the lives of many of his comrades.

Lawrence Carthage Weathers, the son of John Joseph and Ellen Frances Johanna (McCormack), was born on 14 May 1890 in Te Koparu, near Whangarei, North Island, New Zealand. In 1897 his parents, together with their seven children, moved to Adelaide in South Australia. Lawrence was one of three sons and four daughters and their father died at the age of 45. Lawrence attended Snowtown Public School and, according to Gertrude, one of his sisters, he was a high-spirited boy. The family home was in Burunga Gap, and one of his mother's brothers agreed to take him on to his farm as an apprentice. In addition he also promised to treat him as if he was his own son and to help him to set him up in the world. This promise was broken as the young man was just used as a means of cheap labour. As a consequence he was able to send his mother only a few shillings a week. After returning to his own home, he tried his hands at several jobs but without much success. His two brothers also had employment problems, so the three of them decided to try their lot in Europe, and in October 1910 they set off for Germany by boat. Even here there was a problem, as the German crew clearly did not like their Australian passengers, which might have affected Lawrence's opinions later in life. The boys finally ended up in England, where Lawrence worked with a builder for a few months, whose family played an important role in Lawrence's later years.

Returning to Australia, Lawrence became an undertaker, and in 1913 married a domestic servant, Annie Elizabeth (*née* Watson) and the couple lived in Parkside. Three years later Lawrence enlisted in Adelaide Town Hall on 3 February 1916. During the previous year one of his brothers, Thomas Francis, was killed in Gallipoli on 15 June 1915 when serving with the 9th Light Horse (AIF), after having only been in the line for three weeks.

In June Weathers joined the 43rd Battalion, then left for England with the 3rd Division (AIF). In November the division sailed for France, but from January until the end of April 1917 Lawrence was sick and absent from his battalion in hospital. On 10 June, during the Battle of Messines, he was severely wounded during a night operation and did not rejoin his battalion until six months later. He was promoted to lance corporal on 21 March 1918, the start of the German offensive. Two months later, on 26 May, he was gassed at Bois L'Abbé in the Villers-Bretonneux area. He was then away from his unit for another month. Shortly before he won what was to be a posthumous VC in September 1918 he was promoted to corporal.

Many mementoes associated with his epic capture of German prisoners ended up in England at the home of the family who had employed him before the war. The collection included field glasses, officers' canes, etc., that he had taken from the Germans he captured. Weathers' posthumous VC was presented to his widow in Adelaide on 5 March 1920 by Gen. Sir William Birdwood. His other decorations would have included the BWM and VM. All three Weathers brothers met tragic ends. Even Joseph, who had survived the war, was killed by a taxi in a traffic accident in December 1954.

In 1956, after having great difficulty in gathering together the necessary funds for travel, Gertrude Lawrence (one of the Weathers' sisters) travelled to London for the VC Centenary, and took the opportunity of visiting her brother's grave in France.

Lawrence Weathers is commemorated in the Australian War Memorial, Canberra, but his decorations are in private hands. He is also commemorated in the Australian War Memorial, Canberra, the Victoria Cross Park Memorial, also in Canberra and in Sydney in the Victoria Cross Memorial in the Queen Victoria building.

J.F. YOUNG

Arras, France, 2 September

During the hectic fighting of 2 September 1918, no fewer than eleven Victoria Crosses were awarded for gallantry beyond the call of duty. In the Dury–Arras sector Pte John Young was a stretcher-bearer attached to D Company of the 87th Canadian Grenadier Guards Battalion (11th Brigade, 4th Division). The battalion had penetrated the Drocourt–Quéant Line and then had to attack the German-held ridge at Dury. There was no cover and the battalion was an open target for enemy gunners and as a consequence the Canadians suffered very heavy casualties. Young went forward to dress the wounds of some of the injured in this open ground which was still being swept continuously by murderous machine-gun and rifle fire. Despite this, he calmly continued his life-saving work for more than an hour before returning for more dressings. He went out again and again to bring in the wounded over the following days.

Private Young was awarded a VC for his magnificent work, which was gazetted on 14 December 1918 as follows:

> For most conspicuous bravery and devotion to duty in attack at Dury Arras sector on 2 Sept. 1918, when acting as a stretcher-bearer attached to D Company of the 87th Battn. Quebec Regt. This company in the advance over the ridge suffered heavy casualties from shell and machine gun fire. Private Young, in spite of the complete absence of cover, without the least hesitation went out and in the open, fire-swept ground dressed the wounded. Having exhausted his stock of dressings, on more than one occasion he returned, under intense fire, to his company headquarters for a further supply. This work he continued for over an hour, displaying throughout the most absolute

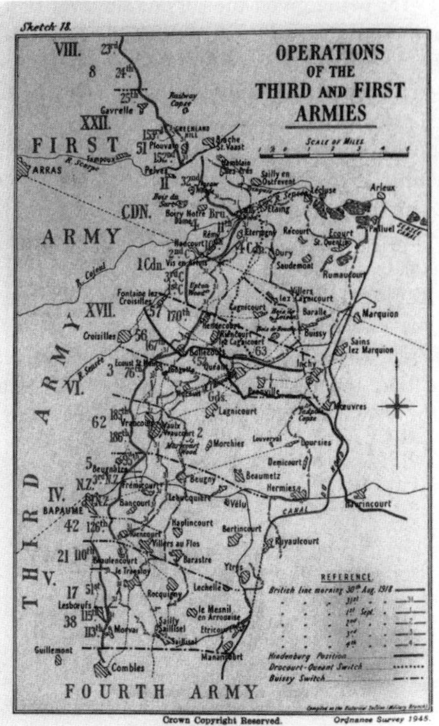

fearlessness. To his courageous conduct must be ascribed the saving of the lives of many of his comrades. Later, when the fire had somewhat slackened, he organised and led stretcher parties to bring in the wounded whom he had dressed. All through the operations of 2, 3 and 4 Sept. Private Young continued to show the greatest valour and devotion to duty.

He was presented with the VC by the King in the Ballroom of Buckingham Palace on 12 April 1919.

John Francis Young was born in Kidderminster, Worcestershire, on 14 January 1893, and later emigrated to Canada where he became a tobacco packer in Montreal. He enlisted in the Canadian Army on

20 October 1915, being given the service number of 177239. After a few months he became a member of the 87th Battalion, Quebec Regiment, and moved to France. Back in Canada after demobilisation Young resumed his work as a tobacco packer in Montreal, and married Ida Thatcher. The couple were to have one son.

John Young was not a well man and died from TB at the early age of 36 on 7 November 1929 in the St Agathe Sanatorium, Quebec. He was buried in Mount Royal Cemetery, Montreal, Section L/2, Plot 2019. He is commemorated in the Canadian Grenadier Guards' Junior Ranks Mess which is called the John Francis Young Club and he also has a plaque to his memory in the Sergeants' Mess.

Young left his VC to his son, John F. Young, of 10479 Laurentide Avenue, Montreal North 459, Quebec, and his two service medals, the BWM and VM, remain in private hands. His VC was acquired in March 2012 for display at the Canadian War Museum in Ottawa.

M. Doyle

Near Riencourt, France, 2–3 September

The main actions concerning the Allied Army's breaking and capture of the strongly defended Drocourt–Quéant line took place over the two days of 2–3 September 1918. As with ten other men, Company Sergeant Major Martin Doyle (1st Royal Munster Fusiliers) won the VC on the first of these days, close to Riencourt, north-west of Quéant. After all his officers had become casualties, he saw that the enemy was encircling part of his unit and he organised a charge which rescued his colleagues and prevented their capture. In addition Doyle also rescued a wounded officer. The Munsters were supporting tanks at the time and later in the day some of the enemy were attempting to enter an Allied tank. Once again Doyle saw them off, but a few minutes later an enemy machine gun opened up and prevented any attempts to rescue members of the tank crew who had been wounded. Seemingly inspired, Doyle once again took on the enemy gun and not only destroyed it but took three of its crew prisoner. Not yet giving up, the enemy staged a counter-attack later in the day but they had underestimated the Munsters and once more Doyle's company not only repelled the attackers but also took many of them prisoner.

The citation for Doyle's very well deserved VC was gazetted on 31 January 1919 and detailed the story as follows:

> On the 2nd Sept. 1918 near Riencourt, as Acting Company Sergeant-Major, command of the company devolved upon him consequent on officer casualties. Observing that some of our men were surrounded by the enemy, he led a party to their assistance, and by skill and leadership worked his way along the trenches, killed several of the enemy and extricated the party, carrying back

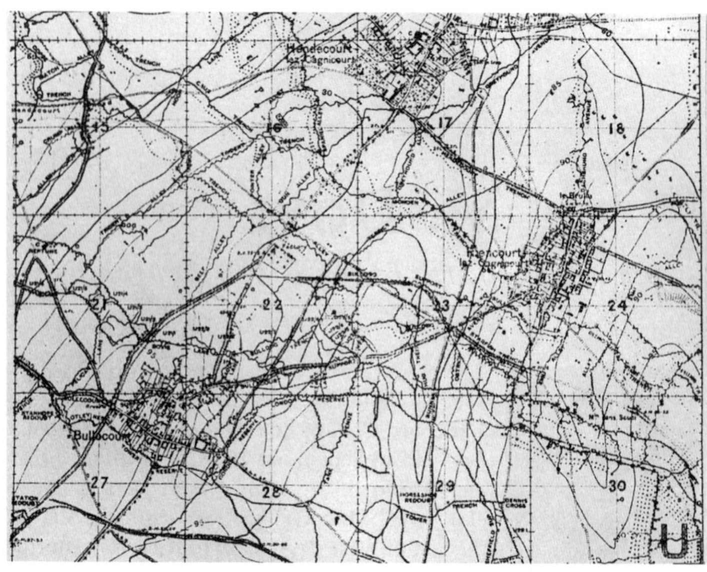

under heavy fire a wounded officer to a place of safety. Later, seeing a Tank in difficulties, he rushed forward under intense fire, routed the enemy who were attempting to get into it, and prevented the advance of another enemy party collecting for a further attack on the Tank. An enemy machine gun now opened on the Tank at close range, rendering it impossible to get the wounded away, whereupon Company Sergt.-Major Doyle, with great gallantry, rushed forward, and, single-handed silenced the machine gun, capturing it with three prisoners. He then carried a wounded man to safety under a very heavy fire. Later in the day, when the enemy counter-attacked his position, he showed a great power of command, driving back the enemy and capturing many prisoners. Throughout the whole of these operations Company. Sergt.-Major Doyle set the very highest example to all ranks by his courage and total disregard of danger.

The above is the 'official' account of how Doyle won his VC, but a contemporary newspaper account told the story in a slightly different way:

A short time later he saw a British tank in difficulties, tipped over in a trench, and immediately rushed forward under heavy

> fire to the aid of the crew. He routed the enemy who were trying to enter the tank and other Germans who were coming up. He then advanced along the enemy trench, shot a German officer who was calling on him to surrender and bayoneted three of a crew of a machine gun. When the enemy counter attacked shortly afterwards …

Doyle was presented with his VC by the King on 8 May 1919, during an investiture at Buckingham Palace.

Martin Doyle was born at Gusserane, near New Ross in County Wexford, Ireland, on 25 October 1894, the son of Larry Doyle and his wife Bridget. He was educated in primary schools at Gusserane and later Cushinstown, joining the Royal Irish Regiment on Boxing Day 1909, with the service number of 9962. He was only fifteen years old, but managed to convince the authorities that he was two years older. After travelling to India with his regiment he won the regimental lightweight boxing title there in 1913. Shortly before war broke out he transferred to the Royal Dublin Fusiliers, with the new service number of 40342, and served with them during the first stages of the war in France from December 1914. In 1915 he was promoted to sergeant and in March 1918 he transferred again, this time to the 1st Royal Munster Fusiliers, with the new number of 10864. By now he had been made a company sergeant major. It is not at all clear why Doyle was a member of three different Irish regiments in the short span of only five years. On 24 March 1918 he won the MM (*LG* 13 September 1918) and in his own words he described the action in a Wexford newspaper soon afterwards:

> We were lying at Hattenfield, held in reserve for a counter attack. The troops in front were driven back after hard fighting and we were called in. We captured Hattenfield and went on to the trench outside, which was to be the limit of our objective. We met parties of the enemy before reaching this trench and drove them before us. We had to cross about 1,000 yards of open country, exposed to terrible shell and MG fire. Our casualties were heavy. Having reached the trench we found that the Germans were dug in not more than 40 yards ahead of us. A big barn stood on the ground between us and a fight ensued to take possession of it. On the enemy side there was long grass which afforded them cover and one of their MGs succeeded in creeping out and taking the barn, from

> which they kept up a heavy fire. I called for volunteers and went over the top with my bayonet at the charge but when I reached the barn I was alone. I bayoneted the two Germans that I found there, seized the machine gun and took possession of the barn.

During the March retreat Doyle was taken prisoner by the enemy who subsequently treated him badly, but as a result of an Allied counter-attack he managed to escape. After he won his MM Doyle received a letter from the then commander of the 24th Division, Maj. Gen. A.L. Daly, in which the general wrote:

> I am very pleased to see that your gallant conduct has been rewarded by the award of the Military Medal, and I offer you my personal congratulations.

Five months later, in August, Doyle was promoted to acting sergeant major.

Apart from his boxing prowess, he was keen on other sports and won a mile race which was open to members of the 57th (West Lancashire) Division in France during 1918.

After the war Doyle attended an investiture on 8 May 1919 in the quadrangle of Buckingham Palace when he received his VC and MM. He was accompanied by other winners of the VC, including Harry Greenwood, James Towers, Thomas Caldwell and John Daykins. On returning home to Ireland he was given a hero's welcome when he arrived back home in New Ross and attended a formal presentation ceremony.

After being discharged from the army in July Doyle married Charlotte Kennedy, also of New Ross, on 25 November. The couple lived at 18 Mary Street and Doyle became an early member of the Regimental Old Comrades' Association (OCA) of the Royal Munster Fusiliers. In June 1920 he attended the VC Garden Party at Buckingham Palace and on 11 November he was a member of the RMF party which attended the unveiling of the Cenotaph in Whitehall. It is perhaps a trifle ironic that he was a member of the IRA at the time.

There is no obvious evidence as to whether Doyle was politically motivated while in the army, fighting on the side of the British Empire, but it is quite evident that once the war had ended he quickly joined the IRA, remaining a member of the organisation until the truce in July 1921. He served with the Mid Clare Brigade in Ennis, while acting as an undercover agent for the IRA. After the 1921 truce, as a member of the newly formed Free State Army, Doyle became involved in the Civil War, serving in Waterford, Kilkenny and in South Tipperary, and was wounded in the left arm during fighting in Limerick.

When peace was restored, Doyle remained in the army from 1925, with the 2nd and 20th Infantry Battalions and the School of Instruction. At one point, in 1924, he was impersonated in Rugby by a man seeking financial gain who claimed to be Doyle VC. Someone who knew the real Doyle during the war was able to disprove the man's false claims.

In November 1929 Doyle attended the VC Dinner at the House of Lords and some years later, in 1937, he was awarded a Coronation Medal and finally left the army in the same year with the rank of company sergeant major. His name was then placed on the list of Reservists until January 1939. Doyle subsequently attended the Armistice Day ceremonies in Dublin in 1938, when accompanied by John Ring, MC, DCM.

For the next two years Doyle worked at the Guinness Brewery in Dublin and at this time his home was at 23 Larfield Park, Kimmage, a house owned by the Irish Soldiers and Sailors Trust.

Martin Doyle died of pneumonia at Sir Patrick Dun's Hospital, Dublin, on 20 November 1940, leaving a widow and three daughters. He was buried in Grangegorman Military Cemetery, Cabra, Dublin, and his gravestone bears the badge of the Royal Munster Fusiliers but not the design of a VC. The grave was paid for by the OCA, the balance of the money raised being presented to Mrs Doyle who outlived her husband by twenty years, and she also received a pension from the OCA. After his death Doyle was awarded by the Irish Government a Military Cross in recognition of his service with the IRA.

In 1984 Doyle's VC was offered for sale by Sotheby's on 1 March, but at the last moment was withdrawn. At the present time it is in the Lord Ashcroft Collection in the Imperial War Museum. As we have seen, Doyle's other decorations included the MM, 1914–15 Star, BWM, VM and 1937 Coronation Medal.

J. McNamara

Lens, France, 2–3 September

At the end of August 1918, when the 9th East Surrey Battalion (72nd Brigade, 24th Division) were in the line in the Lens area to the north-west of the town. It was suspected that the enemy had withdrawn from the town and two officer patrols were sent out to obtain confirmation. They soon had an answer when they were driven back by machine-gun fire from a German working party. A further two patrols were pushed out the next day, reaching as far as the Cité St Auguste road, but they too were driven back by superior forces. Five further patrols were pushed forward during the night and succeeded in linking up with patrols of the 8th Royal West Kents which had reached as far as Fosse No. 1, near where the Bethune and La Bassée roads join up before entering Lens. By now the 9th East Surreys had reached the enemy's front-line posts and became the first British posts in Lens since the town was lost to the enemy four years before in 1914.

During the night of 2 September further posts were established in the enemy front line, which the Germans attempted to capture early next morning. It was at this stage that Cpl John McNamara took an active role in the fighting and the divisional order of 24 November described his actions as follows:

> After a heavy bombardment with guns and 'minenwerfer' the enemy attacked in considerable force. The two officers who were present became casualties almost at once, and Pte. [*sic*] MacNamara proved himself a hero and was the spirit of the defence throughout. He not only did his own task, but he induced the other men by his example to do theirs. He moved about freely, urging everyone to 'stick it', which they did ... Pte. MacNamara

> showed the most supreme courage and powers of leadership and right nobly earned the highest distinction which His Majesty can award.

Corporal John McNamara's VC was gazetted on 15 November 1918, but not as a posthumous one, as follows:

> For most conspicuous bravery, initiative and devotion to duty. When operating a telephone in evacuated enemy trenches occupied by his battalion, Corpl. McNamara realised that a determined counter-attack was gaining ground. Rushing to join the nearest post, he made the most effective use of a revolver taken from a wounded officer. Then seizing a Lewis gun, he continued to fire it until it jammed. By this time he was alone in the post. Having destroyed his telephone, he joined the nearest post, and again displayed great courage and initiative in maintaining Lewis gun fire until reinforcements arrived. It was undoubtably due to the magnificent courage and determination of Private McNamara that the other posts were enabled to hold on, and his fine example of devotion is worthy of the highest praise.

The *Regimental History* has this additional information about the fighting on 3 September:

> In this engagement the two first German attacks were driven off; but a third was made about 1 p.m. in great force and the left posts were temporarily lost, until Lieut.-Colonel Cameron led a party forward and reoccupied them. Among the casualties was the Adjutant, Captain W.H. Lindsay, M.C., who was visiting the posts and was killed while standing up to overwhelming odds in a manner to increase even his reputation for courage and devotion to duty. His body was brought in by Pte. McNamara and Lieut.-Colonel Cameron.

A few weeks later, on 12 October, the 9th East Surreys arrived at the village of Avesnez-lès-Aubert to the east of Cambrai where they billeted for the night. On the following day they moved into billets at St Aubert, where they remained on 14 October. The brigade front line was formed by the 1st North Staffs, and the 8th Royal West Kents and was opposite the village of Haussy on the River Selle.

On the morning of 15 October Col Cameron and two of his officers decided to reconnoitre, and Cameron found a perfect position for bridging the river where the stream narrowed, which was also well hidden by trees. The information gained was conveyed to the brigade and division, and subsequently the 9th East Surreys were ordered to attack and capture the village at 5.15 a.m. the next morning. It was during this action that Corporal McNamara lost his life and was later buried 12 miles east of Cambrai in Romeries Communal Cemetery Extension, near Solesmes in Plot IV, Row D, Grave 17.

A month after his death Col Cameron wrote to McNamara's widow expressing his sympathy, along with that of the whole battalion, and hoping that he would be able to escort Mrs McNamara when the time came for the presentation of the VC to her. On 21 November 1919 the *Daily Telegraph* carried the following report of the proceedings of a 'welcome home' on the previous day to the East Surrey Regiment, known as 'The Gallants' in Kingston-upon-Thames:

> Earl Haig telegraphed his best wishes, adding his thanks to the regiment for all they did in the Great War. The battalion are at present stationed at Clipstone, but a representative party came to Kingston on Wednesday evening and were quartered at the regimental depot. Headed by the band of the 2nd Battn., the men yesterday marched into the town, amid the ringing of bells from the parish church and the cheers of crowds. Colonel Cameron, the commanding officer, was at the head of the troops, who were formed up on a platform in the market place, where they were greeted by the Mayor and Mayoress, and Colonel Brettell, who took the battalion to France in 1915. At the head of the battalion was the Colour party and officers, and on the left, in the leading ranks, the battalion's mascot, a little French boy, Vignolle Serge, aged thirteen years, who wore on his uniform the 1914–15 general service and Victory ribbons, and one red and three chevrons. The lad, whose home was within the war area of France, attached himself to the battalion, and refused to leave them. He was sent five times under escort to his home, but each time made his way back to the battalion, on one occasion getting back before the escort. The Mayoress attached a laurel wreath to the Colours, which were presented to the battalion by the King at Tournai. The whole parade stood at the salute. A speech of welcome was given by the Mayor, who stated that 'The Gallants' were the first to enter Lens and also Cambrai. Colonel Cameron replied on behalf of the regiment. During the proceedings, the fine record of the regiment in the way of decorations was

mentioned, including the winning of the Victoria Cross by Private McNamara, who subsequently laid down his life. Afterwards the troops were entertained at luncheon.

McNamara's VC was presented to his widow by the King in Buckingham Palace on 27 February 1920.

John McNamara was the son of John Thomas McNamara, a blacksmith, and his wife Margaret (*née* Kelly). He was born at 11 Mill Street, Bamber Bridge, Walton-le-Dale, Preston, Lancashire, on 28 October 1887, and as a boy played football for the School Lane Athletic Club. He later worked in School Lane at Orr's Mill, living nearby with his wife in the now demolished 82 Stone Row. A cupola of the mill is all that has been kept of the original mill.

While serving in the army, McNamara's service number was 28939, and he was later commemorated at All Saints' Church, Kingston-upon-Thames. After he had won his VC, residents of his former home town at Walton opened a fund to honour him, and a total of £528 was invested. As he died about five weeks before the war's end this fund was used to help local families of men who had been killed in the war. As each of the children chosen came of age they were presented with a share of the fund, which was finally closed in January 1935.

On 3 September 1997, seventy-nine years after McNamara won his VC, a memorial plaque to his memory was unveiled in School Lane, Bamber Bridge, Lancashire, as part of a special commemorative service. The chairman of Lancashire County Council attended, together with more than twenty members of McNamara's family, as well as members of the regimental association. At the service of dedication and wreath-laying, the plaque, at the entrance to the Old Mill Estate, was unveiled by the head girl and head boy of Brownedge St Mary's Roman Catholic High School.

McNamara's decorations, including his VC, BWM and VM, are held in the Queen's Royal Regiment (West Surrey) Museum in Clandon Park, Guildford.

W.L. Rayfield

East of Arras, France, 2–4 September

Private Walter Rayfield, 7th Battalion (British Columbia Regiment) (2nd Brigade, 1st Division) won his VC on 2–4 September 1918 for several acts of bravery during the fighting for the Drocourt–Quéant Line. After the 14th Battalion (3rd Brigade, 1st Division) captured the village of Cagnicourt with very few casualties, the Bois de Loison was overrun and the Buissy Switch reached. However, at that point the opposition stiffened. On the left of the 3rd Canadian Brigade, the 2nd Brigade attacked with its 7th Battalion, using four tanks on a front of 1,000yds with the 10th Battalion and three more tanks in support. Despite an accurate Allied barrage, the 7th came under heavy fire from advanced machine-gun posts. These were gradually captured and, with the tanks doing good work, the battalion assaulted and took the forward system of the Drocourt–Quéant position with the assistance of seven tanks. The support system and northern end of the Buissy Switch were then taken without much difficulty, with a large number of the enemy surrendering.

Walter Rayfield's VC was gazetted on 14 December 1918. When he received the news of his decoration he was stationed in Germany with his battalion a few weeks after the war had finished, and he was pulled out of bed to be told that his VC was listed in army orders. Later in the day he was escorted out on to the parade ground for the public announcement of his VC. It was the third VC won by the 7th Canadian Battalion, and the citation was as follows:

> For most conspicuous bravery, devotion to duty and initiative during operations east of Arras from 2 to 4 Sept. 1918. Ahead of his company he rushed a trench occupied by a large party of the enemy, personally bayoneting two and taking 10 prisoners.

> Later, he located and engaged with great skill, under constant rifle fire, an enemy sniper who was causing many casualties. He then rushed the section trench from which the sniper had been operating, and so demoralised the enemy by his coolness and daring that 30 others surrendered to him. Again, regardless of his personal safety, he left cover under heavy machine gun fire and carried in a badly wounded comrade. His indomitable courage, cool foresight and daring reconnaissance were invaluable to his company commander and an inspiration to all ranks.

A few weeks later, on 27 September 1918, Rayfield was promoted to corporal, then on 7 January 1919 to acting sergeant. On 8 March 1919 he was presented with his VC by the King in the Ballroom of Buckingham Palace and in the following month he returned to Canada and was demobilised on 25 April.

Walter Leigh Rayfield was born in Richmond, Surrey, on 7 October 1881. He was educated at a private school in London and in Richmond Grammar School. His family emigrated to Canada a few years later and from the age of ten Walter's education was completed in Canada and America, although at this time he lived mainly in Ontario. In America he graduated from Oakland Agricultural College and began a career in California, but he returned to Canada shortly before the outbreak of war.

When the war began in August 1914 Rayfield was involved in the real estate business in Vancouver and when trying to enlist in the Canadian Army he was twice rejected on medical grounds. Eventually though he was successful and enlisted in Victoria, British Columbia, on 10 July 1917, when he was allocated the service number of 2204279 and became a member of the 7th Infantry Battalion CEF. He was 5ft 6in tall.

After Rayfield was discharged in April 1919 he remained in a Vancouver Hospital for some time, presumably as a result of the war. He then took up farming with the hope of improving his health, and was later put in charge of the transfer of shell-shocked and other seriously disabled soldiers to the military hospital under the DSCR.

In November 1929 he travelled to London for the House of Lords VC Dinner, and on the same trip visited Belfast where he laid a wreath in the Garden of Remembrance on behalf of the Canadian winners of the VC. On his return to Canada he moved to Toronto, Ontario, and was later an official of the Toronto Harbour Commission. He was interested in politics and on one occasion stood for membership of the federal parliament but was narrowly defeated. In 1934 he was appointed sergeant-at-arms of the Ontario Legislature, when he 'fulfilled his duties efficiently and to the credit of all concerned'. While acting as a sergeant-at-arms he used to wear a sword, cocked hat and a satin waistcoat, but during his term of office the ceremonial uniform was replaced by a more moden garment. In 1935 Rayfield was made deputy governor of Toronto Jail, later becoming its governor. He was considered to be a very suitable candidate as during his life he had a wide experience in the handling of men. He was also an officer in the Queen's Own Rangers.

In 1939, during the King and Queen's visit to North America, Rayfield was one of the winners of the VC to be presented to the royal couple on 22 May 1939 in the Commons Chamber, Toronto; others were Benjamin Geary, Henry Robson, Colin Barron, Thomas Holmes and Charles Rutherford.

Walter died very suddenly, at home in Toronto on 19 February 1949, and at his own request was buried in the Soldiers' Plot, Prospect Cemetery, in Toronto. Section &. Grave 4196. Apart from his VC, BWM, VM and King George VI Coronation Medal, he was also awarded the Silver Medal of the Crown (Belgium) in recognition of his services. His son, Victor, presented his father's decorations to the Canadian War Museum, Ottawa, in February 1970.

L. CALVERT

Havrincourt near Cambrai, France, 12 September

Sergeant Laurence Calvert was a member of the 1/5th Battalion (KOYLI) TF (187th Brigade) of the 62nd (2nd West Riding) Division. He gained the VC when he saw off the threat from an enemy machine-gun team at the south-west corner of the village of Havrincourt, near Cambrai, on 12 September 1918, the opening day of the Battle of Havrincourt. The citation was gazetted on 15 November 1918 as follows:

> For most conspicuous bravery and devotion to duty in attack when the success of the operation was rendered doubtful owing to severe enfilade machine gun fire. Alone and single-handed, Sergt. Calvert, rushing forward against the machine gun team, bayoneted three and shot four. His valour and determination in capturing single-handed two machine guns and killing the crews thereof enabled the ultimate objective to be won. His personal gallantry inspired all ranks.

Brig.-Gen. Viscount Hampden, the brigade commander who recommended Calvert for his award, later wrote: 'At one time during an attack on Havrincourt it was doubtful as to whether the attack would be successful owing to the determined enfilade machine-gun fire from Boggart's Hole, south of the village.'

Calvert himself later spoke about his VC action at Havrincourt as follows:

> My company were held up by machine gun fire at a place called Boggart's Hole. I attacked the guns single-handed, killed the crew

> of seven Germans and captured the guns; I was recommended for the V.C., and was lucky to get it; I was in action for four days after, during many counter-attacks, but my battalion refused to give ground, and held the village of Havrincourt all the time during heavy shell fire.

In November 1918 when the news came through that Calvert had indeed been awarded a VC, there was no way of honouring him as there was no appropriate medal or ribbon to be had. In order at least to mark this great event Calvert was placed on a saluting base and the whole battalion from the commanding officer downwards marched past him at the salute.

Four months later Laurence Calvert was one of three men to be decorated with the VC in the Ballroom of Buckingham Palace on 29 March 1919. He was accompanied by his mother and brother Walter, who had served in the Royal Navy during the war.

Laurence Calvert was born in Selkirk Place of Dewsbury Road, in the district of Hunslet, Leeds, on 16 February 1892. He was the son of a tin-plate worker named George Calvert, and his wife Beatrice. He was educated at Rowland Road Board School and Cockburn High School. His father died in 1895, and after leaving school Laurence became a coal miner, first at Cadeby and later at the Maltby Colliery. In 1910 he moved to 19 Beech Hill, Conisborough, where he joined the Territorial Army on 17 April 1914 and was with them in camp at Whitby at the outbreak of war. They were immediately mobilised and in April 1915 Calvert left for France as a member of the 49th (West Riding) Division. This division was to serve in France and Belgium for the rest of the war and initially they were concentrated behind the River Lys in the area of Estaires-Merville-Neuf Berquin. Calvert served with the 1/5th Battalion KOYLI and his service number was 240194. When he took part in the Second Battle of Ypres in September he was wounded in the arm and sent home to Brighton, where he recuperated. By early 1916 he was back in France, and in February 1918 his battalion was transferred to the 62nd (2nd West Riding) Division. On 2 September, ten days before gaining his VC, he won the Military Medal near Vaulx for bravery during a 187th Brigade attack against the Drocourt-Quéant Line. After the battalion was relieved it went back to Behagnies. He was also created Chevalier de l'Ordre de Léopold II (Belgium) for his fighting record during the latter months of the war. The award appeared in

Part II Orders, dated 2 February 1919. As part of the occupation the 62nd Division was the only TF Division to enter Germany at the end of the war.

When Calvert arrived home at Conisborough in April 1919 he was welcomed by several thousand people and took part in a procession of a local band and a group of six motor cars. Calvert and his mother were in the first car, which had VC painted in white letters on it. The motor procession drove slowly through the village and arrived at the place of presentation named the Large Hall. He was presented with £520, some war bonds and an illuminated address. His colliery presented him with a gold watch and chain, and various speeches of thanks and congratulation were made.

After the war Calvert continued serving in the army, initially in Germany. When he returned to his birthplace in England in 1919, he was presented with a chiming clock during a presentation at Rowland Road School, Leeds. After a short leave he left for Ireland as part of the British Army force helping to suppress the Sinn Fein movement. He remained there for a year before returning to England on two months' leave. He then left for India with the 2nd Battalion and served there for eleven years and in 1930 was on the North West Frontier.

Calvert married Hellene, a Frenchwoman whom he had met on the Somme, when she travelled out to India in 1922. The couple were to have three children. During his time in India Calvert and his wife returned to England in 1928 for an eight-month leave. Calvert had served in North India (1930–1931) and travelled to much of India during his service in India until he was discharged from the army on 11 December 1932.

Owing to an attack of pleurisy, Calvert was unable to attend the King's Coronation in May 1937. On the outbreak of the Second World War in 1939 he joined the Home Guard, but poor health forced him to resign and instead he became a warden in the local Dagenham branch of the Civil Defence Corps. He and his family then went to live in Yorkshire for a few months but Calvert didn't seek employment, although he did eventually become a commissionaire with a Bradford wholsale merchant. Eighteen months later he and his family returned to Dagenham where he took up a similar post with the National Provincial Bank in London. He stayed with the bank for sixteen years before being forced to retire owing to ill health.

As special guests Laurence and Helene Calvert attended the Coronation of Queen Elizabeth II in 1953 and were given seats outside Buckingham Palace. In the bi-centenary of the King's Own Yorkshire Light Infantry in August 1955 he was among a group of former soldiers presented to Queen Elizabeth, the Queen Mother. In the 1960s a memorial tower, together with bells, were dedicated by the Bishop of Chelmsford in the Essex Regimental Chapel at Warley Barracks, Brentwood. Two of the 400 distinguished visitors were the Lord Lieutenant, Colonel Sir Francis Whitmore and Laurence Calvert VC.

The Calverts' two sons worked at the Ford Motor Company in Dagenham and their daughter, Helene, who had served with the ATS in the Second World War, later lived in New York. Her husband worked for the United Nations.

After a series of protracted illnesses, Laurence Calvert died at his home at No. 73 Oglethorpe Road, Dagenham, on 7 July 1964 when his wife and two sons were at his bedside. His funeral was attended by friends and family, as well as members of the KOYLI. Two buglers sounded the Last Post at the service which was followed by a cremation at the South Essex Crematorium, Upminster on 17 July (Ref 9029). His ashes were placed in the Garden of Remembrance, Rosebed 32, path A. Plaque 714 was later erected to the soldier's memory but is no longer on display.

At his death, Calvert's decorations passed to his wife, and on her death they remained in private hands but in 2010 they were placed on display in the Lord Ashcroft Gallery in the Imperial War Museum.

Apart from his VC and MM, the decorations included the 1914–15 Star, BWM, VM plus MiD Oakleaf, the India General Service Medal with 1 Clasp and North-West Frontier 1930–31, the King George VI Coronation Medal, the Queen Elizabeth II Coronation Medal and the Knight, Order of Leopold II (Belgium). At his home Calvert had always kept a large framed copy of his citation and a copy of his illuminated address of welcome.

Calvert is also commemorated in Victoria Park together with eight other VC holders with local connections close to the City Art Gallery in Leeds. There is also a plaque to his memory in All Saints' Church, Denaby, Conisborough.

H.J. Laurent

East of Gouzeaucourt Wood, Cambrai, France, 12 September

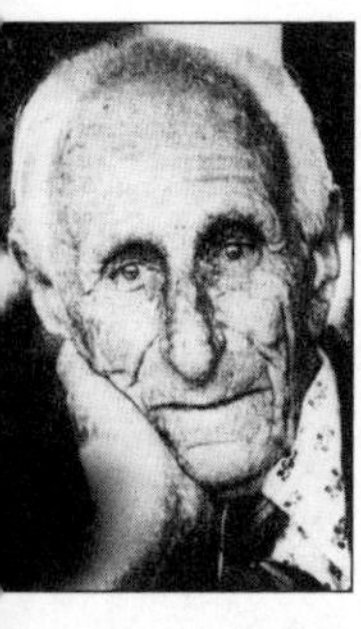

South-west of Cambrai, Sgt Harry Laurent gained the VC as a member of the 2nd Battalion New Zealand (Rifle) Brigade (NZEF), who on 12 September 1918 were holding a position called African Support to the north-west of the village of Gouzeaucourt and east of Gouzeaucourt Wood. A section of a platoon under Sgt Laurent, numbering twelve men, was ordered to push forward as a fighting patrol. They came across a trench line called African Trench, but it was so battered and shallow that they did not recognise it as such and pressed on towards the Gouzeaucourt village. Laurent's party had advanced about 700yds and it was not until they were almost in the village itself that they realised they must have missed their objective, and as a consequence were now well into enemy territory. Laurent could see enemy support lines on and around a sunken road. He made his dispositions, then led a charge with his small group of twelve men. Taking the Germans by surprise, the group killed between twenty and thirty of them and took others as prisoners. The section was now down to seven men and by this time they had become the target, being fired upon from all sides. Their captives also became restless and had to be dealt with afresh.

Laurent's group then came across an enemy company commander at the point of phoning for urgent assistance, but he was quickly dispatched and the phoneline cut. The riflemen then hurried the prisoners, consisting of a large enemy party of one officer, 111 men and two messenger dogs, back to their own lines. Meanwhile the company to the left of Laurent's group had captured the northern part of African Trench to the boundary of the battalion, and had killed many Germans and captured forty-six. During the night the brigade was relieved by the

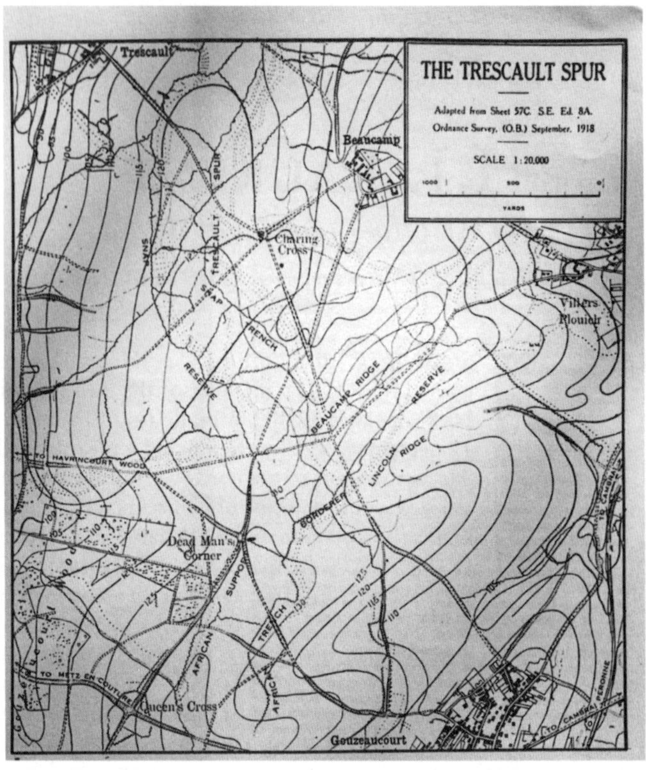

1st Brigade, and later the New Zealanders were driven back to Africa Support when liquid fire was used. It was not until 28 September tha African Trench was fully captured, when men of the 25th Divisio recaptured it but only after two strong attacks.

Sergeant Laurent's VC was gazetted on 15 November 1918 a follows:

> For most conspicuous bravery, skill and enterprise when during an attack he was detailed to exploit an initial success and keep in touch with the enemy. With a party of twelve he located the enemy support line very strongly held, at once charged the position, followed by his men, and completely disorganised the enemy by his sudden onslaught. In the subsequent hand-to-hand fighting which ensued, he showed great resourcefulness in controlling and

> encouraging his men, and 30 of the enemy having been killed, the remainder surrendered, a total of one officer and 111 other ranks in all. The success of this daring venture, which caused his party four casualties only, was due to his gallantry and enterprise.

Laurent was presented with his VC at Buckingham Palace on 26 February 1919.

A report in the *New Zealand Herald* of 11 December 1987 printed an article quoting Laurent's own story of his VC action, when he was leading a small Lewis gun detachment at Gouzeaucourt Wood in a patrol. Unknowingly, they penetrated nearly 800 metres behind the German lines. When they realised this, Sergeant Laurent decided to attack: 'They had a strongpoint with some 30 men and two machine guns. … We put a couple of bombs into the trench and shot up a few and, of course, that was that.' All thirty Germans were killed.

Unknown to the sergeant and the five unwounded men who remained in his detachment, a company of Germans in a nearby underground command post, thinking that they had been overrun, was preparing to surrender.

The hair-raising part of the operation was about to occur.

> I remember that Maurice [Maurice Healy], a fearless fellow, [according to Harry Laurent] called out, "There's thousands of 'em," when they started coming out.
>
> My hair stood on end. You can imagine it. There were just a few of us.
>
> We had just cleaned up 30 in the machine gun post and thought we had nothing more to worry about. And then these blokes streaming up …
>
> We were scared. Those surrendering came up without weapons, and when the colonel in charge saw that he was dealing with a mere sergeant, he spat at Harry Laurent.
>
> He dodged out of the way; Maurice Healy prodded the officer with his bayonet and any move to overwhelm the small Kiwi group was nipped in the bud.

The New Zealanders and their prisoners – including two messenger dogs – then moved back towards Allied lines, with more Germans between them and safety.

> The Germans, seeing the column, began to open up to let them through. When we got nearer they realised what had happened

> and that they were prisoners. They started taking shots at us, but that didn't do any good because they were hitting their own men, wounding and killing them.

Two of his men were injured by snipers and a German was killed by the enemy on the line. 'So they stopped and we walked straight through.'

Meanwhile, another patrol which had gone out at the same time had returned, reporting wrongly that Harry Laurent's section had been lost.

Throughout the event, the sergeant had not fired a shot. 'I never had a rifle. I had a revolver, and I don't think I ever took it out of the holster.' (Author's note: this statement does not tally with the officia citation.)

Harry John Laurent was the son of Mr and Mrs J. Laurent of Hawera and was born at Tarata, Taranaki, New Zealand, on 15 April 1895 He was educated at Hawera District High School. His family was o French descent and the family were farmers. In 1911 Harry joined the Taranaki Rifles, a territorial unit, and took a job working in a chees factory before enlisting with the New Zealand Expeditionary Force on 28 May 1915, with the number of 24/213.

He was 5ft 5½in tall, with auburn hair and blue eyes, and was Presbyterian. He left New Zealand for Egypt with the 2nd Battalion, Nev Zealand Rifle Brigade, on 9 October 1915. He then served in Palestin as a corporal before going to Gallipoli, although he did not disembark there. His unit left for France in April 1916, where he was wounded o 1 October during the Battle of the Somme and admitted to No. 1 Canadia Hospital, Étaples, the following day. He rejoined his battalion later in th month on 28 April. In October 1917 he was promoted to lance corpora then to corporal on 6 November, and to sergeant on 24 November.

Towards the end of the war, on 22 October 1918, he was posted t an officer cadet training unit in England. As the war soon finished h never returned to France. At Christmas 1918 he was awarded ninetee days' leave and was commissioned on 14 February 1919. He returne to New Zealand in August 1919, where he was met by his family, whic included Mr R.M.M.J. Laurent, his grandfather, who was then 93 year old, and who had formerly been a major in the French Army.

Harry Laurent was greeted by the mayor of his home town an presented with a gold watch and chain, the cost of which had bee contributed to by the local citizens. He and his colleagues were warml applauded by a large crowd and both the mayor and Laurent planted oa rees in the Tower Gardens to commemorate the coming of peace. Laurent vas discharged from the army soon after and posted to the Reserve of)fficers. As he had no job to return to he decided to take up farming, and n 1921 he married Ethel (Monty) Homewood, a Londoner, with whom e had three sons, each of whom were later to have military connections. aurent attended the VC Dinner at Wellington on 9 November 1929.

In 1939, at the beginning of the Second World War, he was recalled or service with the home defence establishment and served as area ommander, Home Guard from 1940 until 1942; he then commanded Io. 47 Air Training Corps between 1943 and 1945. He retired with the ank of lieutenant colonel, but not before he was seconded to the Air orce as squadron leader with the 34th Air Training Squadron.

Laurent ceased active duty in August 1945 and was posted to the etired List of Officers in May 1949. In June 1956 he was one of even New Zealand VC holders who travelled to London for the VC entenary Celebrations, and the group's photograph appeared in the *)aily Telegraph* of 12 June 1956. In 1957 he was given a civic welcome y Hawera. Apart from the 1956 review, he also attended several other C commemorations including those of 1970 and 1972.

Ethel Laurent died on 7 September 1986 and her husband died at is son's home at Southland Road, Hastings, in New Zealand, on December 1987 at the age of 92. He was the eldest surviving New ealand VC holder from the First World War. His funeral was held at t Matthew's Church on 14 December and after cremation his ashes ere interred in Memorial Wall, which was named in his honour in e Servicemen's Cemetery, Hawera, Taranaki. He is commemorated the HQ Dunedin Returned Servicemen's Association, New Zealand, nd a street was named after him in Hawera. His decorations, apart om the VC, include the 1914–15 Star, BWM, VM, New Zealand ervice Medal, Coronation Medals for 1937 and 1953 and the Silver ubilee 1977. They are kept in the Queen Elizabeth II Army Memorial luseum, New Zealand. On 2 December together with eight other Cs, Laurent's was one of those stolen but retrieved by the police after reward was offered.

A. Wilcox

North-East of Laventie, France, 12 September

Lance Corporal Alfred Wilcox was a membe of the 2/4th Ox. and Bucks. Light Infantr Battalion (184th Brigade) 61st 2nd (Sout Midland) Division which arrived at Laventie south-west of Armentières, on 11 Septembe 1918. The enemy was holding the line calle the Picantin–Junction Post and the battalio went forward in an attempt to hold an outpos line that was to the north-east of Laventie Headquarters was established in a forme dressing station in Laventie, a house of 'pretentious size' which had nc been destroyed by enemy artillery. In fact, according to the *Regimenta History*, the town of Laventie had 'suffered less havoc than had seeme probable'.

The battalion was ordered to attack Junction Post the following da This post was a grass-bound breastwork, where the enemy offere strong resistance, and the attack was carried out in driving rain. I was here that L/Cpl Wilcox gained the VC, which was gazetted o 15 November 1918 as follows:

> For most conspicuous bravery and initiative in attack when his company was held up by heavy and persistent machine gun fire at close range. On his own initiative with four men he rushed forward to the nearest enemy gun, bombed it and killed the gunner. Being then attacked by an enemy bombing party, Corpl. Wilcox picked up enemy stick bombs, and led his company against the next gun, finally capturing and destroying it. Although left with only one man, he continued bombing and captured a third gun. He again bombed up the trench, captured a fourth gun, and then rejoined his platoon. Corpl. Wilcox displayed in

this series of successful individual enterprises exceptional valour, judgement and initiative.

The *Regimental Chronicle* has the following report on Wilcox's VC:

> During a local operation on the morning of 12th September, 1918, in front of Laventie, the flank platoon of A Company, 2/4th Battalion Oxford and Bucks Light Infantry, was held up by heavy and persistent machine gun fire from a trench about 70 yards distant. Finding it impossible to advance, Lance-Corporal Wilcox crawled towards the trench with 4 men, bombed it, and finally rushed the gun nearest to him, disposed of the gunner, and, being unable to take the gun along with him, put it out of action …

Telling his own version of his action Wilcox later wrote the following:

> My battalion was ordered to take what was known as Junction Post – believed to be strongly held by machine guns. I was in charge of the leading section; my duty was to cut through the wire and locate the posts. Having got to the wire and successfully cut it, I went back for my section, which I had left in a shell hole a hundred yards to the rear, only to find all but one wounded. That one I told to follow me. Getting through the gap I had already cut, and making my way in the trench the enemy was holding, I got into it, and, bombing my way, captured my first gun. Being quite safe from enemy fire, I still proceeded up the trench, capturing a second gun after a hand-to-hand struggle, in which I bayoneted my man; then bombing a third post, killing five. My own rifle by this time being clogged with mud, I had to resort to German stick bombs, which accounted for a fourth post with its gun. I carried on, driving the remainder of the post right away, leaving behind them about twelve dead in all and four guns (one light, three heavy). I then returned to the guns. Finding I could not remove the three latter, I put them out of action, and had to withdraw owing to lack of support and no fire-arms, my own gun having been dumped for the free use of German stick bombs.

Wilcox received the congratulations of Col Flanagan, the battalion commanding officer, who stated: 'Such acts are a credit to himself and all the battalion.' Others who congratulated Wilcox included Gen. Birdwood, Commander of the Fifth Army.

A few weeks later, in October 1918, the 2/4th moved down to the Cambrai Sector to take part in some successful attacks to the east of Haussy on 24 and 25 October, and at St Hubert on 2 November. It was in this last action that Wilcox was wounded.

Wilcox was discharged from the army on 2 May 1919 and six months later he was presented with his VC by the King at Buckingham Palace on 26 November.

Alfred Wilcox, the son of William and Sarah Wilcox of Birmingham, was born in Tower Road, Aston, Birmingham, on 16 December 1884, and attended school at Burlington Street School, Aston.

He enlisted in the 1st Royal Warwickshire Volunteer Battalion in 1902 and, after serving for four years, his job took him to Liverpool where he continued serving as a Territorial for a further three years. After seven full years he retired with the rank of corporal in 1909. On 25 March 1915 he joined the Royal Bucks Hussars and was later dismounted and attached to the 2/4th Ox. and Bucks., going to France in December 1917, with the service number of 285242. In April 1918 Wilcox was promoted to lance-corporal, having survived the German March offensive, when his battalion was holding a section of the line close to St Quentin while surrounded by overwhelming numbers of the enemy. Those who survived were later in action during the retirement of the Fifth Army at Verlaines, La Motte and Marcelcave. At the beginning of the month the 2/4th Battalion had been amalgamated with the 2nd Bucks Battalion, which was refitted and soon in action to the north-east of Robecq on 12 and 15 April. On 11 September Wilcox's battalion arrived at Laventie, to the south-west of Armentières.

Alfred Wilcox had married Ellen Louisa (*née* Clarke) on 6 September 1913 and the couple had a son, Leonard, who was born on 3 April 1916, and a daughter, Doris, born on 10 September 1914. He attended the 1920 Garden Party at Buckingham Palace on 26 June and in 1927 was presented to the Prince of Wales at the opening of the Birmingham–Wolverhampton Road on 2 November. On 9 November 1929 he attended the VC House of Lords Dinner when the Prince of Wales was the host.

For recreation Wilcox was interested in sport and was a keen cyclist. He was also a good swimmer, played football and was a long-distance walker and member of Birchfield Harriers.

On 7 May 1920 a regimental reunion of the 2/1st Royal Bucks Hussars met at a smoking concert which took place in Cannon Street

Hotel. One item on the programme was to drink the health of the regiment's VC, L/Cpl Wilcox, a proposal made by Maj. Mackinnon, and Wilcox made a reply: 'I saw a lot of square-heads, as I call 'em, in front of me, and I went after 'em. If I hadn't been after 'em they'd have been after me, and I used more language than the British Army ever learnt ...'

In 1936 Wilcox took part in a service at Westminster Abbey to commemorate the 16th anniversary of the founding of the Ypres League. Two other VCs attended, Lt M. O'Leary and Sgt E. Brooks (a member of the 2/4th Ox. and Bucks. Battalion). In 1937 Wilcox was with Pte T. Veale and Cpl E. Foster in a poppy fundraising event which took place at the Odeon, Kingston-upon-Thames. During the 1930s Wilcox was president of the Twickenham Branch of the British Legion, but resigned from that position when he moved to Birmingham in January 1939. On 30 October 1938 he attended the Ypres Memorial Service held on Horse Guards' Parade. As a member of the league, he assisted in laying a wreath from the league at the foot of the Centotaph. After the war he attended the Victory Parade in London, held on 8 June 1946.

Alfred Wilcox died of coronary thrombosis at his home at No. 31 Arthur Street, Small Heath, Birmingham, on 30 March 1951. (The house was formerly the Prince Arthur Inn.) He was buried on 3 April at St Peter and St Paul Churchyard, Aston, in an unmarked grave, number 3995. Wilcox's name is listed on the war memorial in the churchyard, and his decorations were purchased for his collection by Lord Ashcroft on 27 April 1999 for £48,000 at an auction sale arranged by Messrs Spink. Apart from the VC, they included the BWM, VM and Coronation Medals for 1937 and 1953. They are on display in the Imperial War Museum.

Wilcox's grave, or the site of it in Aston Parish Churchyard, was finally given a headstone on 12 September 2006, eighty-eight years after he won his VC. His son Vincent Nicholls was one of the family members present at the dedication service.

D.F. Hunter

West of Cambrai, France, 16–17 September

After the capture of the Drocourt-Quéant Line earlier in the month the main objective in the second half of September in the Third Army sector was to capture the outer defences of the Hindenburg Line. Corporal David Hunter was a member of the 1/5th (City of Glasgow) Battalion TF, the Highland Light Infantry (157th Brigade, 52nd Lowland Division), gained the VC in the period 16–17 September 1918. He was in charge of a machine-gun outpost north-west of Mœuvres, west of Cambrai, during an attack when his post became isolated and overlooked. Two days later, when the division retook Mœuvres, they found Hunter and his six men still holding their post. By then they had virtually no ammunition or food left. Corporal Hunter was awarded the VC and his six colleagues the Military Medal. His VC was gazetted on 23 October 1918 as follows:

> For most conspicuous bravery, determination and devotion to duty. When the battalion to which he belonged relieved another unit in the front line, Corpl. Hunter was detailed to take on an advanced post which was established in shell holes close to the enemy. Relief was carried out in darkness, and there was no opportunity for reconnoitring the adjacent ground. On the following afternoon the enemy drove back the posts on Corpl. Hunter's flanks, and established posts in close proximity to and around him, thus completely isolating his command. Despite the fact that he was exceedingly short of rations and of water, this gallant N.C.O. determined to hold on to his post to the last. On the evening of the second day he endeavoured to communicate with the company without result. Neverthless, he maintained his position, and repelled frequent attacks until the evening of

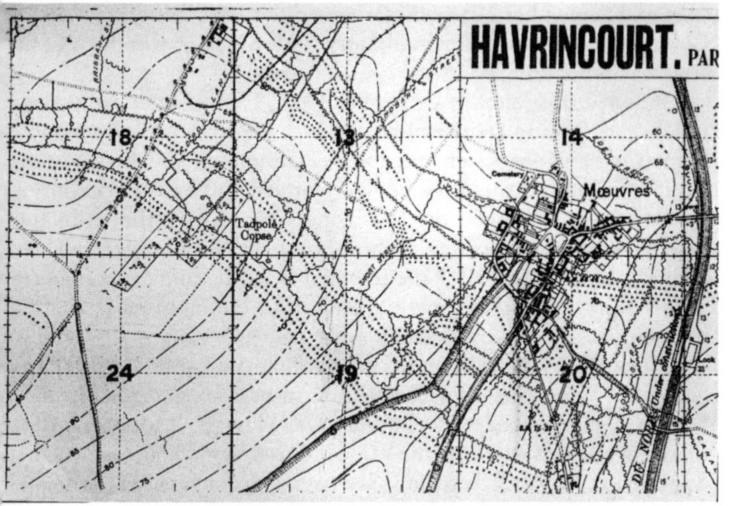

> the third day, when a counter-attack relieved him. Without food and water he had held on to his post for over forty-eight hours. Not only did he withstand constant attacks, but he had also to undergo the barrage fire of the enemy and of our own atttacks, which came right across his post. The outstanding bravery, coupled with determination, fortitude and endurance, displayed by Corpl. Hunter is beyond all praise, and is a magnificent example to all.

Hunter, who by now had been promoted to sergeant, was presented with his VC in the Ballroom of Buckingham Palace on 16 November 1918. He and his six colleagues were later to become known as 'The Seven Men of Mœuvres'.

David Ferguson Hunter was born on 28 November 1891 at Kingseat in Dunfermline, Scotland. After completing his education he became a miner and also joined the Territorials in 1910, the 7th Argyll & Sutherland Highlanders. Two months after war began he volunteered in October 1914 for a Cyclist Battalion, later transferring to the Royal Engineers before serving in France from 1916. Soon after he was wounded and subsequently spent six weeks in hospital.

In mid-September 1918 Hunter joined the 1/5th Battalion (City of Glasgow), the Highland Light Infantry, with whom he won his VC, his service number being 43247.

A few months later, in December 1918, Hunter attended a large public gathering in Dunfermline at which Provost Norval presented Hunter with a gold watch and a wallet containing War Bonds to the value of £250. By this time he had married and had two children. Hunter was discharged the following year and continued to live in Dunfermline, returning to his former job as a miner at Dean Colliery, Kingseat. In 1919 the Imperial War Museum commissioned an oil painting of Hunter which is still in the museum collection in Lambeth.

In June 1920 Hunter attended the Buckingham Palace Garden Party and in the same year sat as a model for a bust being made by Jacob Epstein, commissioned by the Imperial War Museum. It was designed to represent all Scots who won the VC in the First World War, and was first displayed at the Royal Academy, then later in the Imperial War Museum in the mid-1990s as part of an exhibition which commemorated the Victoria Cross and and George Cross.

Hunter left his mining job at Kingseat and was later employed at Steelend, but following an accident gave up his job and became a rural postman in 1924. In November 1929 he attended the House of Lords Dinner for holders of the VC and he also attended almost all the main VC and later VC/GC functions. He had continued to be a member of the Territorial Army, serving with the 7th Argyll & Sutherland Highlanders from 1910 until 1939, and then became a member of the Home Guard. Three of Hunter's four sons served in anti-aircraft batteries and a fourth son was also a member of the Armed Services.

In June 1946 Hunter took part in the victory parade in London, and in 1951 he gave up his postal service after twenty-seven years, returning to the mines at the age of 60 to become a store-keeper for five years at Comrie Colliery. In June 1956, the year of his retirement, Hunter attended the VC centenary celebrations in Hyde Park. During this period his address was No. 40 Haig Crescent, Dunfermline.

In 1957 the government decided that the Highland Light Infantry and the Royal Scots Fusiliers should be amalgamated. On 29 September in Blythswood Square, Glasgow, a massive protest against the amalgamation took place and the government was petitioned by the Lord Provost, when he visited the Home Office for an interview. Mr W. Angus VC, and Mr A.F. Hunter (HLI VC holders) as well as Lord Belhaven and Stenton, took part in the rally and the protest march was led by Angus and Hunter.

In 1962, two years before he died, Hunter was prepared to sell his VC as he was finding it increasingly difficult to get about and his 27-year-old Morris car had recently failed its road test. His family had urged him to sell the decoration, but in the end this was not necessary, as a London car dealer provided a car on condition that the medal was kept by Hunter and not sold. His regiment, the Highland Light Infantry, had been quite prepared to purchase the medal from him but he promised that he would leave it to them on his death anyway.

David Hunter died in Dunfermline Northern Hospital after a heart attack on 14 February 1965, at the age of 73, and was buried in Dunfermline Cemetery. The now-named Royal Highland Fusiliers provided a piper and a detachment to honour their VC at the funeral. Two holders of the VC also attended the funeral, John Carmichael, formerly of the North Staffordshire Regiment, and John Hamilton, formerly of the Highland Light Infantry. Hunter's grave had no headstone and the grave reference is Division E 7510. He was survived by his wife, Elizabeth, his four sons, two daughters and two stepdaughters. His decorations consist of his VC, Imperial Service Medal, BWM, VM, Coronation Medals for 1937 and 1953, and Efficiency Medal 'Territorial'. They are in the care of the Royal Highland Fusilier Regimental Museum, to whom he had promised to leave them.

On 12 August 2004 and partly arranged for by his regiment, a memorial stone was finally placed on his unmarked grave site in Dunfermline Cemetery.

M.V. Buckley

West of St Quentin, France, 18 September

In mid-September 1918 the plan of the Allied advance was to press the enemy vigorously in order to prevent it from destroying roads, railways and bridges as they retreated. The key to this strategy was to be the breaking of the Hindenburg Line. The Australian Corps, and in particular their 4th Division, was to provide a major part of the attacking force, and in time for the operations against the outer defences of the Hindenburg Line, fresh troops had arrived to supplement the depleted front-line units. The first line in this new advance was to be part of the Outpost Line which ran from Hargicourt to Pontruet. The Battle of Épéhy lasted from 12 to 18 September 1918 and on the last date no fewer that six VCs were won.

Sergeant Maurice Buckley (Sexton) was a member of the 13th Battalion (New South Wales) (4th Brigade, 4th AIF Division) and gained the VC at a village called Le Verguier, north-west of St Quentin. The 4th Australian Brigade was on the left flank of 4th Australian Division, having been assigned to capture the main strong points in front of and around Le Verguier, which was well fortified and protected by machine and field guns.

The brigade moved forward on a three-battalion front, with the 16th Battalion concentrated on trying to capture and then mop up the village, while the 13th and 15th Battalions moved round it towards further objectives. The 13th Battalion moved to the south of the village, behind a creeping barrage, and soon cleared seven enemy outposts, mainly due to Sgt Buckley and his Lewis gun team. When some of the smoke and mist began to clear from the battlefield a German field gun and mortar were spotted. Sergeant Buckley dashed forward and shot the crew, then dealt similarly with the crew of the mortar. Afterwards he fired into some dugouts, which turned out to

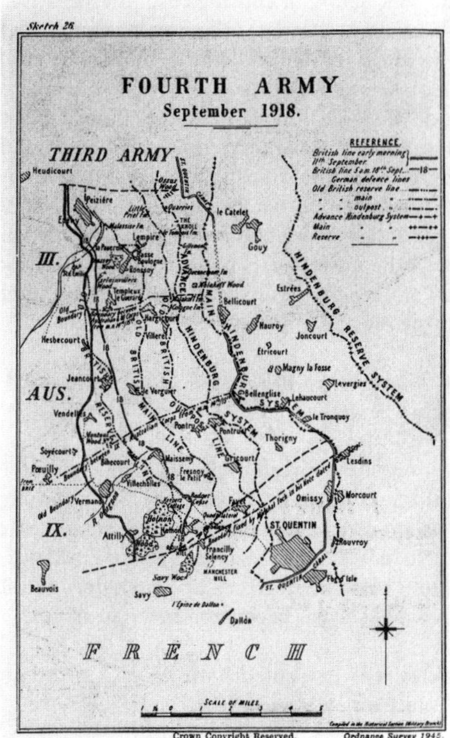

be the headquarters of the German 58th Infantry Regiment, capturing thirty of the enemy. The battalion's success was due in no small measure to Sgt Buckley's bravery.

Sergeant Buckley's VC was gazetted on 14 December 1918, in the name of Gerald Sexton, the name he served under, as follows:

> For most conspicuous bravery during the attack near Le Verguier, north-west of St. Quentin on 18 Sept. 1918. During the whole period of the advance, which was very seriously opposed, Sergt. Sexton was to the fore, dealing with enemy machine guns, rushing enemy posts, and performing great feats of bravery and endurance without faltering or for a moment taking cover. When the advance had passed the ridge at Le Verguier, Sergt. Sexton's attention was directed to a party of the enemy manning

> a bank, and to a field-gun causing casualties and holding up a company. Without hesitation, calling to his section to follow, he rushed down the bank and killed the gunners of the field-gun. Regardless of machine gun fire, he returned to the bank, and after firing down some dugouts, induced about 30 of the enemy to surrender. When the advance was continued from the first to the second objective, the company was again held up by machine guns on the flanks. Supported by another platoon, he disposed of the enemy guns, displaying boldness which inspired all. Later, he again showed the most conspicuous initiative in the capture of hostile posts and machine guns, and rendered invaluable support to his company digging in.

The *London Gazette* of 8 August 1919 published additional information about Sexton:

> The notification of the award of the Victoria Cross to No. 6594, Sergt. Gerald Sexton, 13th Battn. A.I.F., as announced in the *London Gazette* dated 14 December 1918, should read as being awarded to No. 6594, Sergt. Maurice Vincent Buckley, 13th Battn. A.I.F., the latter being the correct Christian names and surname of this N.C.O., which he has been permitted to reassume.

Sergeant Buckley was presented with his VC in the quadrangle of Buckingham Palace on 29 May 1919.

Maurice Vincent Buckley was a son of Timothy Buckley, a brickmaker, and his wife Honora Mary Agnes (*née* Sexton). He was born in Upper Hawthorn, Victoria, Australia, on 13 April 1891, one of five boys and two girls. Timothy Buckley was a native of Cork in Ireland and Honora was born in Victoria. After Maurice left the Christian Brothers' school, Abbotsford, he became a motor trimmer and worked in Warrnambool where he enlisted on 18 December 1914. In June 1915 he embarked for Egypt with the AIF's 13th Light Horse Regiment, but later returned to Australia where on 25 September he was admitted to Langwarren Camp with venereal disease. He deserted on 21 January and on 20 March was struck off the strength.

Buckley remained a civilian for a short time before re-enlisting in Sydney on 6 May 1916, this time using his mother's name. He left for France in October and joined the 13th AIF Battalion on the Somme n January 1917. He took part in many of the major battles of that ear, including Bullecourt, Polygon Wood, Ypres and Passchendaele. In arly 1918 he was at Hébuterne and then Villers-Bretonneux. By now e had been made a lance corporal and in April he became a temporary orporal, before being promoted in June to lance sergeant and in charge f a Lewis gun section. During the Battle of Hamel on 6 July he was vounded and was away from his unit for two weeks.

On 8 August he won a DCM for conspicuous gallantry and devotion o duty on the first day of the great Allied Offensive in the Hamel-Morcourt area, when his company was held up by a German machine un. Buckley's Lewis gun section swiftly silenced the enemy, and the itation was as follows:

> For most conspicuous gallantry and devotion to duty. On four separate occasions his company was suddenly confronted by enemy machine gun fire. On each occasion this N.C.O. in charge of a Lewis gun section, brought his gun into action with great promptitude, quickly silencing the opposition. On one occasion in some tall crops, he stood up in full view of the enemy, firing from the hip until he had put the enemy machine gun out of action. Thoughout the day he displayed initiative combined with coolness.

'hree weeks later, on 28 August, Sexton was promoted to sergeant.

The confusion over Buckley's name began in early 1916 when he nade a mistake over his leave dates, which resulted in him missing the mbarkation. He then deserted the army, but later decided to rejoin in ydney, using the name of Gerald Sexton.

Buckley returned to Australia in 1919, being discharged as medically nfit in December. In 1920 he took up work as a road contractor in ippsland. On 17 March he took part in a St Patrick's Day march Melbourne with thirteen other VC holders, together with 10,000 C Servicemen.

On 15 January 1921, Buckley tried to get his horse to jump over ome railway gates at Boolarra but he misjudged the approach and as thrown from his horse. His head struck the metal road but he ot up and remounted his horse. Later in the day, at around 7 p.m., e was found unconscious having fallen off his horse. He was taken y ambulance to Melbourne and after being operated on in Fitzroy Iospital, Victoria, and seemingly on his way to a recovery, he had a elapse and died on 27 January, of a cerebral haemorrhage.

After a requiem mass in St Patrick's Cathedral, Buckley was buried Brighton Cemetery, Melbourne, (RC Section Grave 114) with full military honours. Buckley's coffin was carried on a gun carriage and ten holders of the VC from Victoria acted as pall-bearers. Past pupil from his former school, the Christian Brothers at Abbotsford, Victoria provided a guard of honour. Buckley's name is commemorated a the Australian War Memorial in Canberra, where his VC and DCM are on display. He was also awarded the 1914–15 Star, BWM and VM. In addition Buckley Court is named after him in Canberra He is remembered on the Victoria Cross Park Memorial, also in Canberra, and in Sydney in the Victoria Cross Memorial in the Queen Victoria building.

L.A. LEWIS

outh-East of Épéhy, France, 18 September

To the north-east of Péronne the Battle of Épéhy lasted from 12 to 18 September 1918 and L/Cpl Leonard Allan Lewis was one of six men to gain the VC on the last day of the battle. The 6th Northamptonshire (Service) Battalion (54th Brigade, 18th Division) was to capture the village of Ronssoy, to the south-east of Épéhy, and L/Cpl Lewis commanded the right-hand section of the line. The 6th Northamptonshires, ssisted by a barrage, moved forward to attack the village until they eached a position where the enemy machine-gun fire was so strong hat there was little hope of further progress. It was at this point that /Cpl Lewis took a hand, when he spotted identified the two enemy achine guns enfilading his battalion. Without waiting for orders he rawled forward, single-handed, and when within range he bombed he two gun teams. The Germans quickly left their positions and ran ut of the emplacement.

According to the *18th Divisional History*:

> Lewis then used his rifle with such effect that the whole enemy party surrendered. Lewis had wounded six of them; the remaining four were brought in unwounded.
>
> It was undoubtably the putting out of action of those two machine guns that enabled the Northamptonshires to resume their advance. Lance Corporal Lewis did not live to know that he had been awarded the greatest of all military honours. Three days later he was killed by a stray shell.

ewis was killed in action on 21 September at Doleful Post near empire, to the north-east of Ronssoy, having taken his section through an enemy barrage while trying to get his men under cover from heav machine-gun fire. While doing this he was hit in the head by shrapne which penetrated his skull. His body was identified nine days later an his pay book removed and returned to his mother. He was buried b Australian troops near Lempire, but the whereabouts of his grave is n longer known and his name is commemorated on Panel 7 of the Vis-en Artois Memorial to the Missing. His posthumous VC was gazetted o 31 January 1919 as follows:

> For most conspicuous bravery at Ronssoy on 18 Sept. 1918, when in command of a section on the right of an attacking line held up by intense machine gun fire. L.-Corpl. Lewis, seeing that two enemy machine guns were enfilading the line, crawled forward, single-handed, and successfully bombed the guns, and by rifle fire later caused the whole team to surrender, thereby enabling the whole line to advance. On 21 Sept. 1918 he again displayed great powers of command, and having rushed his company through the enemy barrage, was killed while getting his men under cover from heavy machine gun fire. Throughout he showed splendid disregard of danger, and his leadership at a critical period was beyond praise.

Lewis' VC was presented to his parents in the Ballroom of Buckinghar Palace on 10 April 1919.

Leonard Allan Lewis, the second son of George and Annie Elizabet Lewis (*née* Gidley), was born in Wood Villas, Brilley near Whitney-or Wye, Herefordshire, on 28 February 1895. George Lewis was a loca man who worked as a jobbing carpenter, but his wife hailed from Lym Regis, Dorset. The family consisted of five boys and four girls, and the small cottage stood on the left bank of the Wye, three-quarters of mile from Whitney-on-Wye station, on the road between Hereford an Glasbury. Soon after his birth Leonard's family moved to a cottage o the River Wye. He attended Whitney-on-Wye school and when he left a the age of 13 he worked as a farm labourer, gardener and next as a bu driver on the GWR motor bus service. At this time he lived in Neath Glamorgan, at No. 17 Creswell Road. His elder brother Edward serve in the Brecknockshire Battalion of the South Wales Borderers, and wa stationed in India.

Leonard Lewis enlisted in March 1915 as a private in the Mechanica Transport Section, the Army Service Corps. For a period of time h was with a School of Instruction, BEF France. While in France he fell ill with jaundice and returned to England, where he was treated in a Red Cross hospital at Longleat, owned by Lord and Lady Bath. After recovering, he joined the Northamptonshire Regiment, at Sheerness as a lance corporal, and returned to France as a member of the 6th (Service) Northamptonshire Battalion, becoming a member of No. 8 Platoon, with the service number 58062.

Leonard Lewis is commemorated at his home church of St Peter and St Paul's, Whitney, which overlooks the River Wye, and his name is listed as one of the men from the locality who had died during the war. His name is also mentioned on the family headstone in the cemetery and on the Brilley War Memorial. His decorations which, apart from the VC, include the 1914–15 Star, BWM, and VM, are in private hands.

The house in which Lewis was born was originally two and called Wood Villas but in recent years it has been turned into one house and hence its name is now Wood Villa.

W.H. Waring

Ronssoy, France, 18 September

Not far from where L/Cpl Allan Lewis won the VC at Ronssoy on 18 September 1918, L/Sgt William Waring of the 25th Battalion Royal Welch Fusiliers (231st Brigade, 74th Division) also gained a posthumous VC during the Battle of Épéhy in the Fourth Army Operations. The RWF *Regimental History* described the battle in the following way:

> The 230th Brigade on the right made good progress all day, although they could not hold onto the final objective. On the left the 231st Brigade met with fierce opposition after the first objective had fallen. The Shropshires (10th) and our 25th Battalion passed through the Devons and Welch Regiment, but their advance, with right shoulders up, should have coincided with the advance of the 18th Division: the 18th Division had, however, met with stout resistance at the commencement of the battle and could not move. On the boundary line between the two Divisions was a formidable quadrilateral work which held two battalions at 500 yards from the second objective, the Red Line. The Shropshires and our 25th Battalion occupied an intermediate trench by the side of the Ronssoy Road.
>
> A further bombardment of the Red line was ordered during the afternoon, and the 10th Shropshires succeeded in making a short advance, but our battalion, with the full weight of the quadrilateral against them, could not conform.

It was at this point that Waring gained his VC which was gazetted on 31 January 1919 as follows:

> For most conspicuous bravery and devotion to duty at Ronssoy on 18 Sept. 1918. He led an attack against enemy machine guns which were holding up the advance of neighbouring troops, and, in the face of devastating fire from flank and front, single-handed, rushed a strong point, bayoneting four of the garrison and capturing 20 of their guns. L.-Sergt. Waring then, under heavy shell and machine gun fire, reorganised his men, and led and inspired them for another 40 yards, when he fell mortally wounded. His valour, determination and leadership were conspicuous throughout.

Waring died of his wounds in the general hospital in Le Havre, twenty days after winning the VC, and was buried at Ste Marie Cemetery, Le Havre, in Plot V, Row 1, Grave 3. His posthumous VC was presented to his parents in the Ballroom of Buckingham Palace on 8 March 1919.

William Herbert Waring, the sixth child of eight born to Richard and Annie Waring, was born at Rock Terrace, Raven Square, Welshpool, in Montgomeryshire on 13 October 1885. His father was a nailmaker. William was educated at Christ Church of England Infants' School, Welshpool, and Boys' National School, Berriew Road, Welshpool. After leaving school he worked in Radnorshire as a labourer in the Elan Valley Reservoir before working for Bushell, a poultry dealer in Welshpool.

In 1904 William joined the Montgomeryshire Yeomanry, becoming a corporal in May 1911 and sergeant in May 1913. Also in 1913 he won a silver watch for being the best shot in his squadron and a few months later, in May 1914, his troop was awarded a silver cup for being the best troop of his squadron. Prior to the war he was a keen and successful amateur footballer in Montgomeryshire and won many distinctions during his career.

His unit was mobilised on 4 August 1914 and his service number was 55014. He trained with the 1/1st Montgomeryshire Yeomanry in Cromer, Norfolk, then served in Egypt and Mesopotamia from March 1916 to April 1918. In March 1917 he had transferred to the 25th (Service) Battalion, Royal Welch Fusiliers, and at his own request he reverted to private. Until his death Waring was to serve with a bewildering number of changes of rank. At the end of October 1917 he was acting sergeant and won the MM in November, after which he was promoted to lance sergeant. He reverted again to private on 29 November and a few days later was a corporal once more. In January he was made acting sergeant, then sergeant at the beginning of March, but on 13 April he reverted to lance sergeant.

William Waring, seemingly a born soldier, was awarded the Territorial Force Efficiency Medal (1908) in addition to his VC, MM, 1914–15 Star, BWM, and VM. In June 1929 William's mother bequeathed her son's war medals to Welshpool Town Council. A replica set of the First World War group are on display in the council chamber. Waring was a member of the Order of Druids and was unmarried. After the war he was commemorated in various places: on the family grave at Christ Church Welsh Baptist Church Burial Ground, and on the local war memorial. There is also a Waring Court named after him in Hightown, Wrexham, and in Afford, Welshpool.

W.A. White

Gouzeaucourt, France, 18 September

At Gouzeaucourt, to the south-east of Havrincourt, Temporary 2/Lt William White, a member of the 38th Battalion, Machine Gun Corps, was one of six men who won a VC on 18 September 1918, the final day of the Battle of Épéhy. His award was gazetted on 15 November 1918 tells the story as follows:

> For most conspicuous bravery and initiative in attack. When the advance of the infantry was being delayed by an enemy machine gun, he rushed the gun position single-handed, shot the three gunners and captured the gun. Later, in similar circumstances, he attacked a gun accompanied by two men, but both of the latter were immediately shot down. He went on alone to the gun positions, and bayoneted or shot the team of five men and captured the gun. On a third occasion, when the advance was held up by hostile fire from an enemy position, he collected a small party and rushed the position, inflicting heavy losses on the garrison. Subsequently, in consolidating the position by the skilful use of captured enemy and his own two machine guns, he inflicted severe casualties of the enemy. His example of fearless and unhesitating devotion to duty under circumstances of great personal danger greatly inspired the neighbouring troops, and his action had a marked effect on the operations.

White was decorated in the Ballroom at Buckingham Palace on 27 March 1919.

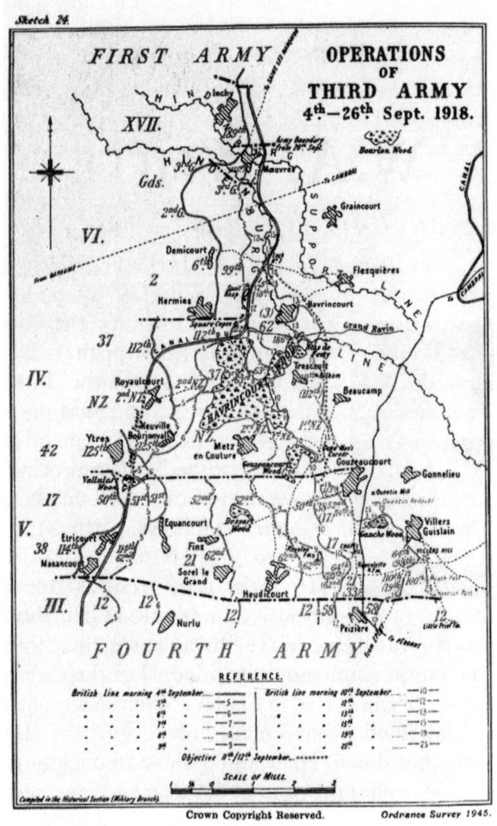

Crown Copyright Reserved. Ordnance Survey 1945.

William Allison White, son of Samuel and Elizabeth White, was born in Mitcham, Surrey, on 19 October 1894. He was educated at Salter's Hill School, West Norwood, and at Lancashire Technical School, Barrow-in-Furness. He joined the Territorial Army on 22 February 1910 as a private in the 4th Battalion (TF) King's Own (Royal Lancaster) Regiment and two years later, in February 1916, he was discharged on the termination of his engagement. He then joined the MGC as a staff sergeant-instructor at the Machine Gun School and was commissioned on 26 June 1917. He was made a full lieutenant on 26 December 1918.

After the war White was invited to unveil a memorial at St Luke's, West Norwood, on 6 November 1921, and one of four VC holders, he also attended the unveiling of the Machine Gun Corps memorial at Hyde Park Corner on 10 May 1925. In fact, he attended almost all of the VC functions, including the House of Lords dinner in November 1929, the victory parade of June 1946 and the VC Centenary in June 1956 at Hyde Park.

On the outbreak of the Second World War in 1939 William White was commissioned as a captain in the Royal Artillery (TF).

In his 80th year William White died at the Priory Nursing Home in Wellington, Shropshire, on 13 September 1974, and his body was cremated in Shrewsbury a week later. His ashes were buried in the family grave at St John's churchyard, Hildenborough, Kent.

In addition to his VC, White had a TD decoration. In 1983 his VC was sold by a Northampton dealer, who had bought it the year before. White's decorations were put up for auction again on 28 July 1993 at Messrs Buckland, Dix and Wood when the asking price was between £14,000 and £16,000. In the end they fetched £18,000. They are now part of the Ashcroft Collection in the Imperial War Museum. Apart from the VC, White's other medals from both world wars included a BWM (1914–1920); VM (1914–19) and MiD Oakleaf, Territorial Force War Medal (1914–1919), Defence Medal (1939– 45), Victory Medal (1939–45), Coronations, 1937 and 1953, Territorial Efficiency Medal (1921), and Army Emergency Reserve Decoration (1952).

J.P. Woods

North-West of St Quentin, France, 18 September

The dates of the Battle of Épéhy were 12–18 September, and on the final day six men gained the VC. Moving from right to left on the battlefield, Pte James Woods was the second man to win a VC in the section of the fighting to the south of the village of Le Verguier to the north-west of St Quentin. Woods was serving in 48th Battalion (South Australia) (AIF), 12th Brigade, 4th Australian Division; the division in which Sgt M.V. Buckley was serving when he won his VC, on the same day during the same action.

On 18 September the 48th Battalion was detailed to lead the attack of their brigade, against the Hindenburg Outpost Line. The battalion was the right-flank guard of the Australian Corps, which was moving forward on a two-divisional front and to the right was the British 1st Division.

An artillery barrage began at 5.20 a.m. At the same time as the 48th Battalion moved off from its start line. The Australians advanced in small groups, reaching the first objective by 6.30 a.m., where trenches and deep dugouts, together with 480 prisoners, were taken, as well as Le Verguier. By 8.30 a.m. the 45th Battalion – which was 40yds to the rear of the 48th – advanced through them to the second objective, which was the former British Outpost Line, consisting of a string of hilltop outpost trenches encirled by wire. The flanking British Brigade to the right was then stopped by the enemy, but the 45th was able to penetrate the disorganised German defence to gain the second objective of hilltop posts, together with several hundred prisoners.

At 10.30 a.m., to the right of the Australian 1st Division, the Australians had both reached and consolidated the Blue Line, a position which overlooked Bellicourt and the St Quentin Canal. However, there were still problems with the British right flank, which was exposed, owing to the fact that the British 2nd Brigade had still to reach their second objective. As a result, two companies of the 48th Battalion were moved up to support the 46th Battalion's frontal assault on the Hindenburg Outpost Line.

Long grass, together with thistles and dense wire, held up Australian progress and by mid-afternoon the 46th's attack was stopped. An hour later the battalion, supported by artillery, made a further attempt to advance, still protected by the two companies from the 48th Battalion on the right flank. To make matters worse for the attackers, a heavy rainstorm began at 10.55 p.m. The right-flank British attack, timed for midnight, failed, but by that time the two protecting companies of the 48th had reached the fork of two trenches. The brigade commander understood that the British on his right flank had withdrawn and was very concerned that the enemy might get around this flank and attack his men from the rear. It was at this stage that a patrol including Pte J.P. Woods, sent out to check on the position of the 2nd Brigade, was fired on by the enemy who were defending positions called Pen and Entrepôt Trenches.

Private James Woods gained his VC when, together with two companions, he found a junction of two trenches held by at least thirty Germans. He then rushed the hostile position, captured one German and wounded another. The rest of the Germans cleared off, leaving behind them four heavy and two light machine guns. When the enemy later began a series of fierce counter-attacks one of Woods' men was wounded. Under heavy fire, Woods then climbed on to the parapet to throw the bombs at the enemy positions which his comrades handed up to him. This enabled him to hold off the enemy until reinforcements arrived. The fighting was very fierce and continued until early morning: each side occupied different points and each erected barricades and constructed obstacles. However, by dawn the enemy was finally flushed out of their positions and into the open.

The right flank of the Allied advance was finally strengthened and the advancing troops had the reward of seeing before them the St Quentin Canal and the village of Bellenglise, together with the main Hindenburg Line. As the struggle between the two sides continued over the next twenty-four hours it became increasingly bitter and savage. As well as winning a VC, the 48th Battalion also won on 18 September a DSO, six MCs, five DCMs, twenty-six MMs, and a Belgian Croix de Guerre. Unsurprisingly casualties were very high and the battalion was too short of men to take an active role in the war again.

Woods' VC was gazetted on 26 December 1918 as follows:

> For most conspicuous bravery and devotion to duty near Le Verguier, north-west of St Quentin, on 18 Sept. 1918, when, with a weak patrol, he attacked and captured a very formidable enemy post, and subsequently, with two comrades, held the same against heavy enemy counter-attacks. Although exposed to heavy fire of all descriptions, he fearlessly jumped on the parapet and opened fire on the attacking enemy, inflicting severe casualties. He kept up his fire and held up the enemy until help arrived, and throughout the operations displayed a splendid example of valour, determination and initative.

Private Woods, who was the smallest Australian soldier to gain the VC in the First World War, was decorated by the King in the quadrangle of Buckingham Palace on 31 May 1919.

James Park Woods was born in Two Wells, South Australia, on 4 January 1891. At the time of his enlistment he was a vinegrower at Caversham in Western Australia. Owing to his lack of height (he was only 5ft 3in tall), he was initially rejected, but on 29 September 1916, after height restrictions were relaxed, he was able to enter the army, where his service number was 3244. He travelled to the United Kingdom in December as a reinforcement for the 48th Battalion and sailed for France on 1 September 1917, joining the 48th in the field in Belgium on 13 September. Having already been in hospital for a short period he was in hospital twice more, in January and July 1918 and after the end of the war he arrived back at Fremantle on 4 August 1919 and was discharged from the army in Perth five weeks later, on 10 September 1919. He then took up a vineyard in the Swan Valley.

On 30 April 1921 in Caversham Methodist Church, Perth Woods married Olive Adeline Wilson, daughter of Mr C.H. Wilson. The couple were to have five sons and two daughters. In October Gordon one of the sons, went missing when flying during the Second World War. After his retirement at the age of 50, Woods' home address was No. 25 Watkins Road, Claremont. Poor health forced him off a property that he owned at Swan Valley, but he had already been awarded a full pension in 1937. He was fond of fishing and cricket and became the president of the Cavershal sub-branch of the Returned

Sailors', Soldiers' and Airmen's Imperial League of Australia. As a member of the Australian contingent, Woods was able to attend the 1956 VC Centenary Celebrations in London in June 1956.

James Woods died in Hollywood Repatriation Hospital, Claremont, in Western Australia, on 18 January 1963, after suffering from respiratory problems which stemmed from the effects of chlorine gas during the war. He was given a military funeral at Karrakatta Cemetery in Perth, Western Australian. The reference is Wesleyan Plot H-A Plot 1. A plaque to his memory commemorates his name in the Garden of Remembrance.

In 1992 the six surviving children donated their father's VC and other decorations to the Australian War Memorial in Canberra. The handover took place at a special ceremony in the Western Front Gallery, in front of a picture painted by Arthur Streeton called St Quentin, which depicted land close to the enemy position that Woods had attacked and held until help arrived. His VC was put on display in the Hall of Valour. His other decorations include the BWM, VM and Coronation Medals for 1937 and 1953. He is also remembered in the Victoria Cross Park Memorial, also in Canberra, and in Sydney in the Victoria Cross Memorial in the Queen Victoria building.

F.E. Young

South-East of Havrincourt, France, 18 September

The area around the village of Havrincour witnessed very severe fighting for possessio of the outer defences of Hindenburg Lin on the culmination of the Battle of Épéhy Second Lieutenant Frank Young gained posthumous VC on 18 September, the fina day of the battle. He was in charge of No. Company of the 1st Hertfordshire Regimen (6th Brigade, 2nd Division) south-east o Havrincourt and close to a copse name Triangle Wood. The enemy positions were to the north-east and after an intense barrage, the foe made a counter-attack against th Hertfordshire positions at about 5.15 p.m. and penetrated their front line posts. However, the attackers were driven back after hard fighting leaving twenty-six men who were promptly taken prisoner.

Young's gallantry was witnessed by several witnesses, includin Maj Clerk, DSO, MC, the second-in-command of Young's battalion who described what happened in the following way:

> Yesterday afternoon the enemy attacked the Battalion in force. 2nd Lieutenant Young was largely instrumental in saving No. 4 Company's Front. The enemy came down on one trench. Frank bombed them out himself. A little later he rescued one of our men who had been taken prisoner. He knocked down one of this lot of the enemy with his fist and scattered the rest, and got our man away. Later he was found to be missing. All the men of No. 4 Company say that they have never seen anything finer than Frank's work that afternoon. He was magnificent. Always the best bomber of No. 4 Company he showed that he has not lost his skill. He impressed everyone during the few days he was with us.

A second witness to Young's gallantry was Sgt R.L. Chalkey who reported that:

> He had met up with Young coming rushing down a trench calling that the enemy was attacking. At that moment a group of ten Germans, led by an officer tried to rush the Sergeant's bombing post. Young, himself shot the officer and threw a couple of bombs into the party which then scattered. He then placed the Sergeant in charge while he rushed round to the right flank.

Private Gould, a third witness, was Young's batman and wrote of an incident when two stretcher bearers in a dugout were captured by two Germans:

> 2nd Lieutenant Young saw them being marched away one German in front and one behind. Without hesitation he leapt out of his outpost, shot the leading German with his revolver and hit the other on the jaw with his fist and knocked him out. ... The two stretcher bearers then made good their escape and Young returned to his outpost.

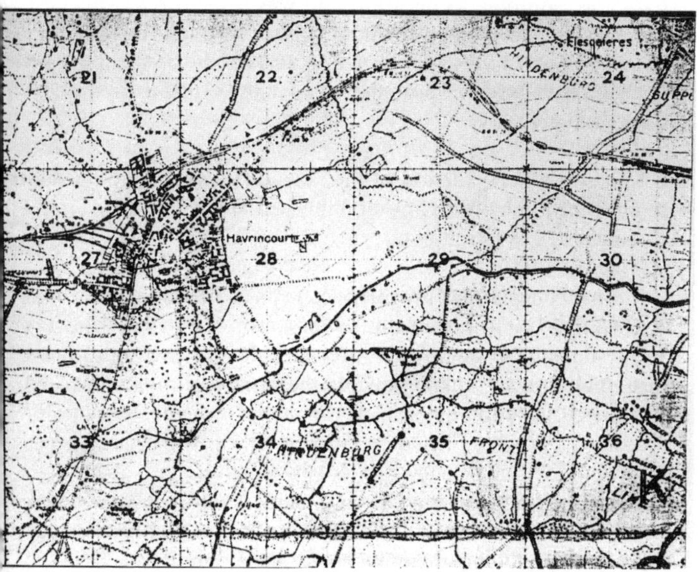

Soon Gould ran out of ammunition and Young sent him back, which left him alone facing the enemy.

A fourth account of the action has come down to us from a Lt H.J. Knee, who wrote as follows:

> No. 4 Company had taken many prisoners. Casualties were small and they had had very good shooting practice. Our post in Femy Line had been overwhelmed at the first onslaught. Some of its occupants had been taken prisoner but two of them had had a remarkable escape. Lieut. Young, son of my first Co. Commander at Tring, and a fine upstanding chap, had scented the danger to our rear if the Boche should be successful in taking our left post. True, Femy was full of glutinous mud, and was not used by us, but still it was not impassable to a determined foe. Young therefore took his stand at the point where the short trench from 'Star' joined 'Femy', that is, soon after the initial assault.
>
> As I was saying, two of our men, having bunked down Femy Line for a short way, fell into the hands of a couple of the Boches and were being piloted back when, as they passed the junction Young sprang out, shot one, bashed the other in the jaw and rescued the No. 3 man who dashed off. On went Young, bombed his way successfully into our captured post, went over the baricade, bombing as he went, and was some forty yards past it before he was most unfortunately shot through the head and killed. His was a very gallant action and had he been supported he could have held our post and saved many valuable lives which were lost later ...

The final and official version of the facts of Frank Young's gallantry were published in his VC citation published in the *London Gazette* of 14 December 1918 as follows:

> For most conspicuous bravery, determination, and exceptional devotion to duty on 18 Sept. 1918, south-east of Havrincourt when during an enemy counter-attack and throughout an extremely intense enemy barrage he visited all posts, warned the garrisons, and encouraged the men. In the early stages of the attack he rescued two of his men who had been captured, and bombed and silenced an enemy machine gun. Although surrounded by the enemy, Second Lieut. Young fought his way back to the main barricade and drove out a party of the enemy who were assembling there. By his further exertions the battalion

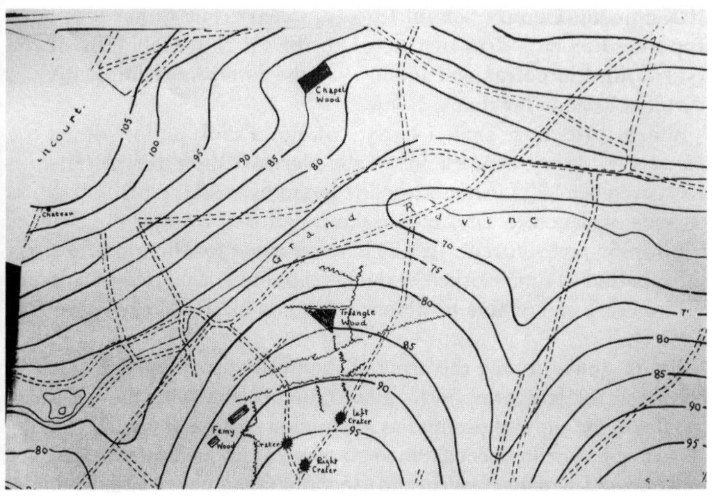

> was able to maintain a line of great tactical value, the loss of which would have meant serious delay to further operations. Throughout four hours of intense hand-to-hand fighting Second Lieut. Young displayed the utmost valour and devotion to duty, and set an example to which the company gallantly responded. He was last seen fighting hand-to-hand against a considerable number of the enemy.

Young was at first reported missing, but nine days later his body was found close to where he won his VC by a party of men from the 1/5th Manchesters who had taken over the line. He had been killed by shrapnel. The group buried the body where they found it and placed a rough wooden cross over the grave. Young's VC was presented to his parents, Captain and Mrs Young, in the Ballroom of Buckingham Palace on 1 March 1919.

Frank Edward Young, son of Sgt (later Capt.) Frank Young and Sarah Ellen Young, was born in Cherat, North-West Province, India (now Pakistan), on 2 October 1895. His father was serving on the North-West Frontier. In 1902 the family returned to England and the father, then a colour sergeant, was posted to the 3rd Bedfordshire Battalion at Bedford. Frank had been educated at the regimental schools, then at Kempston County School for seven years. His father was later appointed to be a drill instructor to the Hitchin Company of the 1st Hertfordshire Regiment and in 1909 the family moved to Elm Villa, Verulum Road in Hitchin.

When little more than 14 years of age, Frank junior joined the Territorial Army, as a bugler in the Hertfordshire Territorials, on 15 November 1909. After school he began by working for W.B. Moss & Sons of Bancroft, later moving to London to work at the Orleans Club in St James Street. In 1911 he returned to Hitchin and for a short period of time worked at the Hitchin Electrical Power Station in Whinbush Road, where he planned to study electrical engineering as a career.

Frank Young joined the army at the outbreak of war when still a private in the Territorial Force, almost literally following in his father's footsteps. He showed promise as a battalion scout and volunteered for service abroad, but was unable to go overseas on medical grounds, not until he had had an operation to sort out some physical disabilities. He left for France as a sergeant in January 1915, with the first reinforcement draft for the 1st Hertfordshire Battalion. By this time his father was battalion sergeant major and Frank joined the unit opposite La Bassée.

Frank Young served in the trenches with the 1st Hertfordshire Battalion, who were part of the Earl of Cavan's 4th Guards Brigade and became known as the Hertfordshire Guards. From 20 January 1915 he served in the trenches with his father at La Bassée and the Battles of Festubert and Loos. Having completed five years' territorial service, Frank was then eligible for home leave. He later returned to France until January 1916, when he volunteered for a bombing instructor's course. He left the battalion for Rouen, where he joined the staff of the Central Bombing School, but at this time an accident forced him to return to England. From May to August 1916 he remained in Cardiff Military Hospital, then was attached to the 3/1st Hertfordshire Regiment at Halton Camp, Wendover, Buckinghamshire. He was recommended for a commission and in January 1917 began cadet training in Oxford. When commissioned on 26 April 1917 he was posted to the 3/1st Battalion at Halton, where his father, by now himself an officer, was also serving. His battalion was broken up in December 1917, and Young was posted to the 5th Reserve Battalion of the Bedfordshire Regiment at Crowborough in Sussex. At about this time he decided to try his luck with the Royal Flying Corps and applied for a transfer. After spending six weeks in a ground training course at Reading he moved to Sleaford, Lincolnshire to begin his flying training.

Unfortunately, following a crash he was so badly shaken that his flying career was at an end, and in July he rejoined the Bedfordshire Regiment in Crowborough. At the beginning of September he was back in Hitchin for what was to be his last leave. Seen off by his father, he returned to France on 5 September 1918 to rejoin the 1st Hertfordshire Regiment. A week later, on 12 September, Young rejoined his unit at the front and his last communication home was a field postcard dated 17 September.

After his body was discovered he was buried in a cemetery 8 miles from Bapaume to the east of Havrincourt, in Hermies Hill British Cemetery, Plot III, Row B, Grave 5. He is commemorated at Hitchin, where his name appears on the base of the town's war memorial outside St Mary's Church, and he is also commemorated by a memorial cross in the Garden of Remembrance, placed there in 1968 along with a similar cross for Flt Sgt Middleton VC.

Young used to live with his parents in a house in Verulam Road, later demolished to make room for the Labour Club. The site was at the rear of what was the former Territorial Club, in front of which stood the local war memorial. Later the memorial was moved to a new site close to the Bedford Road Drill Hall, when the Territorial HQ was changed. Of the 1,050 men from the Hertfordshire Regiment who lost their lives in the war, no fewer than seventy-four came from Hitchin. In 1957 the Young family, two brothers and two sisters, presented Frank's medals to the Hertfordshire Regiment (TA) and they can now be seen in the Beds & Herts regimental collection in the Luton Museum. Apart from the VC, they include the 1914–15 Star, BWM and VM.

If a reader wishes to walk in the steps of this winner of the VC, then he will be able to find the position of Triangle Wood to the south-east of Havrincourt very easily.

J.C. BARRETT

South-West of Bellenglise, France, 24 September

Lieutenant John Barrett was a member of the 1/5th Leicestershire Battalion (138th Brigade, 46th North Midland Division), and on 20 September the battalion went into trenches in the Hindenburg Oupost Line, where they relieved the 14th and 45th Australian Battalions. They were in brigade support at a position called Ascension Ridge, which took its name from a farm of the same name.

Four days later, on 24 September, Lt Barrett gained the VC in the hard fighting for the capture of the village of Pontruet to the south-west of Bellenglise. The rambling village was in a valley and the 5th Leicesters' objective was to take the German trenches in the flank. At dawn the 24th Division to the right was to advance, and the 46th Division on the left was to capture the village and aim for an objective called Forgan's Trench.

The artillery began with a barrage at 5 a.m. and the companies of the Leicestershire Battalion moved off. At the last moment it had been decided to put down a smoke barrage, which unfortunately made it harder for the infantry to see. Moving across the Bellenglise road and into Pontruet from the north, A Company found twice as many Germans as had been expected. Despite the Leicesters causing a lot of German casualties on their route to the village, this was still not enough to allow them to reach their objective. Indeed the village had to be evacuated by the 46th Division later in the day.

The *Regimental History* had this to say of Barrett's exploits:

> Lieut. Barrett found to his surprise a trench across his route. The fog was still thick, and this puzzled him – it had been newly dug during the night – but, as it was full of Germans, he rushed it,

> got inside, and turned towards Forgan's. He was hit doing so. Reaching Forgan's, this party, in which Sergeant Spencer was conspicuous, quickly disposed of the German machine gun posts and their teams, but were then themsleves fired at and bombed from several directions. Undeterred, Lieut. Barrett, though again wounded, drew his revolver and with it held up one bombing party, while Sergeant Spencer dealt with another. A bomb burst close to Lieut. Barrett's pistol arm and put it out of action, and by this time he was becoming exhausted. Calling his N.C.O.s together, he explained what had happened and gave them careful directions as to how to get out, himself quite calm the whole time. Acting on his instructions, those of the party who were left cut their way out; Lieut. Barrett, refusing help, started to crawl through the wire, and was again wounded. He eventually reached the R.A.P. literally covered with wounds. Contrary to the doctor's expectations, however, he not only lived to receive his Victoria Cross, but soon made a complete recovery...

Lieutenant John Barrett's VC was gazetted on 14 December 1918 as follows:

> For most conspicuous bravery and devotion to duty on 24 Sept. 1918, during the attack on Pontruet. Owing to the darkness and smoke barrage, a considerable number of men lost direction, and Lieut. Barrett found himself advancing towards Fagan's [*sic* Forgan's] trench – a trench of great strength, containing numerous machine guns. Without hesitation, he collected all available men and charged the nearest group of machine guns, being wounded on the way. In spite of this he gained the trench and vigorously attacked the garrison, personally disposing of two machine guns and inflicting many casualties. He was again severely wounded, but, neverthless, climbed out of the trench in order to fix his position and locate the enemy. This he succeeded in doing, and, despite exhaustion from wounds, he gave detailed orders to his men to cut their way back to the battalion, which they did. He was again wounded so seriously that he had to be carried out. In spite of his wounds he had managed to fight on, and his spirit was magnificent throughout. It was due to his coolness and grasp of the situation that any of his party were able to get out alive.

Lieutenant Barrett was decorated with his VC in the Ballroom of Buckingham Palace on 13 February 1919.

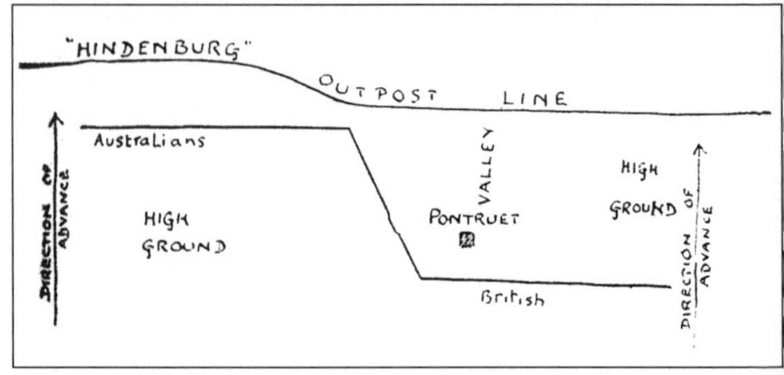

❖❖❖

John Cridlan Barrett was born at No. 30 Regent Street, Leamington Spa, on 10 August 1897, the son of Josephus Teague and Fanny Ada Barrett (*née* Cridlan). He was educated at the Merchant Taylors' School. Although he later began medical studies, these were suspended when he enlisted in the army on 27 January 1916, when posted to the 3/5th Battalion Leicestershire Regiment at Bulwell, Nottinghamshire. Barrett underwent his military training there, before moving to Chesterfield and then Catterick Bridge. On 1 July 1916 he left for France, serving overseas without a break until October 1918.

Barrett served as signals officer to the 1/5th Leicesters from February 1917 until May 1918 and at the beginning of this period he was wounded at Gommecourt. In the following summer he was involved in the fighting in the Lens area. On 27 July 1917 Barrett was made a full lieutenant. In May 1918 he was gassed at Gorre and was in the line when the Germans retreated from La Bassée salient in August.

After the Armistice Barrett continued to serve in the Territorial Army and re-joined the 1st Leicesters after the Territorial Army was reorganised. He later resumed his interrupted medical studies. In 1919, together with L/Cpl Henry Tandey VC, he was given the freedom of the Borough of Leamington. Both men had been born in the spa town. Barrett received a gold wristwatch and Tandey £350 worth of Victory Bonds.

In June 1920 Barrett attended the Buckingham Palace Garden Party for holders of the VC, then in November, the burial of the Unknown Warrior. In April 1920 at a special presentation at No. 27 Devonshire Terrace, Lancaster Gate, Barrett was given a cheque for £330, ogether with other gifts. He was Paddington's second VC and the presentation, made by Gen. Sir Iain Hamilton, was arranged as a mark of appreciation of his bravery.

Barrett studied medicine at St Thomas's Hospital, London, taking degrees MRCS (Eng), and LRCP (Lond) in 1924, after which he became house surgeon. In 1925, while still a member of the Territorial Army, he was promoted to captain in the 5th Leicesters on 1 July 1925, then to major on 1 April 1930. At the end of February 1928 he was made a fellow of the Royal College of Surgeons, and wrote several specialist papers on gangrenous cystitis, malignant tumours and giant prostatic alculi. He was in practice in Watford for a time, before moving to become senior house surgeon at Leicester Royal Infirmary in 1929. In November of the same year he attended the House of Lords VC dinner. n the following year Barrett was made honorary assistant surgeon.

Two years later, in 1932, on the seventeenth anniversary of the Battle of Hohenzollern Redoubt, a commemorative service was held at Loughborough Parish Church. As part of this service a parade was organised with the 5th Leicesters and Maj. Barrett read one of the hurch lessons.

He had many friends in the Leicester area and was keen on sport, particularly golf and swimming, as well as being a keen philatelist. In 933 the Territorials put on an Empire Day display in Loughborough n order to attract new recruits to the Leicestershire Regiment. Displays had taken place in previous years but this was a much larger affair and under the command of Maj. Barrett. During the day the 5th Leicesters paraded through the town and they put on a display in Queen's Park. Here the unit was inspected by its commanding officer, followed by march past and review. Later the ceremony of Beating the Retreat ook place.

In 1935 38-year-old John Barrett became engaged to Ernestine Helen Wright, only child of Mr and Mrs Ernest Wright of Birstall Grange, Leicester. Their marriage took place in August at the church of St John the Divine, Leicester, with the Sergeants' Mess providing a suitable uard of honour. At the time Maj. Barrett was second-in-command of the 5th Leicesters and later in the year his rank was gazetted brevet eutenant colonel. Between 1937 and 1939 Lt Col Barrett commanded he 5th Leicesters.

In February 1937 officers and men from the battalion, numbering 65, attended an annual dinner at the town hall in Lougborough. During he evening Lieutenant Colonel Barrett, whose name was coupled with the toast to the battalion, made a short speech emphasising the mportance of recruiting. He stated that more recruits were now coming forward compared with previous years and that the battalion would shortly be re-equipped and provided with new weapons. The battalion was to continue as an infantry battalion and it later became part of th 148th Brigade of the 49th (West Riding and Midland) Division. On the eve of the Second World War Barrett organised a very successfu territorial ball.

During the war, Barrett was in command of the Surgical Division o No. 30 General Hospital in Iceland for a year, then from 1946 unti 1962 he worked as the Leicester Infirmary's Senior Surgeon, becomin Emeritus Surgeon in December 1962.

In 1948 he set up the Modern Records Department at the Leiceste Royal Infirmary and with the assistance of Mr P.J.F. Hickinbotham set up the Genito-urinary Outpatients Department. Three years late he was appointed a deputy lieutenant for Leicestershire in 1951. A one time he was consulting surgeon to Leicester Isolation Hospital Leicester City General Hospital and Hinckley and District Hospital and from 1958 to 1966 was a member of the Council of the Roya College of Surgeons. In addition, between 1958 and 1960 he was member of the Accident Services Review of Great Britain and Ireland and from 1961 to 1963 president of the Provincial Surgical Club c Great Britain. Between 1967 and 1971 he was also deputy president c the Leicestershire branch of the British Red Cross Society. Barrett seem to have been a born organiser. In 1956 he attended the VC Centenar celebration in London and later other VC/GC functions. Between 195 and 1958 he was honorary colonel of the 5th Leicesters.

In 1961 Barrett appeared in a television programme about hi regiment, as part of a series called *The Fighting Midlands*. At that tim his home was 11 Southerhay Road, Leicester, and it was here that h died on 7 March 1977, aged 79. His funeral took place at St Mary Church, Knighton, Leicester, on 15 March, followed by crematio at Gilroes Crematorium, Leicester. Ref 74560. In his will Barret stipulated that on the death of his wife his VC should go to the Roya Leicestershire Regimental Museum, Leicester, where it is on displa A painting of his VC action by Terence Cuneo was commissioned b the Royal Leicestershire Regiment in 1958. Barrett left £58,703 a his death. In addition to his VC, his medals include the BWM, VM Defence Medal (1939–45), War Medal (1939–45), Coronation Meda for 1937 and 1953 and lastly the Efficiency Medal (TD).

D.J. DEAN

North-West of Lens, France, 24–26 September

/Lt Donald Dean of the 8th Battalion, The Queen's Own Royal West ent Regiment (72nd Brigade, 24th Division) gained a VC in the ghting north-west of Lens during the period 24–26 September 1918. he enemy stoutly defended their positions in the mining area to the orth of Lens when, on the evening of 24 September, Lieutenant Dean, ith half of his platoon, which was part of 'D' Company, took over n advanced post called Canary Trench where two trenches met at he end of a sunken road. Almost immediately Dean's group suffered om a shower of enemy bombs, as well as a frenzied German attack om a north-easterly direction which they managed to drive back by eady fire.

Dean instructed his men to build up the parapets and to improve the arricade which straddled the enemy trench. Enemy machine gun fire ontinued and at midnight another enemy attack was beaten off. Early ext morning, at 6.00, German artillery and mortars shelled Dean's dvance position, subsquently isolating the garrison. The Germans ere determined to capture the post and tenaciously bombed their ay down the continuation of Canary Trench, as well as advancing ver open ground. However Dean's men stood fast and halted the ttack. For the rest of the day Dean's party repaired their defences and t nightfall the other half of the platoon came up on relief, although ean elected to remain in charge. Early on 26 September, enemy erman bombers tried once more, but again they were repelled by rifle re. After this failure the German artillery began a further intensive ombardment. Reckoning his position would be obliterated, Dean ecided to withdraw. His former position was then immediately taken nd Dean then organised a bayonet charge across the open ground. The ermans, having taken the empty position, were no doubt extremely urprised at the group's re-appearance and promptly fled.

Donald Dean's VC was gazetted on 14 December 1918 as follows:

> For most conspicuous bravery, skilful command, and devotion to duty during the period 24 to 26 Sept. 1918, when holding, with his platoon, an advance post established in a newly captured enemy trench north-west of Lens. The left flank of the position was insecure, and the post, when taken over on the night of 24 Sept., was ill-prepared for defence. Shortly after the post was occupied the enemy attempted, without success, to recapture it. Under heavy machine gun fire consolidation was continued, and shortly after midnight another determined enemy attack was driven off. Throughout the night Lieut. Dean worked unceasingly with his men, and about 6 a.m. on 25 Sept. a resolute enemy attack, supported by heavy shell and trench mortar fire, developed. Again, owing to the masterly handling of his command, Lieut. Dean repulsed the attack, causing heavy enemy casualties. Thoughout the 25th and the night of the 25–26 Sept. consolidation was continued under heavy fire, which culminated in intense artillery fire on the morning of the 26th, when the enemy again attacked and was finally repulsed with loss. Five times in all (thrice heavily) was this post attacked, and on each occasion the attack was driven back. Throughout the period Lieut. Dean inspired his command with his own contempt of danger, and all fought with the greatest bravery. He set an example of valour, leadership and devotion to duty of the very highest order.

When Dean's platoon ran out of ammunition after five consecutiv attacks he ordered his men to gather up stones and clods of eart which he then lobbed towards the German machine gunners who f a moment or two thought they were hand-grenades. During the tw days, Dean had a telephone link with his colonel, and after the actio was over he said: 'Anyone on that front could have been awarded t VC. I only got mine because there was a field telephone link with m colonel and I had to tell him what was going on.'

The regimental record of the proceedings was as follows: 'tl defence of "Dean's Post" [no more than an exposed shallow trenc will go down in the history of the Regiment as a fine example courage and leadership. Dean's name will be immortal in our ranks .. T/Lt Dean was decorated in the ballroom of Buckingham Palace o 15 February 1919.

D.J. DEAN

onald John Dean, a son of John H. Dean and Grace Dean, and was orn at Herne Hill, south-east London, on 19 April 1897. His father's usiness was the prosperous brick-making firm, Smeed, Dean & Co. Ltd. onald had an elder brother, Graham, and a younger one, Harold. He lso had a sister, Elsie. Donald was educated at Quenmore College and lso became a Boy Scout.

On the outbreak of war, he attempted to enlist but, as he was nderage, he was not accepted. He decided to join the Kent Special onstabulary instead before trying to enter the army a second time. e succeeded in joining on 19 April 1915, which was his eighteenth irthday, when he gave his age as 19.

At first he served as a private in the 28th County of London Battalion rtists' Rifles), with the service No. 3692, and after completing his itial training at High Beech, Loughton, Essex, he served in France om 10 August 1915. He was with the 1st Battalion Artists' Rifles in e area of St Omer and later at Ploegsteert. Having been commissioned, n 3 October 1916 he was posted to the 11th (S) Queen's Own Royal est Kent Regiment in time for the latter part of the Battle of the omme. He was one of the few junior officers of his battalion to survive e battle. He served with Royal West Kent Regiment until 1918.

On 17 March 1917, Dean was wounded in the neck, arm and leg, and issed the Battle of Messines in June 1917. However, by September he ad recovered and later took part in the Passchendaele battles. During e period between 20 and 23 September he was in the area of Tower amlets and on the 20th he took part in fierce fighting during which e was seriously wounded. He had been hit by three machine-gun ullets and was wounded again in October. After the German Spring ffensive in March 1918, his battalion was disbanded and he joined e 8th (S) Battalion, who moved to the Lens sector in May 1918. He ad recovered from his latest wounds and had returned to the Western ont the month before. At Lens the front line ran through several ining villages and the battalion was billeted in 'Bully' Grenay.

After his VC action on the outskirts of the shattered town of ens, Dean was badly wounded again on 10 October 1918. He was cuperating at home in Sittingbourne when his uncle, John Doubleday, ho lived next door, came rushing into the house. 'You've got the ictoria Cross!' he shouted, which was the first that Dean had heard of . He was also Mentioned in Despatches. Altogether during the war he ad been seriously wounded on four occasions.

Dean then rejoined his battalion and, after his VC investitur on 15 February 1919, he returned home to Sittingbourne to a ver warm welcome from the local residents. The crowd – who were ver anxious to see Lt Dean's VC – were disappointed as he wore it und an overcoat. During the official welcome he was presented with a silv casket by the members of the Sittingbourne, Milton and Milton Rur District Council. During his speech of thanks he opened his coat an briefly displayed the famous bronze medal. In June the following ye he attended the VC Garden Party at Buckingham Palace.

Dean returned to the family brick business and never wanted military career but was keen to retain his links with the army. As suc after the war joined the Territorial Force, becoming a captain in Ju with the 4th Battalion the Buffs (East Kent Regiment).

In 1923 he married Marjorie Emily Wood, the daughter of Mr an Mrs W.R. Wood. His wife came from his home town and their weddir ceremony took place in St Michael's, Sittingbourne. Their firstbor child, Lawrence, died at the age of only 2 months.

From 1 January 1927, Dean was brevet major and full major o 1 April 1930. Between these two dates he attended the House of Lor VC Dinner on 9 November 1929. In 1932 he took a Senior Territori Army Officers' course in Sheerness. At this time his address was Go Court, Sittingbourne.

By 1936, Dean had become the commanding officer of th 4th Battalion the Buffs (East Kent Regiment), and took a promine part in a major service of commemoration for the Buffs in August t following year, which took place at Canterbury Cathedral. In 193 on the outbreak of the Second World War, Dean went to France Officer Commanding No. 5 Group Auxiliary Pioneer Corps, which managed to form into a fighting unit despite having only enough arn for a quarter of his men. He later managed to acquire arms for the re and the group took part in the defence of Boulogne. During the fighti Dean was blown up and incorrectly reported as dead. During this tin his Pioneers covered the withdrawal of the Welsh Guards when the were being taken from the beaches using the Guardsmen's rifles th Dean had acquired for them. Many of his Pioneers came from t backstreets of Glasgow and formed a poor opinion of the Guards as result of this retreat.

After the Dunkirk debacle, Dean was promoted to lieutenant colon and later served in Madagascar, where his job was to organise t return of members of the defeated Vichy forces to France. In 1943 took part in the Sicilian Allied landings and served in Italy. He w Mentioned in Despatches twice. At the end of the war in 1945 he w promoted to full colonel. Subsequently the Buffs and the Royal West Kents amalgamated and became the Queen's Own Buffs, the Royal Kent Regiment. Dean was their honorary colonel for eighteen years and was awarded the Territorial Decoration in 1961. In the same year he was made an OBE. Before that, in 1957, he was made a deputy lieutenant of the County of Kent.

In 1962 he was present at the Ypres Veteran's Annual Shell-Hole Supper that took place at the Wemyss Barracks dining hall in Canterbury. The hall had been transformed to make it into a dugout and 150 people attended, with Lt Col Dean responding to the toast of 'the army' as proposed by Mr W.B. Read. Due as much to Dean as anyone else, two years later the two towns of Sittingbourne and Ypres in Belgium were officially twinned. Dean had always taken a close interest in the Belgian town and was involved in the building of St George's Memorial Church in 1927, arranging for a commemorative plaque to the Royal West Kent Regiment to be placed there. From 1955, when the Friends of St George's was founded, he became the society's vice chairman, which he held until 1979. He was also chairman of the Sittingbourne Branch of the Royal British Legion for a total of fifty years, and in 1983 was awarded the Legion's highest award: a National Certificate of Appreciation. During this period he must have taken part in literally hundreds of Legion ceremonies.

Apart from his military duties, he was also the last of a long line of Kentish brick masters and a member of the family firm of Smeed, Dean & Co. Ltd, who were major brick builders in the Sittingbourne area. He retired from the manufacturing business in 1972 and later opened the Dolphin Yard Sailing Barge Museum at Sittingbourne.

Dean had worshipped at Tunstall Church for many years and had served as a churchwarden for forty-six years. He also served as a local magistrate, and from 1951 he was a justice of the peace. Yet another of his positions was president of the Sittingbourne Horticultural Society.

During his astonishing life, Donald Dean was considered by one and all to be a gentleman who was always ready to take a prominent role in public affairs, and his achievements were quite remarkable. He was one of those men who always managed to get the very best out of people.

In addition to his thirteen British decorations, he was also made a commander, Royal Danish Order of the Dannebrog or Knight Order of Dannebrog.

After two years of failing health, Dean became bedridden and finally died at the age of 88 at his home in Park Avenue, Sittingbourne, on 9 December 1985. He was the last surviving British soldier to have won the VC in the First World War. He was survived by his wife Marjorie after a marriage of sixty-two years and she died nearly three years later, on 29 October 1988. The couple had one son, Michael, who had died in August 1984, one daughter, Susan, and five grandchildren.

Dean's funeral service took place at Tunstall Church on 16 December, followed by cremation at Charing, and his ashes were interred in the family plot at St John the Baptist churchyard, Tunstall, with his name included on the family headstone. At his funeral Dean's cap, sword and medals were carried behind his coffin by two of his grandchildren and the coffin was carried into the church through lines of past and present members of the Sittingbourne Buffs.

On 29 January 1986, a memorial service to give thanks for the life Col Dean took place at St Michael's Church, Sittingbourne, and many local dignitaries attended, together with representatives of the many organisations with which Dean had been connected, from the Artists' Rifles to the Friends of St George's Church, Ypres. In later years a road in Sittingbourne was named after him and there is also a memorial in Central Avenue in the same town. Dean's decorations are privately held and, apart from the VC, they include the 1914–15 Star, BWM and VM from the First World War. From the Second World War they include the 1939–45 Star, the Italy Star, Defence Medal (1939–45) and the War Medal (1939–45), plus MiD Oakleaf. His other decorations included Coronation Medals for 1937 and 1953, a Queen Elizabeth II Silver Jubilee Medal (1977) and TD (1908).

In 1997 the Royal Pioneer Corps Association presented No. 168 Pioneer Regiment with a silver bowl commemorating their spirited defence of Boulogne in May 1940. The family headstone in Tunstall was refurbished in 2008.

SOURCES

The main sources used in the preparation of this book include the five archives listed below, followed by additional material from other places, individuals or archives:

The Lummis VC files at the National Army Museum, London
The Victoria Cross files at the Imperial War Museum, London
The National Archives (TNA), Kew, Surrey
Regimental Museums and Archives
London Gazette 1914–1920 (HMSO)
Stand To! and *Bulletin* are journals published by the Western Front Association. The *Victoria Cross Society* also publish a regular journal.

H.J. Good
Canadian War Museum, Ontario

J.B. Croak
Canadian War Museum, Ontario
Evening Telegram (Newfoundland), 1 May 1991
Legion, July/–August 1991
Punching With Pemberton, vol 3, No. 1, November 1963
The Newfoundland Quarterly (nd)

A.E. Gaby
Australian Dictionary of Biography – online edition

H.G.B. Miner
Canadian War Museum, Ontario
Department of Travel & Publicity (Historical Branch), Canada

J. Brillant
Canadian War Museum, Ontario
Dictionary of Canadian Biography Online
22nd Bn. War Diary

R.M. Beatham
Australian Dictionary of Biography – online edition
This England, Autumn 1984
Cumberland and Westmorland Herald, 5 February 1994

A.P. Brereton
Canadian War Museum, Ontario

F.G. Coppins
Canadian War Museum, Ontario
The World's Highest Paid Army, January 1938

R.L. Zengel
Canadian War Museum, Ontario

T.J. Harris
Strood Rural District Council
Grant, Tony, *A Hero from Halling – Sgt. Thomas Harris, VC,MM.*

T. Dinesen
Canadian War Museum, Ontario
Canada's Viking VC (nd)
The Legionary, August 1968
Victoria Cross Society Volume 7 page 53

R. Spall
Canadian War Museum, Ontario
Stand To! September 2000 Number 59 pages 31–32

P.C. Statton
Australian Dictionary of Biography – online edition
For Valour (nd)

D.M. Beak
Lindsay, Sidney, *Merseyside Heroes* (unpublished)

E.B. Smith
Spinks Catalogue, 12 March 1996
'"Unknown" Officer has uniform which bore the V.C.', *East Anglian Daily Times*, 18 January 1940
Victoria Cross Society Volume 13 pages 38–39

R.A. West
The Tank Museum, Bovington Camp
The Irish Soldier, December 1918
Browne, D.G., *The Tank in Action* (nd)

G. Onions
Black Country VCs (nd)
Birmingham City Council

W.D. Joynt
Australian Dictionary of Biography – online edition
Melbourne Herald, 6 October 1975
The Age, 13 May 1986

L.D.McCarthy
Australian Dictionary of Biography – online edition
The Age, Melbourne, 27 May 1975
The Sunday Times, 25 April 1965

S. Forsyth
The Royal Engineers Journal, December 1965
National Archives, Wellington

D.L. Macintyre
'At King's Park: Legionaries in Historic Park', *The Scotsman*, 1 July 1946
Macintyre, Alastdair- David Lowe Macintryre VC CB (1895–1967) *Victoria Cross Society* Volume 15 pages 46–49

H.J. Colley
Sutton, Chris, *For King & Country: Smethwick's Two V's of the First World War* (Smethwick Heritage Centre Trust 2011)
Smethwick's First VC, 26 October 1918

B.S. Gordon
Australian Dictionary of Biography – online edition
Who's Who in Australia, 1959
Victoria Cross Society page 27 of issue 8 March 2006

R.S. Judson
National Archives, Wellington
Taylor, Richard, J. Reginald, Stanley Judson *Dictionary of New Zealand Biography* – online edition

C.S. Rutherford

Canadian War Museum, Ontario

Article by Eileen Argyris on Capt. Chas. S. Rutherford published in the *Colborne Chronicle* on 27 June 1984.

Charles Rutherford VC, MC, MM – Out of the Shadows (2011)

Charles Smith Rutherford 1892–1989. Canadian Veterans' Hall of Valour

Stand To! Number 27 Winter 1989 – Storey, Edward – 'Last Surviving Victoria Cross Holder from World War 1 Has Died'

W.H. Clark-Kennedy

Canadian War Museum, Ontario

C.H. Sewell

Tank Museum, Bovington Camp *VC Society* Vol 8 pages 48–50

Kennedy, Diana – *Lieutenant Cecil Harold Sewell VC* (*The Sole Society*) December 2002

Sewell, Mike – *Cecil Harold Sewell V.C.* (*The Sole Society*) December 2001

Stockdale, Frank – *Through Mud and Blood to the Green Fields Beyond* (*Tank Corps Motto*)

Cecil Sewell – Tank VC

G. Cartwright

For Valour (nd)

Staunton

Australian Dictionary of Biography – online edition

A.D. Lowerson

Australian Dictionary of Biography – online edition

600 for Opening of Memorial Pool (1966)

Mactier, R.

Australian Dictionary of Biography – online edition

E.T. Towner

Australian Dictionary of Biography – online edition

Business Review Weekly, 4 November 1983

Clune Accounting Systems

Victoria Cross Society Volume 5 pages 34–35

V.M. Currey
Army Newspaper, 2 July 1981
Australian Dictionary of Biography – online edition

.H. Buckley
Australian Dictionary of Biography – online edition

.C. Hall
Australian Dictionary of Biography – online edition
For Valour (nd)

.G. Grant
National Archives, Wellington
Orders and Medals Society, September 1971

.J.P. Nunney
Canadian War Museum, Ontario
Department of Travel and Publicity, August 1962 (Historical Branch, Canada)

. Evans
Gun Fire, York, no. 49
This England, Summer 1983
Lindsay, Sidney, *Merseyside Heroes* (unpublished manuscript)
Reveille, 1 December 1936
Lloyds TSB Group plc

Harvey
The Times, 'One man's tribute to forgotten VC hero 3 September 1984' (Dedication of the headstone to mark the grave off Sergeant Jack Harvey VC, 2 September 1984)

.S. Hutcheson
Wartime letter to a Captain Gwynn as listed in the archives of the Canadian Veterans.
Stand To! Winter 1989 Number 27

.G. Knight
Martin Barker, written communication (2000)
Peter Kefford, written communication (2000)

W.H. Metcalf
Bangor Daily News, 4 September 1998
Stand To! Winter 1989 Number 27

C.W. Peck
Canadian War Museum, Ontario

G. Prowse
Sotheby's Prospectus, 5 June 1992
Victoria Cross Society Volume 19 Derk Hunt-George Prowse VC DCM
Edward Harris
TNA Adm. 339/2/3741

L.C.Weathers
Australian Dictionary of Biography – online edition
For Valour (nd)

J.F. Young
Leslie Hunt, *Our English Heroes* (nd)

M. Doyle
Eamonn O'Toole, *Martin Doyle VC MM*

J. McNamara
Unveiling and dedication of a memorial plaque, School Lane, Bamber Bridge, Lancashire, 3 September 1997

W.L. Rayfield
Canadian War Museum, Ontario

H.J. Laurent
National Archives, Wellington
'Heroism All In A Day's Work', *New Zealand Herald*, 11 December 1987

D.F. Hunter
The Scotsman, 16 February 1965

M.V. Buckley
Australian Dictionary of Biography – online edition
For Valour, Sgt G. Sexton, VC (nd)

V.A. White
Orders, Decorations And Medals, Buckland Dix & Wood, 28 July 1993

.P. Woods
Australian Dictionary of Biography – online edition.
Clissold, B., 'The day that wasn't; 18 September 1918 and the 48th Battalion's Day of Valour on the Hindenburg Line', *Sabretache*, Volume XXXVII, January/March 1996

:E. Young
A. Foster, 'Frank E. Young, Victoria Cross 1895–1918', Hitchin's Soldier Hero
Victoria Cross Society Volume 4 pages 31–32

.C. Barrett
Leicester Mercury, 9 March 1977

).J. Dean
'English Heroes', *This England*, Winter 1986
Stand To! Summer 1989 Number 26 pages 19–21

Bibliography

Arthur, M., *Symbol of Courage: Men Behind the Medal*, (Pan, 2005)

Ashcroft, M., *Victoria Cross Heroes*. Revised edition (Headline/Review, 2007)

Bailey, Roderick, *Forgotten Voices of the Victoria Cross* (Ebury Press, 2010)

Bancroft, J. W., *Devotion to Duty – Tributes to a Region's V. C.* (Aim High Publications, 1990)

Bancroft, J.W., *The Victoria Cross Roll of Honour* (Aim High Productions, 1989)

Bean, C. E. W., *The Official History of Australia in the War of 1914–1918* Volume 3, *The A. I. F. in France* 1916 1929 (Angus & Robertson, 1929)

Brigadier-General R.B. Bradford, VC, M.C. and His Brothers (Ray Westlake Books, nd)

Brazier, K., *The Complete Victoria Cross: A Full Chronological Record of all Holders of Britain's Highest Award for Gallantry* (Pen & Sword, 2010)

Canadian War Records, *Thirty Canadian VCs 1918* (Skeffington, 1919)

Chapman, R., *Beyond Their Duty: Heroes of the Green Howards* (Th Green Howards Museum, 2001)

Clark, B., *The Victoria Cross: a Register of Awards to Irish-born Officers and Men,* (The Irish Sword, 1986)

Dean, Donald & Crowdy, Terence, *Donald Dean VC: The Memoirs of a Volunteer & Territorial from Two World Wars* (Pen & Sword, 2010)

Deeds that Thrilled the Empire: True Stories of the Most Glorious Acts of Heroism of the Empire's Soldiers and Sailors during the Great War (Hutchinson, nd)

De la Billiere, P., *Supreme Courage: Heroic Stories from 150 Years of the VC* (Abacus, 2005)

Denman, T., *Ireland's Unknown Soldiers: The 16th (Irish) Division in the Great War, 1914 – 1918* (Irish Academic Press, 1992)

Doherty, R & Truesdale, D., *Irish Winners of the Victoria Cross* (Four Courts Press, 2000)

Edmonds, Sir J.E. (ed.), *Military Operations France and Belgium* (Macmillan/ HMSO 1922–1949)

Gliddon, G. (ed.), *VCs Handbook: The Western Front 1914–1918* (Sutton Publishing, 2005)

Harvey, D., *Monuments to Courage: Victoria Cross Headstones & Memorials* (D. Harvey, 1999)

James, E. A., *British Regiments 1914–1918* (Samson Books, 1978)

Kelleher, J.P. Comp., *Elegant Extracts, The Royal Fusiliers Recipients of The Victoria Cross*, 'For Valour' (The Royal Fusiliers Association, 2010)

The King' s Regiment 8th 63rd 96th, 'For Valour' (Fleur de Lys Publishing, nd)

Lindsay, Sidney, *Merseyside Heroes* (Unpublished manuscript)

The London Gazette, 1916–1920

McCrery, N., *For Conspicuous Gallantry A Brief History of the Recipients of the Victoria Cross from Nottinghamshire and Derbyshire*, (J. H. Hall & Sons, 1990)

Murphy, James, *Liverpool VCs* (Pen & Sword, 2008)

Napier, G, *The Sapper VCs: The Story of Valour in the Royal Engineers and its Associated Corps,* (The Stationery Office, 1998)

Nicholson, G. W. L. N. *Canadian Expeditionary Force 1914–1919* (Queen's Printer, 1962)

O' Moore, Creagh. General Sir & E.M. Humphris, E. Miss, *The VC and DSO* Vol 1., 1924

Pillinger, D & Staunton, A. *Victoria Cross Presentations and Locations*. (D. Pillinger & A. Staunton, 2000)

The Register of the Victoria Cross (This England Books, 1988)

Shannon, S. D. *Beyond Praise: The Durham Light Infantrymen Who Were Awarded the Victoria Cross* (County Durham Books, 1998)

Smith, M. *Award for Valour: A History of the Victoria Cross and the Evolution of British Heroism* (Palgrave Macmillan, 2008)

Smyth, Sir John VC *The Story of the Victoria Cross* (Frederick Muller, 1963)

Staunton, A., *Victoria Cross: Australia's Finest and the Battles they Fought* (Hardie Grant Books, 2005)

Wigmore, L. & Harding, B., *They Dared Mightily* (2nd edn revised by Williams, J & Staunton, S. Australian War Memorial, 1986)

Williams, W. Alister *Heart of a Dragon: The VCs of Wales & the Welsh Regiments, 1914–1982* (Bridge Books, 2008)

Divisional, regimental and battalion histories have all been consulted where appropriate but unfortunately are too numerous to list here.

INDEX